A Cascading Waterfall of Nectar

Books by Thinley Norbu

A Cascading Waterfall of Nectar

Echoes

Fantasy History of a Himalayan

Gypsy Gossip

Magic Dance: The Display of the Self-Nature of the Five Wisdom Dakinis

The Small Golden Key to the Treasure of the Various Essential Necessities of General and Extraordinary Buddhist Dharma

Sunlight Speech That Dispels the Darkness of Doubt

Welcoming Flowers from Across the Cleansed Threshold of Hope: An Answer to the Pope's Criticism of Buddhism

White Sail: Crossing the Waves of Ocean Mind to the Serene Continent of the Triple Gems

A Cascading Waterfall of Nectar

THINLEY NORBU

With Forewords by

H. H. DRUBWANG PENOR RINPOCHE

KATHOG RIGDZIN PEMA WANGCHEN RINPOCHE

VEN. ALAK ZENKAR RINPOCHE

TULKU THONDUP RINPOCHE

SHAMBHALA
BOSTON & LONDON
2009

Shambhala Publications, Inc.
Horticultural Hall
300 Massachusetts Avenue
Boston, Massachusetts 02115
www.shambhala.com

9 8 7 6 5 4 3 2 1

First Paperback Edition

Printed in the United States of America

♾ This edition is printed on acid-free paper that meets the American National Standards Institute Z39.48 Standard.
♻ This book was printed on 30% postconsumer recycled paper. For more information please visit us at www.shambhala.com.
Distributed in the United States by Random House, Inc.,
and in Canada by Random House of Canada Ltd

Designed by Gopa & Ted2, Inc.

The Library of Congress catalogues the hardcover edition of this book as follows:
Thinley Norbu.
A cascading waterfall of nectar / Thinley Norbu.
p. cm.
Includes bibliographical references and index.
ISBN 978-1-59030-338-2 (alk. paper)
ISBN 978-1-59030-526-3 (pbk: alk. paper)
1. Bdud-'joms-glin-pa, Gter-ston, b. 1835. Snon 'gro bsdus pa. 2. Spiritual life—Rqin-ma-pa (Sect). I. Bdud-'joms-glin-pa, Gter-ston, b. 1835. Snon 'gro bsdus pa. English II. Title.
BQ7662.6.B373T56 2006
294.3'444—dc22
2006000812

Contents

༄། དུས་གསུམ་རྒྱལ་བ་ཡོངས་ཀྱི་སྤྱི་གཟུགས་འཕྱུར་འགྲོའི་སློབ་དཔོན་ཆེན་པོའི་རྒྱལ་ཚབ་གཏེར་ཆེན་དམ་པ་འཇིགས་བྲལ་ཡེ་ཤེས་རྡོ་རྗེའི་དགོངས་པའི་གསང་མཛོད་ལས། ཁྱད་པར་དེང་དུས་འགྲོ་བ་རྣམས་ལ་ཐུགས་བརྩེ་བ་ཆེན་པོས་སྔོན་འགྲོ་བླ་མའི་རྣལ་འབྱོར་འཕོ་བ་དང་བཅས་པ་ཚིག་ཚོགས་ཉུང་ལ་བྱིན་རླབས་ཆེ་བའི་དམ་ཆོས་ཁྱད་པར་དུ་འཕགས་པ་དེ་ལ་བཀའ་དྲིན་ཟླ་མེད་གང་གི་གདུང་སྲས་འཕྲིན་ལས་ནོར་བུ་མཆོག་གིས་ཐུགས་བརྩེ་བ་ཆེན་པོས། བདག་སོགས་སློབ་འབངས་རྣམས་ལ་གསལ་འདེབས་སླ་བའི་ཆེད་དུ་བློ་གྲོས་ཡངས་པོར་འབྱེད་པའི་འགྲེལ་བ་བསྒྲུབ་པ་འདི་ནི། སྐྱེས་འགྲོ་སྤྱི་དང་རང་ཅག་སྒྲ་འགྱུར་བའི་རྗེས་འཇུག་རྣམས་ལ་འདི་ཕྱི་ཀུན་ཏུ་ཕན་པའི་གདམ་ཟབ་མཆོག་ཏུ་གྱུར་པར་ངེས་པས་རང་ནས་དགའ་བས་རྗེས་སུ་ཡི་རང་དང་། དེའི་མཐུས་ལུས་ཅན་ཀུན་གྱི་སྲིད་རྩ་རྨང་མེད་དུ་འཇོམས་ནས་མཐར་ཐུག་དཔལ་ལྡན་བླ་མ་མཆོག་གི་ཐུགས་དང་དབྱེར་མེད་གཅིག་ཏུ་འདྲེས་ནས་འོད་གསལ་འཕོ་བ་ཆེན་པོའི་སྐུར་ཐོབ་པར་འགྱུར་བའི་གསོལ་འདེབས་དང་བཅས། ཤིང་སྤྲེལ་ཟླ་བ་བདུན་པའི་ཚེས་གཅིག་དགེ་བའི་ཉིན་མཆོག་གསུམ་བདེན་བསྒྲུལ་སྔོན་དུ་འགྲོ་བས་དམ་པ་གང་གི་ཞབས་རྡུལ་སྤྱི་བོར་ལེན་པ་དཔལ་སྤྲུལ་པདྨ་ནོར་བུས་སྤེལ།། །།

Foreword

BY HIS HOLINESS PENOR RINPOCHE

THE REGENT OF PADMASAMBHAVA, embodiment of all the Buddhas of the three times, is the great tertön Tragtung Düdjom Lingpa. From the Infinity of Pure Wisdom Phenomena of Tragtung Düdjom Lingpa, full of blessings, this sublime concise Preliminary Practice, including profound Guru Yoga and Phowa, is kindly revealed to all sentient beings of this modern time.

His Holiness Jigdral Yeshe Dorje wrote a brief guide to *The Concise New Treasure Preliminary Practices.* And now Dungse Thinley Norbu Rinpoche, the son of the incomparably compassionate Jigdral Yeshe Dorje, has kindly written this very detailed commentary on this concise Preliminary Practice for all of us students, giving us clear instructions and helping our minds open.

This supreme profound pith commentary will definitely benefit all sentient beings and especially followers of the Nyingma tradition, in this and all future lives.

I, Padma Norbu, with great joy, pray that through this precious Ngöndro commentary all sentient beings may purify the root basis of samsara. May all sentient beings be indivisible with the wisdom mind of the glorious Lama. May they obtain the ultimate clear wisdom light body of Great Transformation.

With this prayer to the Triple Gems and with deep respect to Thinley Norbu Rinpoche, I, Padma Norbu, wrote this on the first virtuous day of the seventh month of the wood monkey year.

སྔོན་འགྲོའི་ཞུ་ཚིག

ན་མོ་གུ་རུ། ཁྲག་འཐུང་བདུད་འཇོམས་གླིང་པའི་གཏེར་གསར་སྔོན་འགྲོའི་ཁྲིད་ཡིག་གོ་བདེ་ཆུ་འབབ་ཀྱི་ཚུལ་དུ་བཀོད་པ། ཞེས་བྱ་བ་འདི་ནི་རྣམ་འདྲེན་ཟས་གཙང་སྲས་པོས་ཆོས་ཀྱི་འཁོར་ལོ་རིམ་པ་གསུམ་དུ་བསྐོར་བའི་བཀའི་དགོངས་པ་འགྲེལ་བའི་བསྟན་བཅོས་ཏེ། དེ་ཡང་སྲས་བཅས་རྒྱལ་བའི་ཡེ་ཤེས་དམ་པའི་རང་གཟུགས་གསང་ཆེན་བསྟན་པའི་བདག་པོ་སིནྡྷུ་རྒྱ་མཚོ་རོལ་པའི་མཚོ་གླིང་དུ་རང་བྱུང་ཐོལ་སྐྱེས་སུ་བྱོན་པ་དཔལ་ཨོ་རྒྱན་སྣང་སྲིད་ཟིལ་གནོན་གང་དང་དགོངས་པ་དབྱེར་མེད་པའི་ཐུགས་སྲས་རྗེ་འབངས་ཉེར་ལྔའི་ཡ་གྱལ། འཇིག་རྟེན་མིག་གཅིག་ཁྲིའུ་ཆུང་ལོ་ཙཱ་བ་མཆོག་གཏེར་གྲུབ་བརྙེས་རིག་པ་འཛིན་པའི་དབང་ཕྱུག་ཏུ་ཞལ་བསྒྱུར་བ། ཁྲག་འཐུང་བདུད་འཇོམས་གླིང་པ་ཞེས་ཡངས་པའི་ས་ཆེན་འདི་ལ་ཡོངས་སུ་གྲགས་ཤིང་གྲུབ་པ་དེ་ཉིད་ཀྱི་སྐུ་ཕྲེང་གཉིས་པ། དོན་དམ་པར་ཀུན་བཟང་གདོད་མའི་སངས་རྒྱས་ཀྱི་ངོ་བོར་བཞུགས་ཀྱང་། ཚུར་མཐོང་གདུལ་བྱའི་སྣང་ངོར་གཏེར་འབྱིན་གྲུབ་པའི་དབང་ཕྱུག་གནས་ལྔ་རིག་པའི་པཎ་ཆེན་གྱི་རྣམ་པར་སྣང་བ། འཇིགས་བྲལ་ཡེ་ཤེས་རྡོ་རྗེ་ཞེས་ཡངས་པའི་རྒྱལ་ཁམས་ཀུན་ཏུ་ཉི་ཟླ་ལྟར་གསལ་བ་མཆོག་གི་གསང་བ་བསམ་མི་ཁྱབ་པའི་ཡོན་ཏན་རིགས་སྲས་ཀྱི་རྣམ་པར་བཞེངས་པ། དགོས་པའི་སླད་དུ་མཚན་ནས་བརྗོད་ན་ ༄སྐྱབས་རྗེ་འཇིགས་མེད་ཆོ་དབང་འཕྲིན་ལས་ནོར་བུ་ཕྱོགས་ཐམས་ཅད་ལས་རྣམ་པར་རྒྱལ་བའི་སྡེ་ཞེས་གྲགས་པ་མཆོག་ནི་ཁྲིད་ཡིག་འདི་ཉིད་མཛད་པ་པོ་ཡིན་ཏེ། དམ་པ་གང་ནི་ཀུན་རྫོབ་ཀྱི་འཕྲིན་ལས། དོན་དམ་གྱི་རྟོགས་པ་སོགས་ཆ་ཐམས་ཅད་ནས་གཏེར་འབྱིན་ཆོས་ཀྱི་རྒྱལ་པོ་དང་རྣམ་དབྱེར་མི་དམིགས་པ་ས་ཆེན་པོ་ལ་གནས་པའི་འཕགས་པ་རྣམས་ཀྱིས་མགྲིན་གཅིག་ཏུ་བསྔགས་སོ། །གྲུབ་པའི་དབང་ཕྱུག་འདི་ཉིད་ཀྱི་མཁྱེན་རབ་ཀྱི་རྩལ་ཡི་གེའི་རྣམ་པར་ཤར་བའི་བསྟན་བཅོས་ཇི་སྙེད་ཅིག་བཞུགས་པ་ལས་སྔོན་འགྲོའི་འགྲེལ་བ་འདི་ཉིད་མཁས་པས་བརྟགས་ན་དོན་

བཟང་བ། ཐོས་ཆུང་རྣམས་ཀྱང་འཇུག་བདེ་བ། སྦྱོར་བ་རྒྱ་མི་ཆེ་བས་འཛིན་བདེ་ཞིང་གོ་སླ་བ། བརྒྱུད་པའི་མན་ངག་གིས་བརྒྱན་པས་བྱིན་རླབས་དང་དངོས་གྲུབ་མྱུར་བ། མདོར་ན་རྗོད་བྱེད་ཚིག་གི་སྦྱོར་བ་ལེགས་ཤིང་། བརྗོད་བྱ་དོན་གྱི་དགོངས་པ་ཟབ་པ། རྒྱལ་བའི་བསྟན་པ་མ་ལུས་པའི་སྙིང་ཆིངས་སུ་གྱུར་པས་ཐར་འདོད་རྣམས་ལ་ལྟ་བའི་མིག་སྦྱིན་པ། སྙིགས་དུས་ཀྱི་ཆོས་གཟུགས་ཡིད་ཀྱི་གླང་ཆེན་རབ་ཏུ་མྱོས་ཏེ་རང་བཞིན་ངན་པ་གཞུ་ལྟར་འཁྱོག་པའི་དུག་གསུམ་གྱི་ཁྲན་མོ་དག་གིས་ཀྱང་ལན་གཅིག་ཀློག་པས་ངེས་འབྱུང་དང་བྱང་སེམས། ཡང་དག་པའི་ལྟ་བས་བསྡུས་པའི་རྣམ་པར་དཀར་བའི་རྟོག་པ་རྒྱུད་ལ་སྐྱེས་ཤིང་། བརྒྱུད་གསུམ་རིག་འཛིན་བླ་མའི་དོན་བརྒྱུད་ཀྱི་ཕ་ཡོག་སྙིང་གི་ཡོལ་གོར་བྲི་བ་མེད་པར་འབྲེལ་བས་རིམ་གཉིས་ཀྱི་རྟོགས་པ་མིག་འཕྲུལ་ལྟར་སྐྱེས་ཏེ་འཇའ་ལུས་འཕོ་བ་ཆེན་པོའི་གོ་འཕང་མངོན་དུ་བྱེད་པར་གདོན་མི་ཟའོ། །དེ་ལྟར་གང་ཟག་སོ་སོའི་བློ་དང་འཚམས་པའི་མན་ངག་གི་བདུད་རྩི་འཛད་མེད་དུ་འཇོ་བའི་གཏེར་གྱི་བུམ་པ་འདི་ཉིད།སྤྱང་རྟོགས་ཀྱི་ཡོན་ཏན་གང་གི་ཆ་ནས་ཀྱང་འཕགས་ཡུལ་གྱི་གྲུབ་ཆེན་རྣམས་དང་དབྱེར་མི་ཕྱེད་པ་མདོ་མཁྱེན་བརྩེ་ཡེ་ཤེས་རྡོ་རྗེའི་སྐུ་ཕྲེང་དང་གདན་ས་འཛིན་པ་༧ཨ་ལག་གཟན་དཀར་རིན་པོ་ཆེ་ཐུབ་བསྟན་ཉི་མས་ཐུགས་བསྐྱེད་ཀྱིས་གཅིག་ལས་དུ་མར་འཕྲུལ་བའི་པར་བསྐྲུན་དགེ་ལེགས་ཀྱི་སྣང་བ་གསར་དུ་བཞད་པའི་དུས་སུ། ཀཿཐོག་རིག་འཛིན་ཆེན་པོའི་མཚན་ཙམ་སྤྱི་བོར་འཛིན་པའི་གྱི་ན་བ་པདྨ་དབང་ཆེན་གྱིས་ཤིང་མོ་བྱ་ལོའི་སྟོན་ཟླ་ར་བའི་དམར་ཕྱོགས་མཁའ་འགྲོ་འདུ་བའི་དུས་བཟང་ལ་མཁའ་འགྲོ་བདེ་ཆེན་རྒྱལ་མོའི་ཚོགས་མཆོད་དང་འབྲེལ་དགའ་དད་རྗེས་སུ་ཡི་རང་གི་ངང་ནས་བྲིས་པ་ཛ་ཡནྟུ།། །།

Foreword

BY KATHOG RIGDZIN PEMA WANGCHEN RINPOCHE

Homage to the Guru.

This easily understood commentary, flowing like a cascading waterfall, on *The Concise New Treasure Preliminary Practices* of Tragtung Düdjom Lingpa, is in the category of shastra. Shastras are defined as texts written by sublime beings about Buddha Shakyamuni's teachings, mainly the three turnings of the Wheel of Dharma.

The embodiment of all the Buddhas and Bodhisattvas is Guru Padmasambhava, who manifested on the Island of Sindhu Lake. Padmasambhava's twenty-five disciples, King and subjects, are the indivisible wisdom mind of Guru Padmasambhava. The light of the world, the great translator Khye'uchung Lotsawa, most realized Vidyadhara, is one of these twenty-five wisdom-mind disciples of Guru Padmasambhava. Khye'uchung Lotsawa manifested as Tragtung Düdjom Lingpa, who is known as the great Vajrayana master of this great earth. The second reincarnation is His Holiness Düdjom Rinpoche, in essence the originally pure nature of Buddha Samantabhadra. In the eyes of ordinary sentient beings, His Holiness Düdjom Rinpoche is perceived as a great tertön and most realized compassionate wisdom being, as well as a Mahapandita who mastered the five major sciences. His Holiness Düdjom Rinpoche's inconceivable secret wisdom qualities illuminate all countries of the world like the light of the sun and moon.

The author of this commentary is a son of His Holiness Düdjom Rinpoche's wisdom body, speech, and mind. Jigme Tsewang Thinley Norbu Chogley Nampar Gyalway De is the author's full name. All sublime beings agree that Thinley Norbu Rinpoche's everyday activities and ultimate realizations are indivisible with his father, His Holiness Düdjom Rinpoche, the great king of treasure revealers. Most realized Thinley Norbu Rinpoche's wisdom is manifested here in a written form. If learned people analyze this book they will find profound sublime meaning. Ordinary people will find this book easy to read and understand, without too many complex details.

This commentary is endowed with the upadesha and full blessings of the wisdom lineage and will bring swift accomplishment.

In brief, this commentary (written in Tibetan) uses beautifully chosen words to express the meanings, and the meanings are the profound wisdom knowledge of Buddha. This commentary contains the essence of all the teachings of Buddha, shining a wisdom light for those of us seeking liberation.

Even a person of this degenerate age with an outer Dharma form and the inner corrupted mind of a crazed wild elephant, overpowered by bad habits of the three poisons, by reading this commentary once will realize the benefits of renunciation and bodhichitta. Positive thoughts of Dharma will rise in one's mind. The ultimate wisdom blessings of the three lineages coming through the awareness holder Guru will fill one's heart. The two stages of realization will be swiftly attained, and without doubt one will attain the great transformation of rainbow light body.

Alak Zenkar Rinpoche, the present seat holder and incarnation of Do Khyentse Yeshe Dorje, whose wisdom quality of realization equals that of the ancient Mahasiddhas of the holy land of India, requested that I write this for the occasion of celebrating the new virtuous phenomenon of printing many copies from one master copy of Thinley Norbu Rinpoche's treasure vase filled with the inexhaustible nectar of pith instructions for all sentient beings.

I, Pema Wangchen, merely holding the name of Kathog Rigdzin Chenpo's tulku as a blessing on my crown chakra, wrote this joyfully on Dakini Day with the special offering tsok of the Queen of Great Bliss, during an autumn month of the wood bird year.

May the teachings be victorious!

Foreword

BY ALAK ZENKAR RINPOCHE

ALTHOUGH I NEVER MET His Holiness Düdjom Rinpoche in person, I have a strong feeling of meeting him when encountering Thinley Norbu Rinpoche, the true son of his body, speech, and mind. He is the son of Kyabje Düdjom Rinpoche's Body, and their physical resemblance becomes more and more striking with the passing of time. He is the son of Kyabje Düdjom Rinpoche's Speech, as when I read some of these two great teachers' writings, I am struck by the resemblance in the clarity and depth. He is the son of Kyabje Düdjom Rinpoche's Mind, as I became convinced that their wisdom, compassion, and ability are indistinguishable.

In this commentary upon the renowned Preliminary Practices composed by Kyabje Düdjom Rinpoche, Dungse Thinley Norbu Rinpoche bestows instructions suited to all kinds of practitioners, endowed with high, medium, or ordinary faculties. In a text that is concise, yet of great depth, Thinley Norbu Rinpoche offers us all the pith instructions needed to practice in an authentic way the various stages of the path. These instructions will be vastly beneficial to practitioners of all levels and will engender deep confidence in their minds. Such essential instructions are truly sufficient if one is fortunate enough to put them into practice, and sadly wasted if one ignores them. I am therefore deeply thankful to Thinley Norbu Rinpoche to have granted them to the practitioners desirous of seriously engaging in spiritual practice.

Foreword

BY TULKU THONDUP RINPOCHE

The Outer and Inner Preliminary Practices
With supplementary training on Transference of Consciousness
Embody all the teachings of the Buddha,
The treatises of the omniscient lineage masters, and
The quintessence of all instructions that lead us
to Buddhahood in one lifetime.
—Paltrul Rinpoche

A Cascading Waterfall of Nectar is a great original work and the enlightened vision of one of the greatest realized Nyingma masters of our age, Thinley Norbu Rinpoche. Its incisive reasoning and scriptural citations deepen our understanding of the holy Dharma. It condenses different paths of training taught by the Buddha to fulfill the needs of diverse audiences into a single volume. Profound philosophical standpoints and meditative trainings of sutras and tantras and especially of tranquil stillness (*Zhi gnas*) and true seeing (*Lhag mthong*) are presented with interpretations by different Buddhist masters of the past. The absolute teachings on the primordially pure great emptiness nature (*Ka dag*) and self-accomplishing clear light vision (*Lhun grub*) of Dzogpa Chenpo are the heart of this volume.

The main body of this book is a commentary by Thinley Norbu Rinpoche on *The Concise Preliminary Practices* (*sNgon 'gro bsdus pa*) of Düdjom Tersar, new treasures revealed by Düdjom Lingpa (1835–1903). Born in Serta Valley of Golok in East Tibet, Düdjom Lingpa founded the Düdjom Tersar tradition. Thinley Norbu Rinpoche is the eldest son of the reincarnation of Düdjom Lingpa, Kyabje Düdjom Rinpoche (1904–1987).

Although called "Preliminary Practices," the text is actually a manual of stages of mind training that leads even beginners to the ultimate goal, Buddhahood.

The Buddha said, "Mind is chief, and the forerunner of all happenings." If our mind is in peace, whatever we say and do will be the expression of that peace. Then whatever we do will turn into peaceful and beneficial services for others. So training the mind is essential to improve our life and those of all humanity.

According to Buddhism, the true nature of our mind is enlightened, and the realization of the true nature is instantaneous. But to reach that point, we must rely on others' support and go through the stages of training that the Preliminary Practices fully provide.

In Buddhism there are three major paths of training, called vehicles (Skt. yana). The Hinayana teaches students to avoid sources of emotional afflictions by, for instance, living in solitude or celibacy. The Mahayana teaches followers to take the responsibility of serving all mother-beings and to deal directly with sources of emotional afflictions like anger by applying antidotes like compassion. The Vajrayana teaches adherents to accept and transform all as wisdom and wisdom power by realizing everything as the enlightened nature and qualities.

The Preliminary Practices embody all three vehicles. The text begins with the four Common Outer Preliminary Practices to inspire us to Dharma and to renounce mundane life. We meditate on the preciousness and rarity of our human life; the impermanence of life and the world; the principle of karma, in which everything happens due to causation; and the suffering inherent in samsara, mundane life.

When we realize the truth of samsara, we will want to liberate ourselves and others. For this we rely on enlightened ones who are beyond samsaric control. We invoke the blessings of the compassionate and enlightened refuges and meditate on the five Uncommon Inner Preliminary Practices for the sake of all mother-beings:

We commit ourselves to Dharma and become Buddhists by taking refuge in the Buddha as the guide, the Dharma as the path, and Buddhists as our supporting community.

We establish the foundation of the Mahayana by developing the enlightened aspiration of taking responsibility to bring happiness to all mother-beings and lead them to enlightenment, and by putting such aspirations into practice through the six perfections.

We accumulate merits, the force of positive conditions, by offering the whole of existence as the mandala, the assembly of pure offerings, to the refuges.

We purify all negative conditions by visualizing the source of purification, Vajrasattva, above us, developing strong regrets for whatever evil we have committed, and making a commitment not to repeat it. Then, saying prayers, we meditate on washing away our afflictions in the form of filth from our body through the stream of the Buddha's blissful blessing nectar without leaving any trace behind.

The heart of the Inner Preliminary Practices is Guru Yoga, a training based on pure perception of Vajrayana and realization of the true nature of the mind of Dzogpa Chenpo. We visualize ourselves as Vajrayogini, and Guru Rinpoche in front of us as the source of blessing. We pray and meditate on the sevenfold devotional trainings: paying homage, making offerings, purifying impurities, rejoicing over all virtue, praying to the Enlightened Ones to teach and have a long life, and dedicating all our merits for the enlightenment of all.

We receive the blessing lights of Guru Rinpoche's vajra body, speech, mind, and wisdom, purifying the obscurations of our body, speech, mind, and the basis of all, thus enabling us to attain the four Buddha-bodies.

At the end, Guru Rinpoche melts into a ball of five-colored light and merges into us. Our mind and Guru Rinpoche's enlightened mind become indivisible. With that realization and confidence, we rest in contemplating the true nature of the mind, the union of the primordially pure emptiness nature and self-accomplishing clear light qualities of Dzogpa Chenpo. When we perfect such realization, we attain the fully enlightened state, Buddhahood with three Buddha-bodies and five primordial wisdoms.

As a supplement to the Preliminary Practices, the meditation on the transference of consciousness (*'Pho ba*) is an important training. If we are unable to perfect our realization in this life, we could still take rebirth in a pureland by meditating on the transference of consciousness and attain enlightenment there.

The second part of this book is another commentary by Thinley Norbu Rinpoche on the "Fulfillment (*bsKang ba*) Liturgy of the Dakinis" by Kyabje Düdjom Rinpoche, who was a great tertön, a celebrated scholar, and the Supreme Head of the Nyingma school of Tibetan Buddhism for decades. This commentary explains the meaning of this text and illuminates vast bodies of important tantric teachings.

Author's Preface

In general, each Buddhist tradition, from the Hinayana up to Mahamudra and Mahasandhi, has preliminary practices, or ngöndro (*sngon 'gro*), that are supposed to precede main practices such as the practices of visualization and completion stages. As an example of the importance of the preliminary practices, if someone wants to build a special house or temple, the most important part of the construction is the foundation in order for the building to be stable.

Even though the main target of attaining fully enlightened Buddhahood is the same in different Buddhist traditions, there are different methods and different objects of prayers or visualization. The preliminary practices presented here are from the Nyingma, or Old Tradition. In the Nyingma tradition, there are two categories of teachings: kama, the tradition of oral transmission, and terma, the treasure tradition. The oral transmission tradition is an unbroken lineage from the beginning from Samantabhadra or Vajradhara up to now. The treasure tradition is revealed by treasure holders.

Some Buddhist doctrinaires do not believe in the treasure tradition, which often includes prophecies; those nonbelievers have very limited faculties. From the Hinayana up to the Mantrayana, including in the Golden Age, there have been predictions about sublime beings who would appear in particular places at particular times in the future to impart the teachings of the Buddha. Of course, individual hypocrites can appear anywhere and anytime, but the Mantrayana teachings and treasure traditions, including where, when, by whom, and what kind of teachings would be revealed, have been predicted by sublime beings, including Buddha Shakyamuni. These are not just ordinary oracle blurting.

The first commentary in this book, *An Easily Understood Commentary Flowing Like a Cascading Waterfall on "The Concise New Treasure Preliminary Practices" from the Section of Teachings of the Infinity of Pure Wisdom Phenomena of Tragtung Düdjom Lingpa*[1] is on the brief root preliminary

1. The commentary was published in Tibetan under the title *khrag 'thung bdud 'joms gling pa'i*

practice prayer from the treasure of Tragtung Düdjom Lingpa.[2] Before Tragtung Düdjom Lingpa emanated in Serthang in Golok, in East Tibet, more than thirty sublime beings who came before him, including the Great Treasure Revealer Rigdzin Düddul Dorje, very, very clearly predicted that he would be born and what he would reveal. Whoever wants to know about this in more detail can read the prayer about the emanations of Kyabje Düdjom Rinpoche called *The Pearl Rosary*, written by Kyabje Düdjom Rinpoche, and the commentary on it that I have written, called *The Ruby Rosary That Is Joyfully Accepted by Vidyadharas and Dakinis as the Ornament of a Necklace.*[3]

Even though the present writing is called a commentary on the preliminary practices, it actually includes discussion of many main practices, so whatever is read can be read thoroughly, and it will be beneficial.

This book also contains *A Commentary on the Meaning of "The Continuously Blossoming Rosary of the Lotus Assembly Palace" Called The Light Rays of the Youthful Sun,* which I have written for the root text prayer of Kyabje Düdjom Rinpoche.[4]

In preparing the English-language edition of this book, some new words have been made in order to talk about Buddhism. Sometimes making the language too correct in English is very awkward, since in English there are no terms for a subjectless, objectless spiritual state or immaterial openness light, and it is very hard for those using proper English to understand the meaning. Even professors and scholars in universities, translators of Tibetan, and those studying Asian religion for many years have misinterpretations, because they get lost without making some kind of object or subject or certain identification, and when they don't have a nondual view, it is very hard for them to believe in a nondual state. In Western terms there is either a totally eternalist concept, with object and subject, or a nihilistic concept, with nil, so there is no idea about dharmadhatu, forever stainless space,

dag snang ye shes drva ba'i chos sde'i khongs su bzhugs pa'i gter gsar sngon 'gro bsdus pa'i khrid yig go bde chu 'babs kyi tshul du bkod pa bzhugs.

2. *Düdjom Tersar Ngöndro* (*bdud 'joms gter gsar sngon 'gro'i ngag 'don bsdus pa bzhugs, A Recitation of the Concise Preliminary Practices of the New Treasures of Düdjom*), by Tragtung Düdjom Lingpa (khrag 'thung bdud 'joms gling pa), the previous manifestation of Kyabje Düdjom Rinpoche (skyabs rje bdud 'joms rin po che).

3. Published in Thimphu, Bhutan; Taipei, Taiwan; and Chengdu, China.

4. The commentary in Tibetan is *tshogs khang pad ma'i rgyud mang gi don 'grel nyi ma gzhon nu'i 'od zer zhes bya ba bzhugs.* The root text prayer of Tsok Khang Dechen (tshogs khang bde chen, Assembly Palace of Great Exaltation) is *mkha' 'gro'i bskang bsdus pad ma'i rgyud mang zhes bya ba bzhugs.*

which is the origin of pure phenomena. So one has to be careful to avoid obscuration from overly fancy words or proper English, because nondoer speech does not exist in English.

I hope and pray that from the
illuminating rays of the sun of the holy Dharma mandala,
breezes of compassion emanate to cleanse all clouds of obscuration
so stainless wisdom sky is seen.
Thinley Norbu

An Easily Understood Commentary

Flowing Like

A Cascading Waterfall

on "The Concise New Treasure Preliminary Practices"

from the Section of Teachings of the

Infinity of Pure Wisdom Phenomena

of Tragtung Düdjom Lingpa

WELL, THEN,

> Philosophy is characterized by making categories,
> But synthesizing into the essence is upadesha.[1]

Thus it is said. Without following the tradition of philosophy, avoiding elaborations of describing many divisions and categories, this explanation is given like a cascading waterfall for the benefit of all new practitioners according to the tradition of upadesha in a way that is easily understood.

Namo in Sanskrit, or *phyag 'tshal lo* in Tibetan, means **homage.**[2] To whom? To the root **Lama.**[3] Who is that? The **deceitless, constant protector.** This is one's only root Lama, the constant protector, the embodiment of the Three Jewels, who shows self and all sentient beings the unmistaken, deceitless path leading from the white phenomena of the temporary happiness of higher states of gods and human beings until attainment of the ultimate white phenomena of the immortal bliss of the state of Buddha. **I beseech you to know me** means that from the three doors of faith—clear faith, enthusiastic faith, and confident faith—one requests to be held by the great kindness and compassion of the root Lama, praying from the heart.

Why is it necessary to rely on an undeceiving Lama? Are there deceivers? There is no doubt there are a great many. Who are they? They are those who are never worthy of trust because they represent all the causes and results of the suffering of samsaric phenomena. Where do they come from? They are from among all those who hold the various doctrines of eternalist views of this world. Each kind of eternalist has its own way of recognizing the meaning of its own gods, with different ways of describing how its gods created the world and different ways of worshiping its gods. Although there

1. Sanskrit *upadesha* is *man ngag* in Tibetan, which means pith instructions from the Guru.
2. The words of the root text are in boldface type.
3. bla ma; Skt. Guru.

are many differences among them, in synthesis, almost all eternalists decide that the ultimate basis of truth is believing only in their own god, and believing that no greater god exists beyond their own. Each is convinced that the essence of their god is permanent, and that their god has created the impermanent universe, all living beings, happiness, suffering, and so on. They believe that if their god is pleased, then the world will be a place of happiness. If their god is displeased, then the world will be a place where mistakes are made and torment and punishment are delivered.

To examine this logically according to Buddhist theory: if the essence of a god who created the world were permanent, unchanging, and enduring, it would be impossible for that god ever to perform actions to benefit or harm the world. Just as it is impossible for continuous showers of rain to fall from a cloudless, empty sky, so is it impossible for a god whose nature is forever unchanging and permanent to benefit or harm a world that is always changing and impermanent.

One might ask: "If, according to Buddhist doctrine, the state of holy Dharmakaya[4] is permanent, then how can Rupakaya[5] manifest from that?" Dharmakaya is not permanent in the same way as the imagined gods of eternalism. Buddhism does not focus on or define a particular, permanent god. According to the Buddhist view, the emanations of Rupakaya occur from the permanent, uncontrived nature of Dharmakaya, which is always inconceivable openness. No particles of substance exist in dharmadhatu,[6] which is perfectly pure and completely beyond the limitations of the two extreme views of eternalism and nihilism. The nature of Dharmakaya is the essence of Rupakaya, and Rupakaya is the inexhaustible self-manifestation of Dharmakaya. From the beginning, the qualities of Rupakaya cannot be separated from Dharmakaya by conceptualization. Acceptance of this view can therefore never be considered the same as the eternalist belief in a separate, distinct original source of all conceptual phenomena.

Those who hold the eternalist view believe that pleasing the gods leads to happiness for mankind, while displeasing the gods leads to suffering. If the gods' pleasure and displeasure are dependent on the root and contributing circumstances of other beings, this means that gods are not able to transcend changing phenomena. If a god relies on other beings, and if those

4. chos sku, completely pure formless form.
5. gzugs sku, enlightened embodiment of form, which includes Sambhogakaya and Nirmanakaya.
6. chos kyi dbyings, space of phenomena.

beings are impermanent, it means that the god is not permanent or unchanging. This reasoning demonstrates that the concept of establishing the essence of gods as permanent is a mere fabrication that cannot actually exist. If pleased gods deliver happiness to the world and displeased gods deliver suffering to the world, how can they possibly be pure or perfect? Even ordinary worldly beings respond to whoever is kind to them by returning their kindness to benefit them, and to whoever is unkind to them by returning their unkindness so as to take revenge on them, identifying them as enemies and so on. All beings react in this manner, from the power of aversion and attachment, as is obvious to everyone. Therefore, even though such activity seems to be temporarily beneficial for beings, if it is performed without great compassion, then helping other beings with the expectation of a result in return is only a worldly phenomenon. It is not appropriate to refer to this as the activity of gods.

Eternalists may think that Buddhists, too, say that happiness occurs when a deity is pleased and suffering occurs when the deity is displeased. According to the general Mahayana tradition, Buddha nature is within the minds of all beings in the same way that oil permeates a sesame seed. Once that nature awakens, until all habit is completely exhausted and the state of Buddha is attained, there will be gods and demons, depending on the good and bad habits of mind. Therefore, there will be suffering, and there will also be happiness. Accepting that, the way to attain constant bliss is to recognize that one's own mind is Buddha. Until one has completely perfected confidence in that state, one must rely on deities and the Three Jewels, believing with faith.

According to those who hold eternalist views, a permanent, unchanging, enduring god is established as always existing separately over there, and self and all sentient beings are established as existing separately over here, so eternalists always try to make a connection between gods and sentient beings without having any basis of a view that would enable this to occur. From a Buddhist view, trying to create this connection with eternalist beliefs is like hoping for water from a mirage. It is not possible. According to Buddhist beliefs, receiving the attainment of bliss and happiness from deities comes when one's own dualistic mind is purified into the power of truth of inherent wisdom deity, which blossoms subjectively through belief, faith, merit, and meditation. Finally, inherent subjective deity becomes indivisible with sole nonduality, which is called the result of the fully enlightened state, without falling to either objectivity or subjectivity. The immeasurable quality of this state of immaculate self-discerning wisdom is not known by any concept that belongs to egoism. It is forever wisdom body, wisdom mind, and wisdom pureland. Known by an omniscient stainless knower but not known by any obscured concept, it is inconceivable phenomena. This is different from the idea of a permanent, unchanging, enduring god who exists separately and who presents gifts, like one person giving a gift to another person. In the same way, the experience of suffering actually comes from the reflection of negative habit, which comes from one's own deluded mind. There is no particular enemy or demon who comes from elsewhere to impose harm. Therefore, according to Buddhist tantric teachings, everything taught about deities benefiting and harming is explained simply as the manifestation of one's own pure and impure mind appearing to itself. Unlike the doctrine of the eternalist view, whatever phenomena appear—including the entire universe and sentient beings, happiness and suffering, and so on—are thus not the creation of any god, nor do compassionate Buddhas and male and female Bodhisattvas ever punish sentient beings as in the eternalist way of thinking.

Nihilists, on the other hand, do not believe that all the phenomena of life come from root and contributing circumstances, thinking instead that everything just happens, like mushrooms suddenly springing up in meadows. Nihilists only accept root and contributing circumstances that occur within substance, and only believe in what their senses experience within this momentary life. They believe that mind ceases at the time of death, that there are no previous or future lives, and that there is definitely no karma of cause and result. In contrast to the nihilist view, just because one cannot see something does not mean it is non-existent. For example, a blind person cannot see, but others with clear vision can see. If something is unheard, it does not mean that it cannot exist. For example, a deaf person cannot hear, but others with a clear sense of hearing can hear. So even if an object is unseen or unheard by some, it can still exist and be known by others.

Although Buddhists do not accept the eternalist view that all appearances are created by gods, many sublime beings have affirmed that eternalism is much more optimistic and positive than nihilism. The eternalists' belief in a god gives them a positive goal, and through believing, they can ultimately find enlightenment. Even though their point of view is different from Buddhism, since eternalists are believers, their belief can someday cause their Buddha nature to open and they can believe in Buddha.

Among humans, nihilists are the most pitiful, because without belief there is no hope of stepping toward positive phenomena in the future. Even so, it cannot be denied that nihilists will be reborn within the realms of cyclic existence, since they have continuous mind and its habit. Since theirs is not a positive spiritual habit of belief, they must unavoidably follow the karma created by their disbelief. The positive potential of their Buddha nature and spiritual qualities of mind may remain dormant for many lives, so that it may take many eons for them to realize their Buddha nature.

According to the Mahayana, it cannot be said that nihilists always remain nihilists or eternalists always remain eternalists, because they can change through the influence of previous positive karmic connections, prayers, or blessings. Even inexperienced Buddhists can apostatize due to their previous nihilist habit of only expecting material answers, so that from a lack of experience and practice, when they do not get material answers, they give up. This shows that dharmata has not been realized. Sometimes beings who were misdirected as nihilists can gradually or suddenly rekindle the root circumstance of Buddha nature through contributing circumstances, such as spiritual teachers, and can step toward the path of enlightenment. All beings have the potential to transcend the limitations of nihilism and eternalism and to attain enlightenment.

According to the tradition of Buddhism, until the continuity of dualistic mind is purified in nondual unending wisdom awareness, there will be past and future lifetimes and karma and karmic results that unavoidably arise from mind through interdependence. Omniscient Rongzompa said:[7]

> Those who hold the view of eternalism believe that the great god Brahma is permanent, powerful gods are permanent,[8] ego is permanent, the nature of the elements is permanent, and particles of substance are permanent. From those beliefs in permanence, they claim that the impermanent world is compounded; they say that gods are permanent but can create phenomena that are impermanent.[9] Those who hold the view of nihilism believe that there are no karmic causes or karmic results, and that there is no need to do anything in a spiritual way about believing in practice,

7. The great omniscient master Rongzom Chökyi Zangpo (rong zom chos kyi bzang po; Skt. Dharmabhadra).

8. This permanence refers to eternalist gods such as the creator God of Christianity, Allah in Islam, and devas in Hinduism.

9. There are countless eternalist points of view and explanations of them, but the essence of any kind of eternalism can be synthesized into these few words.

worship, prayer to be reborn in a pureland, or enlightenment, because there is no thought of what is beyond the appearances of this momentary life, and there is no special quality to gain from the effort of activity. All of these various views are synthesized by Buddhism and called worldly views[10] because without giving up the view of a personal I or an existing self, there is no power to transcend the world. In this way, one always goes under the blanket of attachment to ego, so that negative karma cannot be transformed. Thus, karma cannot be changed, and then the result of karmic life cannot be changed. If one cannot be released from karma and its karmic life, then there is no liberation. This is what Buddhists believe.[11] In Buddhism, the outer and inner aspects of this material world are explained as the characteristics of cause and result that come from interdependent relative truth, agreed on by both the Great and Lesser Vehicles. It is said:

> All aspects of this outer and inner material world
> Were not created by gods,
> Were not made by a doer,
> Have not occurred naturally,
> Have not occurred without a cause,
> And are not changed by time.
> They only occur through the characteristics
> of the root and contributing circumstances
> of interdependent relative truth.
> Cause depends on result.
> Result depends on cause.
> Not occurring independently,
> Whenever root and contributing circumstances
> join together, then there is a result.

10. Eternalists and nihilists do not characterize their views as worldly. It is by Buddhism that these are synthesized and called worldly views.

11. We cannot practice unless we understand what nihilism is, what eternalism is, and what Buddhism is, and recognize the differences between them. If we do not understand these distinctions, it is like shooting arrows in the dark with no target. It is most important to analyze the differences, which does not mean that we are being sectarian. These are points of view, and without a point of view, we cannot practice.

If root and contributing circumstances do not join,
then nothing occurs.
It is impossible for root circumstances to be obstructed.
They only depend on the arising of contributing
circumstances.
So, when the passions and karma
And their suffering are all transcended,
Including one's own skandhas without anything remaining,
Then one attains the space of enlightenment.

Thus, that is the Buddhist belief.

Thus Rongzompa said.

In each eternalist religion, a supreme god is almost always considered to be the ultimate source of truth. There is always some uncertainty about eternalist beliefs, however, and it cannot be decided that any eternalist doctrine is definite or surely true. Although eternalism is based on belief in what will always exist, because beings and gods are always separated in eternalism, the connection between beings and gods can change. Therefore, the convictions of eternalists can change, which causes many different beliefs about gods, so that nothing can be decided on as sure.

Although followers of eternalist religions believe their god is supreme, which of course the followers of any religion must think, individuals have different views at different times and sometimes voluntarily change their views and religions. According to history, not just individual eternalists but eternalist doctrines have changed, adjusting to worldly social ideas of different times. Even when eternalists say they have one god, their views about their god are not necessarily the same; some views can be the same, and some can be different. Not only do followers of different eternalist religions have different views, such as Jews believing that the Messiah is coming and Christians believing that the Messiah already came; followers within the same eternalist religion have different views. In Islam, for example, some extremists believe in Allah's message to worship by sacrificing human beings, while others are against this extremist position. Even though eternalism is based on the sureness of permanence, if something is said to be definitely sure about one eternalist doctrine, it cancels the sureness of another doctrine, so any sureness creates more unsureness. Furthermore, if a god is considered to be a creator, then one cannot make something sure, because the possibilities for creation are supposed to be open so that something else can be created according to what beings wish. Therefore, from a Buddhist view, descriptions of eternalism must be left open and flexible, not trying to make them certain but letting them depend on differences in individual faculties and views.

There are many different eternalist gods, including the gods of religions that recognize one god and the gods of religions that have many gods, but it is unnecessary to name each one here or to describe each of their doctrines. It is taught in the sutras and shastras, as synthesized by Kunkhyen Rongzompa, that eternalists consider their gods to be absolute. From a Buddhist view, it is unnecessary to try to decide which of these gods is absolute, since whatever eternalists think is absolute is actually just beings' phenomena appearing according to time and place and is totally uncertain. With this uncertainty as its basis, eternalist history about gods cannot prove what is true or absolute. The many different histories about eternalist gods are not ultimate or believable because they only occur according to beings' phenomena. Beings concretize these histories, but they do not exist as reality in a solid way. It is also unnecessary to describe the differences in the characteristics of gods, to determine whether a god is mortal or immortal, or to pay attention to whether a god is worshiped by few or many. If each god were analyzed in detail by studying historical accounts and making endless conceptual observations, pretending to be scholarly, it would be materializing due to the lack of recognizing the nature of manifestation. This is what ordinary intellectual scholars do, and then they become attached to these details. If one materializes each detail, there are endless details, just as there are endless conceptions, but no wisdom.

If one becomes stuck in history, one is caught somewhere, even though history will not always be the same but can change. In Buddhism, the Yogachara, Madhyamika, Mahamudra, and Mahasandhi each have particular special explanations, but all teach about not remaining in two extremes. This is special because it is never caught anywhere. Being caught in the material, one believes in time, history, and beliefs held in common with others, but absolute truth is not established by the beliefs of everyone else. There is no majority or minority to accept or reject what is less or what is more. These do not matter; they are self-deceiving. For example, people think they can choose the right person for president, but the person they choose will change. Who is ultimate? Also, it is not certain when a majority elects a president whether that selection will later be considered a mistake and the beliefs of the majority will be considered false and deluded. According to delusion, delusion is believed to be the truth and becomes what is called true, but that truth does not exist from the beginning.

When a believer believes in a god and then compares gods to decide which god is greater and which is greatest, if the believer believes that one is lesser and one is greater based on historical recognition that has been given to these gods, it means the believer is accepting what others believe. If a god is considered to be lesser because the god is worshiped less often by fewer people than other gods, and a god is considered greater because a majority believes in that god, the importance of these gods is being determined only materially and is therefore deceptive. In this case, what seems to be eternalism is actually a misinterpretation of nihilism, which is disbelief in anything beyond the present reality of ordinary worldly perception and agreement with others. Actually, eternalists are not sure about anything; as much as they try to ascertain anything, their beliefs still do not connect with a point of view that provides certainty. This applies to the beliefs of all eternalist doctrines.

The Buddhist view is always flawless and absolute because it is always based on the state of immeasurable stainless space. From that state come the ultimate pure Buddhafields of Sambhogakaya, and from that state come the infinite manifestations of Nirmanakaya. Buddhism is beyond eternalism, but Buddhism never denies phenomena, which are always unobstructed and can arise according to time and place. That does not mean they arise only in one way, because they are never stuck in time and place. The Buddhist view is beyond time and place because there is always stainless, immeasurable empty space, so it never falls to time and place; it also never falls to nothingness because phenomena appear in time and place as manifestations wherever beings' phenomena occur, not fixed by conceptualization or materialization. There is not only nothingness because there is always, and always can manifest.

Buddhist teachings begin in a beginninglessly pure way, so the path is naturally clean and easy. In Buddhism, whatever eternalist beliefs are held are not denied, although Buddhism does not accept the eternalist's supreme view or totally believe in eternalist characterizations of gods. The Buddhist view is that anything can appear to benefit beings according to their different faculties, without attempting to assure that anything is definite. Therefore, when Buddhism explains eternalist and nihilist views, and that eternalism has many different views, while Buddhism does not accept these views as ultimate, there is no objection to whatever gods appear according to eternalism, which depends on time and individual capacity. Also, since Buddhism teaches that there is manifestation, although these manifestations are fully enlightened, they can appear in any impure or pure aspect depending on time and individual beings' faculties resulting from previous karma.

Generally, in Buddhism, gods are considered not ultimate but temporary because gods themselves cannot give up a self. That is why Kunkhyen Rongzompa identifies eternalist gods as worldly deities. As long as there is a self, there are always passions, there is always karma, and there is always change. There is nothing absolute. There is no view of how to reach the fully enlightened state that is connected with eternalist gods, whose histories occur within different times and places. Whether time is brief, long-lasting, or many eons, it is a temporary appearance that belongs to beings, depending on beings' habit or manifesting from Buddhas according to beings' faculties. Even though time and place do not exist and are just conception, whoever has not realized the fully enlightened state believes in a reality of time and place. Buddhas have no time or place, but Buddhas manifest within time and place for the benefit of beings. They are called fully enlightened because there is nothing trapped in time. Buddhas' inconceivable wisdom is forever abiding in unwavering stainless Dharmakaya, never remaining in the habit of a certain place.

Buddha has purified self, so that is why Buddha is fully enlightened. Because eternalism does not give up the view of an existing self, whether a god is considered intermediate or supreme, there is still the cause of passions and karma, even though the way the appearances of gods arise seems positive according to history or an individual's experience and excels beyond the appearances of ordinary human beings. Since self is not purified, self produces cause and effect. Whenever there is cause and effect, a possessor comes, and there is samsara no matter what aspect of gods arises.

This is the basic Buddhist view about the characteristics of gods. The contrast between eternalist and Buddhist views of gods is comparable to the contrast between the Western geographical system, which from a Buddhist perspective only concerns one small part of the phenomena of this world, and the Buddhist geographical system, which is about all phenomena and is related to sentient beings according to time and place. In the Buddhist view, one cannot make anything certain and sure. It is actually not good to try to make any kind of doctrine into something certain and sure, because if something is thought to exist only in a definite way, its reliability will eventually fail.

It is important not to compare eternalist gods, but to differentiate between the characteristics of wisdom, and then it will not be necessary to deny any gods' doctrines, which are infinite. They have existed before, they exist now, and they will exist in the future because of beings' phenomena, which are the general source of eternalist beliefs, and what arises is believed depending on beings' time and place. The eternalist belief that a god is absolute is only conceptual within time and place. Even if one tries to determine what is absolute according to an eternalist view, whatever is found will be conditional, compounded, and temporary because it is conceptual. Even though there is belief in permanence, where does anything exist permanently? If something exists permanently, it cannot manifest anything because it is frozen, without mind, spirit, or wisdom. Even when considering absolute truth, by excessively concretizing absolute truth due to inflexibility, it will become diminishable and will not turn to a pivotal state or quality.

As the supreme Nyingma wisdom scholars Dharmabhadra, Kunkhyen Longchenpa, and Mipham Rinpoche explained based on the teachings of Buddha Shakyamuni, the fully enlightened state is Buddhahood, which is omniscient. At that time, it does not matter who is considered to be great, greatest, or absolute, since this measurement does not go beyond conception. In Buddhism, there is nothing more omniscient than Buddha, yet this is not an eternalist view. What is Buddhism? In brief, it is beyond eternalism and nihilism, and neither of these views is accepted or denied. As Kunkhyen Longchenpa said:

> Self is Samantabhadra, other is Samantabhadra, eternalism is Samantabhadra, nihilism is Samantabhadra.
> In the expanse of Samantabhadra, there is no self, other, eternalism, or nihilism.

Buddhism always accepts that different doctrines occur to benefit beings according to their faculties, but Buddhism does not take the side of permanence as eternalists do. Also, Buddhism does not take the side of nothingness as nihilists do, because there are always phenomena. As much as there is inconceivable empty space, that much do appearances arise, so Buddhism never remains in a nihilist view. Buddhism explains that the nature of truth is inconceivable, beyond expressibility, so a certain time or direction cannot be made for it in a certain way. Individually or according to the shared agreement of complementary groups, a time or direction can temporarily be made if one wishes, but it actually is not going to be that way, because it is compounded by substance habit and conceptualized, and will diminish. As it says in Sutra:

> Instantly for some beings,
> Slowly for some beings,
> Depending on what beings want,
> Buddha emanates whatever time is ripening.

One is supposed to believe this. General beings have different particular phenomena, so whatever is believed in eternalism only follows beings' phenomena. One cannot say any of these beliefs are absolute; whatever is said jumps between eternalism and nihilism. The activity of Buddhas always benefits beings, whether individually or collectively, yet it is beyond either eternalism or nihilism because it is manifestation. It is said:

> The consciousness of mind appears like time.

Time can occur as one instant or as many eons, but whether time seems to be short or long only depends on beings' habit. Even though it is said that there are many exact times, exact time does not exist. All time only depends on beings' habit of time, including any order of time as agreement between beings' concepts about whatever appears to be earlier or later. When history is created, it is predominantly about what is agreed on by a majority of people in particular times and places, but a reality of time does not exist that can be fixed. Even though fixation does not exist, beings create it, and then whatever is agreed on by a majority is thought to be absolute. It actually is not absolute, because this agreement can change, and a majority can become a minority. Just as there is no reliability of time, since time does not exist and is only conceptual, the histories of the gods of different eternalist religions do not exist and are all conceptual. Within time and place, arguments occur from the conceptions of order and disorder of majorities and minorities who try to solidify time and place, but it is easily recognized these arguments are only conceptions about time and place. Whatever appears will vanish, and whatever is not appearing will appear.

Time and place occur as the creations of karmic conception and habit, so arguing about time and place is absurd.

Fully enlightened Buddhahood does not have even an iota of samsaric phenomena because it is stainless, but it manifests as immeasurable phenomena such as Buddhafields without remaining in samsara even one moment because it is Dharmakaya, and at the same time it manifests for beings within ordinary phenomena, excelling beyond the ordinary. It is beyond eternalism and nihilism because it is inconceivable. This is not made up to be inconceivable by conception; it is totally beyond conception, even logically. One cannot judge these inconceivable manifestations or materialize them as occurring only in a certain way within time and place.

According to the Buddhist view, one cannot say the qualities of gods are certain. There are many gods, including worldly gods, pure worldly wisdom gods, and enlightened wisdom beings.

There are countless different beings, different faculties, and different stages of realization, so there are many categories of wisdom. There is wisdom that relies on compounded circumstances such as accumulation when all root and contributing circumstances gather together perfectly and wisdom occurs, and there is also self-manifesting wisdom that does not rely on compounded circumstances. Buddhist theory explains the difference between worldly wisdom, which surpasses ordinary intelligence but is not like the holy wisdom of sublime beings because it is still worldly; pure worldly wisdom, which is connected with holy wisdom and is the wisdom of Bodhisattvas who have wisdom mind and wisdom activities but are not fully enlightened, so even though it is not fully enlightened Buddhahood, holy mind and holy activities always occur to benefit beings; and the fully enlightened wisdom of Buddha, which is only beginningless wisdom.

From a Buddhist view, although eternalist gods are generally considered to be related to beings' phenomena and therefore connected to the stage of worldly wisdom, they can also be connected to the stage of pure worldly wisdom or the manifestation of enlightenment. When full enlightenment is reached, the same as Buddha, there are no stages, but continuous manifestations of wisdom appear to benefit beings unintentionally, including manifestations that can appear in the aspect of other doctrines' gods or deities and manifestations of Buddhas. Fully enlightened almighty wisdom can always manifest unobstructedly. As what? As anything, including, as nihilists wish, in ordinary beings' reality form, and also in eternalist gods' form.

Therefore, Buddhism accepts worldly wisdom gods, but not in the same way that eternalists do, because Buddhism distinguishes between stages of wisdom and their relation to sentient beings, eternalist gods, and enlightenment, recognizing the qualities of impurity, impure purity, and extreme purity that differentiate these categories. These qualities cannot be discerned by ordinary beings. Even though Buddhas are fully enlightened, since they can manifest as impure or pure, worldly gods and sublime beings are not necessarily totally separated since deciding who is worldly and who is sublime is uncertain unless it is based on wisdom.

Pure worldly wisdom is wisdom that occurs when entering the path of enlightenment and starting to practice so that wisdom mind is developing. It is not totally ordinary because wisdom is blossoming, yet it is not fully enlightened because it is still remaining in habitual samsaric phenomena. Wisdom has not fully expanded, but because it excels beyond ordinary beings, it is pure; yet residual habit still remains, so it is worldly, while excelling beyond the ordinary. Buddhism teaches that pure worldly wisdom is spiritual but not completely spiritual since it does not excel beyond worldliness if compared with the state of Buddha, which has no worldliness. Pure worldly wisdom is mixed, having both worldly and holy wisdom mind and activity. It is performing in samsara, but at the same time, it is not like other beings' extremely ordinary samsaric phenomena, because there is wisdom. Also, one cannot say that an aspect that seems to be mixed with worldliness cannot be enlightened, since enlightenment can manifest within worldliness. Enlightened wisdom beings can manifest in the aspect of pure worldly wisdom.

The beginningless wisdom of Buddhas is not ordinary beings' wisdom. When the state of full enlightenment is reached, there is no name of worldliness. One cannot only conceptualize this. Fully enlightened Buddhahood is full wisdom and full wisdom activity. Buddhas' mind is wisdom, but Buddhas such as Guru Rinpoche and many others emanate in samsara to benefit beings. Buddhas teach faith, meditation, and realization, manifesting in the state of impure worldly wisdom to guide others, but the mind is fully enlightened Buddhahood. This wisdom excels beyond samsara, but is performing in samsara. Buddha Shakyamuni manifested in samsara in order to guide beings by showing a history and an order of stages of how to enlighten, but Buddha does not have any conception of order. If there is no conception, there is no stage. When Buddhas emanate, they have to emanate according to beings' phenomena, showing histories to other beings, such as that of Buddha Shakyamuni learning, studying, and enduring hardship for six years so others can follow the example of these histories and open Buddha nature through practice, as Buddha taught according to Mahayana, until finally reaching the fully enlightened state in which there is no fixation of time, place, or direction, where all Buddhas abide. So, Buddhas manifest within pure worldly wisdom. Full enlightenment has no pure worldly wisdom, but the fully enlightened can still manifest anything, whether in male or female form or as any kind of being, in any world or realm, while their mind is fully enlightened. This way of excelling is not like stone; it does not appear and just remain as it is. Whatever excels does not stay in one state. Whatever is shown is like magic and will change miraculously. That is why whatever manifests cannot be made a certain way.

The power of manifestation is inconceivable, and it cannot be made conceivable. Even if one tries to make it conceivable to understand it or explain it, inconceivability means that there is nothing that can be conceived of in an ordinary way. It would be very tiring to try to describe the many different levels and qualities of all the different gods and deities, placing them within a framework of stages and trying to make them into something real or to determine whose qualities are greater. Whatever god is considered, too much materialization transforms into nihilism. It is enough to consider that manifestations of fully enlightened Buddhas appear in infinite forms to help beings.

It says many times in Buddhist sadhanas, and as the main key in many Vajrayana teachings of sublime beings including Nagarjuna, never to remain in one side. Never falling into eternalism, which is the view of always and does not change, or into nihilism, which is belief in whatever is present, all Buddhist views are beyond these two extremes; they cannot be made into something sure. Even though Buddhism talks about views, because Buddhism never falls to any extreme, there is no certain point of view, which has immeasurable meaning.

The state of Buddhas is always from beginninglessness between the two extremes, which is not creating a third neutral state; it has no determined expression, yet without determination it always unobstructedly manifests. By establishing this nature from the beginning, in which phenomena are not denied because manifestation is accepted, there is no danger of falling to nihilism because nothing is materialized. Without remaining in eternalism or nihilism, there is immeasurable manifestation, as the system of the Three Kayas shows. There is nothing stuck, because certain and uncertain manifestations occur endlessly as infinite forms, sounds, and wisdom only to benefit beings.

It is said in *The Jewel Treasure of the Dharmadhatu:*

> This is called the self-manifestation of enlightened mind.
> Its unobstructed emanation can occur as anything,
> With concept and without concept, as the existent phenomena of outer elements and inner beings,
> Including all varied phenomena.
> Even as all these arise, they naturally do not exist substantially.
> There is no such thing; there is not any permanent material nature.
> Just like the water of a mirage, a dream, an echo,
> Miraculous emanation, the reflection of form, a town of gandharvas, and the illusions of the eyes.
> It is just appearing. While it is appearing,
> There is no base, there is no substance; just recognize it as only sudden temporary appearances arising from time to time.
> It must be realized that phenomena are not always, but occasional.

If one materializes and conceptualizes, one cannot realize wisdom. To decide that something will always be the way it is, even though nothing solid exists, is the view of always. If one looks at one's own ordinary mind, it does not stay in a solid state in that way. One's own ordinary mind is going to change; there is not just one conception. To decide that there is nothing other than what is perceived is the view of nothing. If one looks at one's own ordinary mind, it is not inert; something continually appears. Buddhism's view is beyond the view of always and beyond the view of nothing. All samsaric phenomena are called samsara; all of the immeasurable enlightened state is coming from stainless dharmadhatu. This is the treasure of samsara and the treasure of enlightenment. This treasure never moved from anywhere to anywhere. It is seeing the nature of wisdom. There is no need to worry about anything if one synthesizes that all immeasurable samsara and enlightenment are coming from dharmadhatu. It is the treasure of samsara and enlightenment, but it is extremely pure itself, and has never moved from wisdom. This view is very important. There is no certain view. To try to make it certain can be damaging. If one recognizes this, one is not going to be stuck in some small matter. That means liberation.

Mind is not only material; it is immaterial and empty. It is not only empty now, but always empty. Since it is always empty, it is not nothingness but always wisdom inseparable with immeasurable emptiness. Since it is immeasurable emptiness, wisdom is always present, timelessly and directionlessly, inseparable with emptiness. How can one believe in making what does not exist into something real and certain? Buddha Shakyamuni said this is like babies grasping at rainbows.

The essence of immeasurable phenomena is emptiness. How can what gods are be made into absolute truth? With attachment to materialism, one always creates materializations. No matter what the absolute truth of eternalism may be, according to Dzogchen's point of view, although histories exist of gods and deities over many generations, they are still momentary. That is why worshiping a god is not ultimate, whether the god is worshiped by everyone or not. As Kunkhyen Longchenpa showed:

> In brief, from the self-accomplished openness of inner space,
> Even whatever arises of the unobstructed manifestation of samsara
> and enlightenment,
> Just as it arises, does not materially exist.
> Even whatever is dreamed from the emanations of sleep
> Actually does not exist and is just the bed of self-awareness ecstasy.
> Let the great expanse of equanimity's splendor pervade.

All immeasurable phenomena can be synthesized into the two categories of samsara and enlightenment. To take the immeasurable phenomena of samsara and enlightenment into the path of enlightenment by sustaining the effortless beginningless openness of dharmadhatu, what is found? Just as they arise, they do not exist in reality because they are manifestation. Whenever the phenomena of whatever one has, says, or thinks arise, even if one thinks of them for many eons, they are just arising; there is no reality. Even whenever one sleeps, it is still sustaining in dharmadhatu, because even sleep is the unobstructed state. Whenever dreams arise, there is no dream, because one is just staying in sole awareness mind. Like a bed, one is there relaxing. In unobstructed space, whatever comes, just as it arises, there is nothing exact, not any reality.

In summary, the outer container of the universe and the inner essence of sentient beings, all states of happiness and suffering, and so on that depend on the interdependent connection between root circumstances and contributing circumstances are rooted in the mind of duality, which creates everything. Since that is so, if one wonders where this mind of duality originates, it is as said in *The Prayer of Great Strength:*[12]

> Simultaneously born ignorance
> Is the dispersion of mindless unawareness.
> All-naming ignorance
> Is clinging to the duality of self and other.
> These two, simultaneously born ignorance and
> all-naming ignorance,[13]
> Are the cause of delusion for all sentient beings.

Thus it says. The cause from which delusion occurs is ignorance. Ignorance is the essence of stupidity, coming from the circumstance of the lack of recognition of awareness. From that, the way in which the phenomena of samsara are established is explained according to the traditions of Buddhism, such as the Vaibhashika,[14] Sautrantika,[15] Yogachara,[16] and so on, each of which has its own beliefs about the way in which outer and inner phenomena are established as material or immaterial. According to the special tradition of the Great Perfection,[17] Great Omniscient Longchen Rabjam said:

> The sun of absolute self-manifesting awareness
> Is obscured by both white and black clouds of virtue and nonvirtue.
> Misery comes from the lightning-like mind of attachment
> to the effort of accepting and rejecting.
> From the rainfall of deluded appearances of happiness and
> suffering continuously descending,
> The seeds of samsara grow in the field of crops of sentient
> beings of the six realms.
> Alas! Compassion arises for all pitiful, helpless ones.

12. *smon lam stobs po che.*
13. Simultaneously born ignorance: lhan cig skyes pa'i ma rig pa. All-naming ignorance: kun tu brtags pa'i ma rig pa.
14. Particularists, or bye brag tu smra ba.
15. Specialists in the scriptures, or mdo sde pa.
16. Practice and Conduct, or rnal 'byor spyod pa.
17. Dzogpa Chenpo; rdzogs pa chen po.

Thus, as said, recognizing the self-manifesting appearances of the spontaneous presence of the basis of appearances to be the natural emanation of the great empty basis of original purity, or not recognizing this, is the difference between the appearances of Buddhas and sentient beings. If one wonders how this can be, it is because the originally pure Buddha is the most exalted, not remaining in the indifferent stupor of alaya, the basis of all.[18] The undeluded self-manifestation of the basis of Dharmakaya is recognized as self-manifestation. The inconceivable qualities of the appearance of self-nature are not dormant in alaya and are always stainlessly discerned. Without clinging, distinctions are discerned in the self-openness of liberation from the beginning. Whatever appears is only the unimpeded, uncompounded manifestation of self-awareness, which does not arise from any other compounded root or contributing circumstances. Awareness is always unchanging because it abides forever in pure self-nature. These are the six most exalted aspects of the supreme Kuntuzangpo.[19] All of this is upadesha that does not come from general teachings. Results do not come from causes. The state of Buddha does not come from dualistic mind. These are the three self-occurring dharmas through which the state of immutable space from the beginning is held forever.

All sentient beings who have not recognized their own naturally occurring self-manifestation of great empty original purity grasp at the appearance of the five lights. The five lights are the source of inconceivable myriad appearances of enlightened body and wisdom. Clinging to these five lights creates dualistic mind, and then the ordinary objects of form and body as the basis of delusion occur. The self-sound of dharmata does not occur from root circumstances and contributing circumstances, but sentient beings grasp at it, and ordinary speech as the basis of delusion occurs. Owing to dependence on that, all deluded appearances such as self, others, cyclic existence, enlightenment, happiness, suffering, and so on, are experienced. In *The Wish-Fulfilling Treasure*,[20] it says:

> Whatever deluded appearances exist come from the three habits.
> The habit of objects causes the vessel of the universe, and
> Relying on that, form and the objects of the five senses occur.

18. kun gzhi.
19. Skt. Samantabhadra.
20. *yid bzhin mdzod.*

> The habit of consciousness causes the eight groups
> of consciousness, and
> Relying on that, positive and negative karma occur.
> The habit of the body causes the bodies of the six classes of beings.
> Relying on that, the branches of the extremities and the smaller
> branches of fingers and toes occur.
> These are the three habits that settle on alaya, the basis of all.
> If there is addiction to these habits that have been placed on alaya
> from beginningless time,
> These appearances will occur for many lives.

Thus it is said.

As it says in the speech of Omniscient Rongzompa, *Entering the Way of the Great Vehicle:*[21]

> According to the lower vehicles, the characteristic of alaya is that it is where the root cause and the effect of all flawed phenomena are curdling, like the ripening place of fruit, and it is also the support of all the phenomena of flawlessness, like having medicine in a vessel of poison. Thus it is explained.
>
> According to the higher vehicles, the characteristic of alaya is that from the beginning, it is abiding in the pure essence of enlightenment, so it is called the basis of enlightened mind. Because of temporary obscurations imposed by the passions and negative habits, it is like gold covered by stains or a precious jewel lodged in the mud; it is only temporarily that its qualities do not appear. The nature of the essence of enlightenment never diminishes. It is said in *The Vajra Ornament:*[22]
>
> > The jewel that blazes like a lamp,
> > Although sunk in the mud of a defiled place,
> > Has self-manifesting natural qualities of light
> > That illuminate the sky.
> > Likewise, the precious jewel of the mind's nature,
> > Although sunk within a defiled body in existence,

21. *theg chen tshul 'jug.*
22. *rdo rje bkod pa.*

By its natural light of wisdom
Illuminates the space of dharmata.

It is just as said.

In brief, whatever the case, all black and white phenomena are only the appearances of the consciousness of the basis of all. All those appearances are controlled by the power of compounded habit. The way they appear is not the way they really are. If one understands that all phenomena are naturally enlightened, it will be unnecessary to search for the path of Buddha elsewhere.

Thus Rongzompa said.

In the *Uttara Tantra*,[23] it says:

The body of Buddha is manifesting within the minds
of all sentient beings.
There is no difference between the nature of Buddha's
wisdom mind and sentient beings' minds.
All beings hold the lineage of enlightenment.
So therefore, all beings are always the essence of Buddha
for these three reasons.

Thus, the meaning of these three reasons is revealed. If this is not recognized, it can be called not having awakened the Buddha essence; or, according to the common tradition of Tantra, it can be called not recognizing one's own nature as the wisdom of simultaneously born absolute truth. According to the Great Perfection, it can be called not recognizing the self-manifesting appearance of the natural emanation of self-occurring awareness. Since it is not recognized, it is held as other, and delusion starts. In essence, the wisdom of the all-encompassing compassionate qualities of Nirmanakaya,[24] which simultaneously abides within one's own continuous mind, becomes dormant, so that the appearance of enlightened body is obscured.

When one fixates on one's own light as that of another, the habit of grasping increases. This is like the rays of the sun warming the earth, from

23. *rgyud bla ma.*
24. sprul sku, miraculous emanation form.

which the subtle substance of heat arises. From that comes the gross substance of vapor, which turns into gross cloud formations. The cloud formations gather and become extremely dense and turbulent, then cool, turning into the obvious physical object of the extremely gross substance of rainfall. In the same way, externally through earth and water, and internally through flesh, which is the element earth, and blood, which is the element water, and so on—the skandhas of form and feeling occur, increasing the secret passion of desire.

Because of the dormancy of the natural, clear qualities of Sambhogakaya,[25] which are pure sound, light, and radiance, its manifestation of pure sound, light, and radiance is fixated on, and grasping mind occurs. As this habit increases, it appears externally as fire and wind, and internally as physical warmth and breath, and so on. With dependence on this, the skandhas of perception and intention occur, increasing the secret passion of hatred.

Instead of Dharmakaya's quality of the essence of wisdom emptiness, when there is fixation on empty nothingness, Dharmakaya becomes dormant within alaya. As this habit increases, it appears externally as space, and internally as the relative essential fluid of enlightened mind. Depending on this, the skandha of consciousness occurs, increasing the secret passion of ignorance.

In this way, the basis of the Three Kayas becomes dormant, which is the condition through which the passions of the three root poisons occur. All gross and subtle passions increase from the passions of the three root poisons, one after another. From this interdependency of the gathering of root and contributing circumstances of the subtle outer and inner elements, the sentient beings of the formless realm occur. From the interdependency of root and contributing circumstances of the outer and inner elements becoming slightly more coarse, the sentient beings of the form realm occur. From the interdependency of root and contributing circumstances of the outer and inner elements becoming very coarse, the sentient beings of the desire realm occur. The three realms occur in this way.

All sentient beings of the three realms experience various kinds of happiness and suffering that are all untrue. As an example, some magicians, although skillful in the combination of substance and incantations, if lacking awareness, may feel attachment to believing that the sight of their magic

25. longs sku, immeasurable qualities of flawless, inconceivable exaltation form.

display, whether good or bad, is real. Then they may experience various kinds of happiness and suffering with attachment or aversion. Likewise, all sentient beings hold to the manifestation of pure self-awareness as real and true. The unceasing chain of cyclic existence continues as the mind, deluded by self-grasping, holds with attachment to the objective appearances of form, sound, smell, taste, touch, and the objects of all phenomena, in a state of perpetual deception for many lifetimes.

For example, when the sense of the eyes becomes attached to any beautiful form, there is deception, like a moth attached to the light of fire and jumping into it to its death. When the sense of the ears becomes attached to pleasant words, sounds, and a good reputation, there is deception, like a deer who hears the sound of a hunter's flute and in that moment of distraction is killed by the hunter's sharp arrow. Being attached to the delicious smells that entice the sense of the nose, there is deception, like a honeybee that is attracted to the sweet smell of a flower and, after alighting there, does not notice when the flower closes, smothering it to death. When the sense of the tongue is attached to flavorful tastes, there is deception, like a fish that is attracted to the delicious taste of bait on a hook. By biting, the fish is hooked and dies. When the sense of the body becomes attached to physical sensations, there is deception, like an elephant who is attracted to the feeling of mud, so it submerges itself in the mud in such a way that it cannot get out and dies there. In this way, wherever one is born in cyclic existence, whether in high or low realms, there is ultimately only the cause and result of suffering, with nothing that is reliable other than deception. It is for this reason that, instead of always engaging in the deceptive phenomena of cyclic existence, it is necessary to engage in methods that bring about the undeceiving state of the freedom of constant bliss.

As mentioned earlier, within the continuity of mind of all sentient beings, the empty essence of Dharmakaya, naturally clear Sambhogakaya, and all-pervasively compassionate Nirmanakaya abide as dormant. In order to achieve a state that is without deception, one must be able to fully manifest the qualities of the Three Kayas that abide in the basis. To do this, one must train in the three aspects of wisdom, which are the wisdom of hearing, the wisdom of contemplating, and the wisdom of meditating. Those who are expanding their perception through the three wisdoms are called those who are entering the path, or practitioners. Whoever is a practitioner must first, from the beginning, rely on the guidance of a fully qualified, sublime Lama. It is said:

Before a Lama appeared,
There was not even the name of Buddha.
Even all of the one thousand Buddhas of this eon
Became enlightened by relying on a Lama.[26]

So it is said.

If one relies on an individual who appears to be a Lama and seems to be teaching Dharma yet who enjoys worldly stimulation, logic, and controversy, Buddhahood will not be obtained. One must meet a Lama who has completely perfected the qualities of enlightened wisdom mind, who is capable of directly introducing one to the nature of mind, which is completely omniscient Buddha, pure from the beginning, by removing the temporary film of obscurations.

Then, first, in the beginning, it is said that one must be skillful in knowing how to examine a Lama. It is mentioned in all the sutras, tantras, and shastras that it is absolutely necessary first to find a Lama who has all positive characteristics, and then to rely on this Lama. In one way, however, if the student who is examining a Lama has not trained extensively by hearing and contemplating the teachings, or if the student has some training but has developed arrogance so that no qualities can penetrate, like water being poured over an iron ball, then the meaning of what is heard is of no benefit to the mind and becomes another cause for increasing negative habit. If the character of the student is like that, then it is as the monk Sunakshatra[27] said to the Buddha:

> I have remained in your company as your attendant for twenty-four years. Other than the fathom of light surrounding your body, I have not seen even a sesame seed's worth of qualities. Although lacking this fathom of light, I find myself to be more learned in Dharma than you are. Since we are therefore equal, I will serve you no more.

Speaking in this way, he abandoned the Buddha. Likewise, however much a disciple examines a teacher, that much fault can be seen, and then blessings will not be received. Thus it is explained:[28]

26. Modern people do not like to rely on a Lama, due to nihilist self-esteem and egotism, but it is necessary to rely on a Lama.
27. In Tibetan, Lekpe Karma (legs pa'i skar ma), Noble Star.
28. The following three categories about siddhi (attainment) belong to practitioners.

However long it takes a logician to examine through
conceptualizing,
That is how long it will take to receive siddhi.

That is how it is. Therefore,

If one is learned in the actual meaning of dharmata,
That learned one is close to attaining siddhi.

Thus, this indicates that it is best to decide on this and stay firm with that decision. Otherwise:

If one is foolish, yet one's faith is firm and
one is engaged in approaching the path of enlightenment,
One is close to connecting to siddhi.

The meaning of this is that one should not just examine one's Lama but should rely solely on faith and pure view. If so, this will be beneficial in not delaying the accomplishment of Dharma. If one thinks, "How can I know how this Buddha nature blossoms?" it is as said in *Uma Jukpa*:[29]

Although it is still the time of being an ordinary person, having
heard of the nature of emptiness,
Extreme joy arises again and again from deep within.
From this extreme joy, the eyes are wet with tears
And the hair in the pores stands on end. Whoever is like this,
That person has the seed of Buddhahood.
That person is an actual suitable vessel,
And to that person, the truth of the holy meaning should be shown.

And so it is.

No matter what, in the general tradition of Mahayana, the mind of the Lama being relied on must be permeated with bodhichitta.[30] In the new and old traditions of Mantrayana, there are many teachings on the various individual qualifications of a Lama. In brief, a Lama who teaches Tantra, gives transmissions, and teaches upadesha must have the treasure of the tantras,

29. *dbu ma 'jug pa.*
30. Here, *bodhichitta* means compassion.

transmissions, and upadesha of the tradition of the Great Perfection, must have perfected the four rivers of the descent of the lineage of actual speech in the Nyingma Vajrayana lineage, and must have the capacity to accomplish and fulfill the wishes of disciples. A Lama must especially be skilled in the meaning of the tantras of Vajrayana and in how to accomplish the four activities, must fully contain the meaning of the developing and completion stages and upadesha, and must have the signs of accomplishment of confidence. As it says in *The Stages of Magical Manifestation:*[31]

> One needs to find and rely on a Vajra Master who has
> the eight natural qualities.

So it is said.

If one's own perceptions are impure, or as an indication of the degenerate age of time when it is difficult to find a flawless Lama whose faults are all exhausted and whose qualities are all completed, it is said to rely on a Lama with fewer faults and greater qualities. In *Reliance on the Absolute Meaning,*[32] it says:

> By the force of the time of degeneration,[33] the faults
> and qualities of the Lama will be mixed.
> One cannot always find flawlessness.
> After examining to see if the qualities are greater, then if they are,
> All disciples may rely on that.

Thus it is said.

From *The Embodiment of Wisdom Mind:*[34]

> Even if a Lama has worldly faults,
> If it is certain he is expert in guiding on the path of enlightenment,
> Even though it may be difficult to deal with that Lama,
> Whatever difficulties occur, be tolerant.

Thus it is said.

31. *sgyu 'phrul lam rim.*
32. *don dam bsnyen pa.*
33. rtsod dus; Skt. kaliyuga.
34. *dgongs 'dus.*

In sublime teachings, it is said that if a disciple is on the path of accumulation, the Lama should at least be on the path of joining. If a disciple is on the path of joining, the Lama should be on the path of seeing the true nature.

In the middle, after one has examined the Lama, one should be skilled in knowing how to rely on the Lama. As said in *The Treasure of Qualities:*[35]

> If a disciple with a bad attitude pretends to be smooth
> with his tongue,
> Depending on the Lama like a musk deer,
> By regarding the precious Dharma as musk obtained,
> He discards samaya,[36] very joyful to hunt again.

Thus, by keeping this close to the heart, with conscientiousness and complete rejection of wrong intentions, it is necessary to rely on the Lama with the four pure perceptions intact. As said in *The Sutra of the Adornment of Stalks:*[37]

> Son of the lineage, you must perceive yourself as a sick patient, perceive Dharma as medicine, perceive constant emphasis on practice as the urgently needed cure, and perceive the virtuous spiritual guide as the most skillful doctor.

Thus it is said, and:

> KYE![38] Son of the lineage, concerning your virtuous spiritual guide, your mind should be like the solid earth, willing to take on any burden without becoming discouraged. Your mind should be like a vajra, irreversible and unaffected by harm. Without breaking your Lama's word, have the mind of a true disciple. Whatever your Lama asks of you, listen with the mind of a servant. Without arrogance, be like the best of the herd with a broken horn.

Thus, as it is said, one must rely on the Lama.

35. *yon tan mdzod.*
36. Tantric vow.
37. *sdong po bkod pa'i mdo.*
38. A sound of calling or invoking.

The Lama should be respected whether his appearances or activity seem good or bad, because of the Lama's general great kindness of turning one to the direction of holy Dharma and especially introducing one's own awareness mind. It is as said:

> The Lama is equal to all Buddhas.

Thus, as it is said, it is necessary to view the qualities of the Lama as equal to that of all Buddhas. The reason for this is that by seeing one's own Lama as Buddha, there is no doubt that the interdependent connection is made for one to obtain the qualities of Buddha in the future.

It is said in the speech of the Buddha that even Bodhisattvas who have attained higher stages cannot perceive the inconceivable qualities of Buddhas. One might think that seeing one's own Lama, who appears with an ordinary human form and behavior, as equal to Buddha's qualities is an exaggeration and not true, making something that is unequal seem equal. Absolutely do not have that wrong conception. Rely on the antidote of strengthening and increasing faith. If one wonders why this is so, all phenomena included in cyclic existence and enlightenment are due to the strength and power of the habit of deluded perception, which make every deluded phenomenon seem to definitely exist separately outside of oneself. These phenomena are nothing except the habits of conception, whether they are bad or good, that are impressed on alaya. All appearances are like the reflections in a mirror, which reflects exactly what is placed before it. They are only one's reflections reflecting in one's own mind. Except for this, no independently existing phenomena come from somewhere else in reality. If one wishes to obtain the result of seeing existence as pure self-manifesting appearances, the state of Buddha, then this must occur now, while practicing on the path. Instead of building negative habit, one has to develop positive habit until fully enlightened stainless Buddhahood, beyond habit, is achieved. The only method is to see one's Lama as Buddha, training one's mind to have pure perception. Other than this, there is no other method even of the size of a sesame seed. It is also for this reason that there are so many amazing accounts of the inspiring life stories of the great Buddhas and Bodhisattvas of the past relying on their Lamas. If one can follow their examples of how to rely on the Lama, then it is as said in *The Adornment of the Qualities of the Pureland of Manjushri:*[39]

39. *'jam dpal zhing gi yon tan bkod pa.*

> Since all phenomena rely on contributing circumstances,
> Depend on the peak of the best intention.
> Then, for whoever prays,
> The result will ripen accordingly.

As said, if one has the best intention, there is no need to doubt the result.

Finally, being skilled in learning about the Lama's wisdom mind and activity means learning about however the Lama sustains his conduct and activity and whatever pleases the Lama's mind. Accordingly, one trains in only extremely pure intention and conduct. Instead of doing that, promoting one's own fame and wanting to be respected by others will not bring one close to approaching even the direction of the Lama's enlightened mind. Even though one does not understand the activities and conduct of the Lama, imitating the Lama's activities and pretending to be learned without having knowledge, not being accomplished but pretending to be accomplished, not being realized but pretending to be realized and the lineage holder and principal heart disciple of the Lama, and so on, one fools oneself by misusing Dharma, all of which is what is called an unsurpassed lie. Without fooling oneself in this way, solely for the aim of benefiting the teachings and all sentient beings, one should show true respect, honor, and devotion, like a lotus bud that is inside pure and outside pure. Relying on the Lama in this way is very important. The reason is that

> The Lama is greater than all Buddhas.

Before, there were many Buddhas in this world, but we could not see them, owing to our lack of karmic connection, so we were wandering in samsara and suffering like patients who have unceasing pain. It was only our own Lama who showed us the direction and path that lead to constant bliss, at a time when no one else was caring for us. Therefore, it is the essence of the teachings to hold the view that the Lama's kindness surpasses that of Buddha. It says in *The Sutra Requested by Maitreya:*[40]

> All liberation and seeing of wisdom by Hearers, Solitary Realizers, and unsurpassed Buddhas, whatever accomplishment they have, must be recognized as the result of relying on a virtuous spiritual guide. Maitreya, recognize that whatever benefit and

40. *byams pas zhus pa'i mdo.*

> happiness all sentient beings have is the result of the root of their virtue, the source of which is the virtuous spiritual guide.

Thus it is said.

Also, it says in *The Sutra of Stainless Sky:*[41]

> Ananda, Tathagatas cannot be seen by all sentient beings, but the virtuous spiritual guide can be seen by all and reveals Dharma, which sows the seeds of liberation. More than all Tathagatas combined, cherish and hold the highest regard for the virtuous spiritual guide.

Thus, there are limitless teachings on this point. So therefore, as Guru Rinpoche said:

> With unchangeable faith, blessings enter in any circumstances.
> With a mind free from doubt, all wishes are accomplished.

Thus, as said, one definitely has to believe this.

The Four Common Outer Preliminaries

Now, the four common outer preliminaries.

Precious Human Birth

First, the contemplation on the difficulty of obtaining a precious human rebirth. As the root verses read: **The eases and obtainments of this precious human rebirth are extremely difficult to find.**

As previously explained, when samsara starts with the delusion of sentient beings, alaya is the basis of all ordinary phenomena. Kuntuzangpo never abides in alaya and is thus forever sublime. To describe this in relation to the condition of human birth: in alaya, pure wisdom vital energy and impure karmic vital energy are dormant. When alaya is not transformed in stainless Dharmakaya, pure wisdom vital energy is dormant and

41. *nam mkha' dri ma med pa'i mdo.*

impure karmic vital energy arises or moves. Then one mind becomes dualistic mind. This is the basis of the mind of ordinary beings, which creates deluded phenomena. In the first instant, the objectifying mind that creates objects arises, so that the outer phenomena of all form, sound, smell, taste, and touch appear, including all outer elements of rivers, mountains, trees, and all male and female beings. Then, in the next instant, the analytical mind arises that perceives these phenomena as pleasing or displeasing and creates attraction or aversion toward objects. Then the various karmic habits of subtle mind become grosser and grosser.

Kuntuzangpo never wavers from his unwavering state. That is why Kuntuzangpo is called the primordial Buddha. Beings have the potential of the unwavering state of Kuntuzangpo, but when beings waver from this state due to not abiding in Dharmakaya the same as Kuntuzangpo and instead remain in alaya, they create the ordinary five skandhas and ordinary five elements from the basis of alaya, but they can return to the pure, inconceivable wisdom elements, as later explained in Guru Yoga. If one obtains a precious human birth, hears the great teachings of Mahasandhi, and meets and receives the blessings of precious Dzogchen teachers who can teach how to purify and transform all ordinary body, speech, and mind through Guru Yoga practice with light initiation on the path of the Three Kayas, one can return to the state of the result of the Three Kayas, which is the original primordial Buddha, the same as Kuntuzangpo.

Rigdzin Jigme Lingpa prayed for us:

> From alaya, karmic vital energy arises.
> The habit of mind that, by being trapped in the womb,
> Occurs as flesh, fluid, warmth, and breath, the elements
> of the skandhas,
> I offer to you. May I attain rainbow body.

Many people feel discouraged, thinking that it is very difficult to attain rainbow body because it takes so much time for thögal[42] practice to transform the ordinary karmic body into rainbow body. This discouragement is due to being lazy for many lives and expecting an instant material answer. Of course, if one has total faith and belief, and practices, one can attain

42. thod rgal, the natural revelation of passing simultaneously to the direct clear light manifestation of Buddhas, which is Sambhogakaya and Nirmanakaya, through direct transmission.

rainbow body in this life or the next life, as many saints in India and Tibet have done, including Guru Rinpoche and Vimalamitra. Even in this life, in this karmic body, one is not supposed to discourage oneself. Do not hesitate, thinking that it is difficult to attain because one has to transform one's karmic body into rainbow body. There are many choices. According to trekchö,[43] for one who can realize the teachings of Mahasandhi, one's own wisdom mind is always the origin of wisdom body, so even if one did not transform one's karmic body from lack of thögal practice in this life, one who can practice trekchö can attain fully enlightened wisdom body. Longchenpa said in *Jewel Treasure of the Dharmadhatu:*[44]

> The power of the skill of the garuda's wings
> Is already perfected while in the shell, although
> temporarily it does not appear.
> Whenever the trap of the shell breaks, he simultaneously
> soars in the sky.
> Likewise, for good practitioners, the previous deluded
> habit body has been cleansed through practice.
> Whenever the shell of the remainder of the karmic
> body has been torn,
> Self-accomplished awareness wisdom self-occurs and expands,
> And wisdom body and wisdom mind phenomena
> pervade, filling the stainless sky of dharmadhatu.
> Recognizing this is liberation in the wisdom body of
> Samantabhadra.
> From that state, out of immeasurable, unconditioned, effortless
> compassion's manifestation toward the ten directions,
> The emanation of wisdom body and activity benefits all beings.

In taking rebirth, the root circumstance is dualistic mind and the contributing circumstance is impure karmic vital energy. When beings are wandering in an in-between state searching for birth and see parents in union, first the objectifying mind arises and grasps, and then the analytical mind arises with attachment and desire. When the three conditions of the father's white essence (corresponding to semen, which predominantly

43. khregs chod, the natural revelation of cutting through all substantial and insubstantial phenomena, which establishes the great stainless emptiness of Dharmakaya.
44. *chos dbyings rin po che'i mdzod.*

produces bone), the mother's red essence (corresponding to blood, which predominantly produces flesh), and consciousness join, it is the beginning of a living being. This may appear similar to a nonreligious, biological description of the male's sperm and female's egg coming together. A biological description, however, does not consider the karmic vital energy of grasping mind joining with the father's liquid and the mother's substance from the being's karmic connection with parents. The Buddhist view is that it is only when these three conditions are gathered together that the mother becomes pregnant and all of the elements develop into a being's form. These elements include the outer element of earth corresponding to the inner element of flesh, the outer element of water corresponding to the inner element of bodily fluids, the outer element of fire corresponding to the inner element of warmth, the outer element of air corresponding to the inner element of breath, and the outer element of sky corresponding to the inner element of consciousness.

The nihilist view is that whenever a sperm enters an egg, a living being begins, but there is nothing said about a karmic connection with parents because there is no belief in the continuity of mind. According to the Buddhist view, a being with dualistic mind's karmic vital energy, through having a strong connection with parents from previous karma, becomes attached to them so that form can develop. There are also countless other beings who are trying to take rebirth but do not have a karmic connection and cannot connect with these parents in time, even though they may be present at the time of conception and attempt to enter into a body. This may sound like nihilist explanations of many sperm competing to enter an egg, but in a nihilist explanation there is no thought of or belief in a karmic connection or the intangible vital energy of dualistic mind. Therefore, nihilists only say that many sperm try to penetrate an egg, but do not consider the root circumstance of mind and contributing circumstance of karmic vital energy. They only notice that out of many sperm, just one sperm goes into the egg, and that other sperm that are close to that one sperm can be killed by it, and that these sperm even fight with each other. Mysteriously, when nihilists express the idea that the one powerful sperm entering the egg can damage other sperm, seeing this sperm as a powerful killer and seeing other sperm as being killed by it, they inadvertently express qualities connected with mind. This is like a Tibetan proverb saying that if one asks a question of others, they won't say anything, but if one just waits, they are going to blurt. So, naturally, even though nihilists do not accept the continuity of mind, nor karma or enlightenment, which are connected with mind, nihilists sometimes come out with an acknowledgment of the existence of mind without realizing what they are saying.

The main point is that nihilists do not think that continuous mind exists, but think that the forms of human beings are made by sperm entering eggs, which naturally results in life. They do not believe that mind begins until the senses are completely developed. They do not think that embryos see or hear in the same way as adults, and they do not think that when the mother is pregnant, consciousness is dormant but arising, or that consciousness begins to function as the sense organs ripen.

There are different ideas about consciousness and when it occurs. Some eternalists believe that life, which is the support of consciousness, begins at conception and are strongly opposed to abortion for this reason. This may seem similar to the Buddhist view, but Buddhists do not consider conception to be the moment when the mind begins. Buddhists think that mind is continuous, and that consciousness is only either dormant or actualized. The power of consciousness depends on the power of the elements of the senses. Buddhists believe that consciousness begins to be actualized when the sperm joins the egg, and that mind is there. When the objects of the senses can be located, consciousness has started to function. Buddhists do not think that the moment of conception when the sperm enters the egg is all that matters, because Buddhists believe that the continuity of mind is unbroken whether mind exists within form or not, and is based on karma unless enlightenment is attained. This is the reason why Buddhists believe in creating virtue, which always follows mind. When the elements of beings are exhausted and they die, even though the gross five skandhas no longer exist, the mind is continuous. Therefore, beings take rebirth in a realm corresponding to the habits that have been created or else attain the state of enlightenment, depending on the individual's karma. Ordinary nonreligious people think that when one dies, everything is finished and vanishes. Because there is no belief in the continuity of mind, they are disengaged from accumulating virtue.

Since Buddhists believe that mind is continuous, when one dies, it is one's previous individual karma that determines whether one has to be reborn or can be enlightened. This is not like ordinary nonreligious people thinking that life comes from a sperm joining with an egg, and that it disappears at death. Buddhism teaches how samsara started and how to arrive at enlightenment.

When sublime beings manifest, they take birth in order to benefit other beings. When they see parents in union, their minds are visualizing the seat of wisdom deity, and when they abide in the mother's womb, they bless it as a palace and pureland through their great prayers and visualization. That is why, although sublime beings seemingly take birth, they have special wisdom energy and the power to guide and help ordinary beings.

Returning to the eight eases of obtaining a precious human birth, they are as follows: If one is born in the hell realm, because of the intensity of suffering from heat and cold, there is no ease to practice Dharma. Not being born there at this time is the ease of not taking that rebirth. If one is born in the hungry spirit realm, because of the intensity of suffering from hunger and thirst, there is no ease to practice Dharma. Not being born there is the ease of not taking that rebirth. All animals are constantly intent on harming one another and in particular are subject to stupidity, so that there is no capability to practice Dharma. Not being born in the animal realm at this time is the ease of not taking that rebirth. Although one is born in a central land where Dharma is flourishing, if one is born with the wrong view of totally disbelieving in the karma of cause and result, previous and future lifetimes, abandoning nonvirtue and accumulating virtue, and so on, then the mind is not suitable for Dharma practice, so there is no ease. Not being born in that state is the ease of not taking that rebirth. If one is born as a barbarian, then there is no discernment between virtue and nonvirtue, and so no ease to practice Dharma. Not being born in that state is the ease of not taking that rebirth. If one is born mentally dull, either the senses are flawed or there is a lack of intelligence necessary for understanding how to discern what to accept and what to abandon. Not being born in that state is the ease of not taking that rebirth. Although born as a human being, if one is born in a realm where a Buddha has not come, then that is a dark age where there is no appearance of Dharma and even the sound of Dharma cannot be heard. Not being born in that state is the ease of not taking that rebirth. If one is born as a long-life god, then with a long life that is distracted by desirable objects and sensual pleasures, there is no freedom to practice Dharma. Not being born in that state is the ease of not taking that rebirth. These are the eight eases.

Now, generally, in this lifetime, a human body has been obtained. Especially, rebirth has been taken in a central land where there is Dharma. All five senses—the sense of the eyes, the sense of the ears, the sense of the nose, the sense of the tongue, and the sense of the body—are intact. Karma is not reversed,[45] because of not having a strong inclination to engage in nonvirtue. There is faith in the teachings of the Buddha. This means that the five personal obtainments that depend on oneself have been acquired.

The Buddha came to the world. The Buddha taught Dharma. The teachings of the Buddha still endure without having diminished. There are others who are followers of the teachings of the Buddha. These followers in turn can guide others. These are the five obtainments that depend on others.

The five personal obtainments and the five obtainments that depend on others are together the ten obtainments. The eight eases and the ten obtainments complete a precious human body. Contemplate how difficult it is to attain a precious human body by considering the example of peas dropping over a needle and the rarity of a single pea staying on top of the needle. Contemplate the difficulty of obtaining a precious human life by considering the number of other sentient beings compared with human beings. Contemplate the difficulty of obtaining the cause of a precious human body by considering how few human beings are actually concerned with accumulating the causes of becoming a practitioner of virtue. So, at this time, having obtained this precious human rebirth just this once, without allowing it to be wasted, it is necessary to practice purely the sacred and perfectly pure sublime path of Dharma. Thus, as Jigdral Yeshe Dorje, the manifestation of Padmasambhava, says in *The Lamp Illuminating the Path of Liberation:*[46]

> Continuously having the suffering of fear and destitution, however much occurs during this and future lives, all these are due to the fault of wasting the precious human rebirth in meaningless distraction. All qualities and happiness of higher rebirth and enlightenment come only from not wasting the precious human rebirth.

In *The Sutra of the Adornment of Stalks,*[47] it is said:

> KYE! Sons of the lineage, however much there is wandering in existence, it is due to not appreciating the precious human body

45. Reversed karma is wanting to engage in nonvirtue. So karma that is not reversed is not doing unvirtuous actions with intention.

46. *thar lam snang sgron.*

47. *sdong po bkod pa'i mdo* (also known as *sdong pos brgyan pa'i mdo*).

> that is difficult to find, which is adorned with the eighteen qualities of the eases and obtainments. Relying on nonvirtuous teachers causes a burning fire of suffering. I myself appreciate the eases and obtainments. That is why I am liberated from existence. All of you must do the same.

Furthermore, Buddha said:

> KYE! Sons of the lineage, whoever has the eases and obtainments will be blessed by the great descent of the rain of perfect Buddha Dharma. Also, the benefits are incalculable.

Thus it is said. One must think that the benefit of obtaining a precious human being's rebirth is immeasurable, just as Buddha said.

IMPERMANENCE

Second, the contemplation on impermanence.

As the root verses read: **Whoever is born possesses the phenomena of impermanence and death.** Thus, wherever one is born, then from birth, without depending on measuring the numbers of more or less beings, impermanence is the conditional phenomenon of death. As the Great Pandit, Ashvaghosha,[48] said:

> Whether on earth or else in the heavens,
> Once born, was there ever anyone who did not die?
> Did you ever see anyone?
> Did you ever hear of anyone, or did you have any doubt?

Thus, as said, here in this universe, has one ever heard of any being who never died and is still living at this time? Did anyone ever see any such being with their eyes, or ever hear about them, or have any doubt? There is no escape from death, so therefore, such decisive questions are asked by the learned one. However one thinks, whether considering the outer container of the universe or the inner essence of beings, it is all conditional phenomena that are destructible. From *The King of Samadhi Sutra:*[49]

48. rta dbyangs.
49. *mdo ting nge 'dzin gyi rgyal po.*

> Before, many eons ago, the world occurred,
> And again, after occurring, it dissolved, and there was no world.
> As it was, it will be, coming and going.

Thus it is said.

Although thinking it is true that taking birth leads to death, one might still speculate, according to the strength or weakness of one's health and whether one is old or young, that one is young and healthy, and for this reason may assume that one will continue to live for a while. It is impossible to predict that. As it says in *The Voice of My Root Guru, the Emanation of Samantabhadra:*[50]

> Some infants still crawling meet with death. Some youths meet with death. For some, death comes when they are old, frail, and decrepit. Others may not even have the opportunity to take medicine or to try to protect themselves from sudden, untimely death. Some are ailing for so long that their bodies are stuck to the bedsheets while their dead eyes continue to gaze longingly at the living, with only skin covering their bones, and then they die. Some suddenly die of a stroke without even finishing their meal, conversation, or work. There are even those who die by suicide. There are many conditions for death. The power of life is weak in comparison, like a butter lamp in a windstorm. Even today at this very moment, death could suddenly occur, so that by this time tomorrow, rebirth as an animal with horns or a beak could have already happened. The time of death is extremely uncertain, and so is the future place of rebirth. It is important to be concerned about this.

Since the circumstances of death are so uncertain, it is important to have confidence in the immeasurable teachings that are given. As it says in *The Speech on Impermanence:*[51]

> For all who are born,
> Death is staying before them.
> Since even I have not transcended that,
> Dharma must be practiced from today.

50. *kun bzang bla ma'i zhal lung.*
51. *mi rtag pa'i gtam.*

Thus it is said, and, from *The Sutra of Parinirvana:*[52]

> For whoever harvests fields, the best is to have found a field with crops. Among the tracks of all groups, the best is to have found the tracks of the excellent one. Among all perceptions, the best is the perception of impermanence and death. Why? Because the perception of the three realms will be diminished.

Thus it is said. Then, in this case, the meaning of reversing the mind that identifies with the three realms is as follows. According to the Hinayana vehicle, knowing the passions and their karma are exhausted so there is no cause to be born again is the attainment of the Arhat state. According to the great vehicles of cause[53] and result,[54] the mind of the desire realm is exhausted in the wisdom mind of Nirmanakaya, the all-encompassing compassion of empty bliss. The mind of the form realm is exhausted in the wisdom mind of Sambhogakaya, the spontaneous presence of empty radiance. The mind of the formless realm is exhausted in the sphere of the wisdom mind of the empty awareness of Dharmakaya. In this way, the sublime permanent state of deathlessness places one in the state of the Victorious Ones of the Three Kayas. The meaning of this is in *The Sutra of Revealing the Three Kayas:*[55]

> Dharmakaya is the permanence of the essential nature as it is.
> Sambhogakaya is constant permanence.
> Nirmanakaya is uninterrupted permanence.

Thus it is said. Also, in the *Uttara Tantra,* it says:

> The lord of Dharma annihilates the demon of death,
> And since this is unborn, it is the permanent protector of the world.

Then, from *Uma Jukpa:*

> Body of peace, the wish-granting tree, ever radiant,
> Like a wish-fulfilling jewel with no conception,
> Permanently endures in this world until all beings are liberated.

52. *mya ngan las 'das pa'i mdo.*
53. Mahayana.
54. Vajrayana.
55. *sku gsum bstan pa'i mdo.*

Thus, Dharmakaya and Sambhogakaya are permanent. Nirmanakaya is both pure and impure, according to the purity or impurity of the vessels of water of various beings' capacities, which reflect clearly or unclearly the image of the moon that appears in the sky. Just as the actual moon does not really enter the water to become self-characterized within water, the nature of phenomena is likewise beyond the nature of permanence and impermanence, and so is called the permanence of the uninterrupted continuity of Nirmanakaya. Therefore, since the result of meditating on impermanence is the attainment of the deathless, permanent, sublime state of the Victorious Ones of the Three Kayas, be diligent.

Karma

Third, the contemplation on the undeniable karma of cause and result.

The root verses read: **The cause and result of virtuous and nonvirtuous actions cannot be denied.** Thus it is said.

To think that there is nothing wrong with death is as said in *The Treatise on the Heretic's View of Nihilism:*[56]

> Like a dead fire's ashes that have been carried away by the wind,
> How can they be born again?

As said, this belief of those who hold the reverse view of not accepting past and future rebirths or anything other than this life alone is absolutely mistaken. This is because once a sentient being exists, there is mind, which is an unceasing continuity that does not stop just because of physical death. Since mind is continuous, it creates habits based on alaya and then has to follow powerlessly after those karmas and habits. For example, when the appearances of waking reality cease at the time one falls asleep at night, the body while dreaming still remains lying on a small bed that fits its size while the mind experiences countless appearances that are as vast as the universe, all based on fluctuating between happiness and suffering. These appearances are similar to daytime reality. Definitely, one's body did not get up from the bed and go outside in order to experience these countless phenomena of happiness and suffering, and neither are these countless varied aspects of phenomena coming from outside into one's small bed. It is impossible for

56. *mu stegs chad lta ba'i gzhung.*

them to fit. This experience is solely the result of the deluded phenomena of the habits of appearances of daytime reality or the magical deceptions of the habits of past and future lives, only occurring in one's own mind.

In *Entering the Path of Bodhisattvas,*[57] it says:

> Therefore, all fear and
> Incalculable suffering
> Have occurred from the mind.
> These are the words of Buddha.
> All hell beings and their weapons
> Were not intentionally made by someone else.
> Who has created the ground of burning iron?
> From where did all those fires originate?
> Buddha said that this and everything like it
> Is the result of the negative mind.

Also, in *Gone to Lanka,*[58] it says:

> The mind has no reality phenomena.
> Whatever is seen outwardly is all seen incorrectly.
> This mind disturbed by habit is the source of all appearances,
> So that outer phenomena are seen as occurring objectively.

Also, from *Entering the Way of the Great Vehicle:*[59]

> Furthermore, it is said that the pureland of the Conqueror Shakyamuni, the four continents of this world, is impure. According to that, Living Shariputra said, "In this land of the Buddha, I can see the distinction of high and low, narrow gorges, canyons, ravines, marshland, and swamps."
>
> Tsangpa Ralpachan, who came from the Pureland of No Suffering, replied, "Living Shariputra, do not say that. It is your own mind that is high and low. The pureland of the Buddha is not impure in any way. I see this pureland of the Buddha as the

57. *spyod 'jug.*
58. *lang kar gshegs pa*; Skt. *Lankavatara Sutra.*
59. *theg pa chen po'i tshul la 'jug pa.*

place of the highest god realm.[60] The basis is a perfect arrangement of precious jewels, and I see it as being extremely pure in every way." It was then that the Buddha revealed to the mandala of his assembly of disciples the pureland of the Buddha of the eastern direction, as a glorious manifestation with the perfect arrangement of precious jeweled ornaments.

Then the Buddha spoke to Shariputra: "Are the sun and the moon completely impure, since the blind do not see them at all?"

Shariputra replied, "It is not the fault of the sun and moon. It is the fault of those who are blind."

Then the Buddha said, "Likewise, my pureland is always like this eastern pureland of the perfect arrangement of precious jeweled ornaments, but all of you did not see it. It is like the example of all the sons of the gods, who, although eating nectar out of one jeweled vessel as their food, each experience the taste of the nectar differently, according to their accumulation of merit. Likewise, even though beings are born in one pureland of the Buddha, according to how karma is purified, the pureland of the Buddha will also be seen as pure or impure."

Thus the Buddha said, as it occurs in sublime teachings.

Until the continuity of dualistic mind is purified, one must only follow karma and habit. Therefore, one must believe in the undeniable truth of the karma of cause and result. Lord Atisha said:

Until conception is exhausted, there is karma,
So you must believe in the result of karma.

Also, Omniscient Longchenpa said:

Until grasping mind ceases in stainless space,
The karma of cause and result manifest,
Compounded by the mind, and performed by the mind.
All these phenomena occur in mind.
The mind names the appearances of the mind,
So therefore, in order to subdue the mind of delusion, be diligent.

60. gzhan 'phrul dbang byed.

Thus he said.

From a lack of understanding about the order of cause and result, some may wonder why there are those who make the effort to abandon negativity in this life and accumulate virtue but still experience suffering. Then there are those who have no faith or confidence in the karma of cause and result, yet who are happy and successful in this life. Because of this, if one thinks that the karma of cause and result is therefore untrue, this is a sign of not knowing the order of cause and result, owing to the strength of nonbelieving nihilist habit. Some people who abandon negativity and accumulate virtue but still suffer in this life are cleansing the suffering from previous lives. This is said by sublime beings to be a sign that in the future they will no longer need to experience this suffering. Then there are those who are fearlessly accruing negativity in this life and yet experience very positive happy phenomena. This is exhaustible virtue, which is the result of small virtuous causes accumulated in previous lives. Once the result of virtue has actually appeared in this life, as soon as the result of happiness is used up, they again must follow whatever negative causes they have created from previous lives.

When the result of suffering and unhappiness from nonvirtuous actions and the result of benefit and happiness from virtuous actions accumulated in this life are experienced as ripening in this immediate life, this is called the karma of obviously experienced phenomena. Even if the result of sinful actions accumulated in this life does not ripen in this immediate life, suffering will be experienced in the next life, and likewise, even if the result of virtuous actions accumulated in this life does not ripen in this immediate life, the result of happiness will be experienced in the next life. This is called the karma of what will be experienced in the next rebirth. If the time does not arrive in this life or the next life for the ripening of the result of suffering from the cause of nonvirtue and the result of happiness from virtue, it is certain that it will be experienced in another future life. This is called the karma of what will be experienced in far future lives. In this way, according to how the cause of either **virtuous or nonvirtuous karma** is accumulated, the **result** will ripen **undeniably**. From *Revealing Karmas:*[61]

61. *las brgya pa.*

For all who have a karmic body,
Even if one hundred eons of time pass,
When the time of all accumulation arrives,
Its result will definitely ripen without waste.

Thus it is said. Also, it is said in *The Treasure of Qualities:*

Like a bird soaring high above the earth,
Even though its shadow is momentarily inconspicuous to sight,
Since beings with bodies have not abandoned gathering and separation, when the bird lands,
As circumstances gather and the time is right, the shadow becomes very conspicuous.

As it is said, therefore, until one reaches the state of Buddha, in which all karma, causes and results, and good and bad habits are fully purified, one must carefully abandon even the slightest tendency toward the accumulation of nonvirtue, and one must be diligent in even the smallest effort to accumulate excellent virtuous actions that are in accord with the holy Dharma.

The root of the passions is the view of an existing self. From the self, passions arise, and from passions, various kinds of karma are accumulated. All of these actions are like these examples. If a root is poisonous, its fruit is poisonous. If a root is medicinal, the fruit will also be medicinal. If a seed is bitter, the fruit will be bitter. If a seed is sweet, the fruit will be sweet. Likewise, from nonvirtuous causes come the results of suffering and unhappiness. From virtuous causes comes benefit that is the source of happiness. Since positive and negative actions undeniably bring the experiences of happiness and suffering, it is necessary to believe this. As Nagarjuna[62] said:

From nonvirtue come all lower rebirths and suffering.
From virtue come all higher rebirths and always having happiness.

Thus it is said.

For this reason, the state of higher rebirth as a human or god is due to the ten virtues. The ten virtues are to abandon killing and protect the lives of others; to abandon stealing and be diligent in offerings and alms; to abandon

62. klu sgrub.

sexual misconduct and maintain pure conduct; to abandon lying and speak the truth; to abandon slander and strive to bring harmony and rapport; to abandon harsh speech and speak pleasantly; to abandon gossip and be diligent in reciting mantras, prayers, virtuous speech, and so on; to abandon coveting and increase the intention to be generous; to abandon harmful thoughts and increase the intention to benefit others; and to abandon wrong view, believing in the karma of cause and result and the Three Jewels.

From *The Jewel Rosary:*[63]

> Abandoning the taking of lives, stealing, and sleeping with the mate of another; abstaining from lying, slander, harsh speech, and idle words; being without greed, harmful thoughts, and completely abandoning wrong view, these are the white path of the ten virtues.

Thus, as said, the ten virtues, and especially the vows of individual liberation, Bodhisattva training, and secret mantra samaya, and every possible activity one can accomplish in the direction of virtue, lead to the state beyond suffering, enlightenment.

From *Entering the Path of Bodhisattvas* by Shantideva:

> Virtue that is intentionally accumulated will accompany
> you wherever you go.
> That and all virtue like it will ripen as the actual object
> of others' respect.

Thus it is said.

Furthermore, in the path of the Great Vehicle,[64] all phenomena are realized to be without true existence, like magic, and within that awareness, undefiled by consideration of a self, total dedication to benefiting others is the principal activity. Therefore, if it is necessary to use any of the seven nonvirtues of body and speech in order to fulfill the needs of sentient beings and benefit the teachings of Buddha, it is permitted and should be considered an action that needs to be performed without fear. As it says in *Entering the Path of the Bodhisattvas:*

63. *rin chen phreng ba.*
64. Mahayana.

> Whoever always sees with compassion even has permission
> to do that which is prohibited.

From *The Arrangement of the Three Jewels:*[65]

> If wealth is received as in a dream from the illusions of a magician,
> Even if one uses this wealth,
> There is no negative karma or its effects.
> Like this, to practice the wisdom of nonattachment
> Goes to the state beyond suffering, the supreme peace.

Thus it is said. Also:

> For whoever has the confidence to see phenomena like dreams
> or the nature of magic,
> Even though that person is relying on desire,
> It is essentially empty and intangible,
> So there is no negative karma or its effect.

It is as said. Likewise, this also holds true for the other nonvirtues of body and speech.

In all cases, the basis or root of the karma of cause and result is the subjective mind. Once there is a subjective mind, there is a conditional object. Therefore, because of grasping at the reality of each reality object and reality subject, the result of various positive and negative interdependent reality phenomena arises. Whatever arises, there is actually not even an iota of true existence. There is nothing. One has to decide that there is only empty appearance. As Mahapandita Dharmabhadra, revered by Indian and Tibetan scholars and saints, said:

> Contributing circumstances present themselves as though they exist, so I do not say that results will not appear. Thus, I never deny anything anywhere, so there is no reason to misconstrue this speech. It is only from interdependent relative truth that phenomena just appear. Beyond that, there is no need to produce an independent reality cause and reality result. So, I see no reason to fabricate this.

65. *dkon mchog brtsegs pa.*

Thus, as said, through actually realizing the meaning, it is necessary to completely purify the subjective and objective mind, because all appearances of existence and enlightenment arise interdependently, depending on positive and negative karmic causes and results. Where does that need to be purified? Within the unmoving nature of awareness, the great sole inconceivability. As Great Omniscient Longchenpa said:

> Never moving from the basis of present awareness,
> With this experience, existence will be emptied.
> Free from the habit and karma of returning to existence,
> The even nature of cause and result is called the equality of samsara and enlightenment.
> Without remaining in existence or enlightenment, one arrives at the essence of enlightenment.

Thus, as said, it is most important to abide in this, the immutable state.

Suffering

Fourth, the contemplation on the faults of existence and the aspiration to engage in Dharma.

The continuous character of the three realms of samsara is an ocean of suffering. By remembering this, may my mind turn to the holy Dharma. Thus the root verses say.

The hell, hungry spirit, and animal realms are the three lower realms. The deva, asura, and human realms are the three higher realms. If synthesized, the beings of the six realms make up the three realms of existence: the formless, form, and desire realms.

As mentioned during the explanation of the eight states of ease, hell beings suffer from heat and cold, hungry spirits suffer from hunger and thirst, animals suffer from stupidity, devas suffer from the inevitability of death and their fall to lower realms, and asuras suffer from jealous warfare.

On the seventeen levels of the form realm and the four extremes of the sense sources[66] of the formless realm, as well as others, all the worldly devas who dwell for extended periods of time in samadhi are unable to see without error the truth of dharmata that transcends the world. When the power

66. skyed mched mu bzhi. These are the four unenlightened states called Limitless Space, Limitless Consciousness, Leaving Nothing, and Indeterminate.

of their worldly samadhi is exhausted, once again they fall into the lower realms of existence to experience suffering.

In general, human beings suffer from the four great rivers of suffering, which are birth, old age, sickness, and death. Furthermore, humans especially have the suffering of the anxiety of encountering enemies, the suffering of the prospect of separating from loved ones, the suffering of sudden unwanted events, and the suffering of not being able to acquire what is desired. Future suffering that begins before previous suffering has finished is called the suffering of suffering. Even though at present one may be extremely content and happy, this happiness can suddenly change to suffering with the occurrence of some circumstance of suffering; this is called the suffering of change. Although suffering may not be conspicuous in the present, whatever thoughts or actions have occurred are the seeds of suffering that have been planted. This is called pervasive compounded suffering. Since there is no one in existence who is not bound by the chains of these three types of suffering, therefore, wherever one is born within the three realms of samsara, the continuous character of suffering is vast and deep like the ocean. By remembering this nature of suffering, may my mind wish only to reach the constant state of bliss and turn to the holy Dharma, which is the sublime path to liberation.

Thus, also, as it says in *The Prayer to Kuntuzangpo:*[67]

> The basis of all is uncompounded.
> The self-occurring, all-pervasive expanse is inexpressible.
> There is no name for either samsara or enlightenment.
> To see this nature is Buddha.

Thus, as said, one must rely on mindfulness until stability is achieved. The phrase "The basis of all is uncompounded," according to sutra, refers to the basis of all varieties of habits. According to Mantrayana, it is the absolute basis of all from the beginning, or joining the absolute basis of all.[68] There are many categories, but it is not necessary to include explanations of all of them here. The essential meaning of what is being presented here about alaya is as said in *The Extremely Extensive Tantra:*[69]

67. *kun bzang smon lam.*

68. These three aspects of the basis of all are: bag chags sna tshogs pa'i kun gzhi, the basis of all varieties of habit; ye don gyi kun gzhi, the absolute basis of all from the beginning; and sbyor ba don gyi kun gzhi, joining the absolute basis of all.

69. *rgyud rgyas pa.*

Not the basis of all conception,
Natural non-existence is the basis of absolute truth.
It is called the space of phenomena, dharmadhatu.
That is wisdom as it is.

As said, this should not be misunderstood as the basis of all varieties of habit, which is alaya. It should be understood as the basis of the ocean of nondual wisdom, which is Dharmakaya. Until the stability of abiding in the basis of wisdom, Dharmakaya, is attained, it is necessary to depend on mindfulness. Without mindfulness, forget about accomplishing the absolute goal of holy Dharma. Even temporary worldly concerns and activities cannot be accomplished. As the Glorious Protector Nagarjuna said in *Harmonious Letter to a Friend:*[70]

If mindfulness fades, all phenomena collapse.

So it is said. Also, Bodhisattva Shantideva said:

All those who wish to guard their minds
Must do so knowingly with mindfulness.
This must be protected even if death occurs.
I implore you with palms pressed together to protect mindfulness.

Thus, there are many such teachings. Also, Phadampa,[71] Holy Father, said:

When enlightenment comes, mindfulness becomes cleansed. That is wisdom.

Thus, as said, the objects that support mindfulness are virtues, and the supporter of mindfulness is the mind. One needs to reach the pure state in which both of them are transformed into one pure taste of nonduality.

In conclusion, these outer common preliminary practices of the contemplations on the difficulty of obtaining a precious human rebirth, the impermanence of life, the karma of cause and result, and the faults of cyclic existence are the four thoughts experienced by the mind that are necessary to practice. These practices are not taught for the purpose of causing additional depression, suppression, fear, sadness, discouragement, and so on.

70. *bshes pa'i spring yig.*
71. pha dam pa.

These habits of suffering have already existed from previous lives until now, gathered and accumulated like a high, solid mountain, so that now in this life, there is this suffering. This is not taught to revive all this suffering so as to make it more firm in this and all future lives, so that one will be tormented by thinking of this suffering, become even more discouraged, and continuously cry about it. Instead, by thinking about these four thoughts and remembering the characteristics of the suffering of samsara, one will become extremely tired of samsara with heartfelt aversion, and will think that one has obtained the good opportunity of having a precious human rebirth in this life and will not waste any time. The four thoughts are taught to hold the mind steady in the direction of virtue, which is always beneficial and creates happiness, encouraging and inspiring one to attain the state of Buddha. If one wishes to be kind to oneself, one must not search for excuses such as this and that about why one is unable to have the freedom to accomplish Dharma. It is necessary to accomplish Dharma purely. Buddha said:

> I will show you the path to liberation.
> You must know that liberation depends on you.

As said, one can know the meaning from this speech. These four thoughts experienced by the mind for Dharma are called common outer preliminary practices. Why? Because engaging in these practices is held in common by all vehicles, including the Hearers and Solitary Realizers of the Hinayana, the Bodhisattvas of the Mahayana, and so on, for the purpose of developing renunciation of cyclic existence so that the mind will turn in the direction of holy Dharma. Thus, these are called the common outer preliminary practices.

The Uncommon Inner Preliminary Practices

Next are the uncommon inner preliminary practices. In this case, the meaning of "uncommon" is that Mahayana and Vajrayana practices are revealed.

Refuge

First, there is refuge.

Then, the lower objects of refuge are as follows. As said in the sutras:

> All people who are overcome by fear will mostly seek refuge in mountains, forests, and groves of trees. Those objects of refuge are not ultimate, for in depending on them, there is no freedom from all forms of fear.

As said, mountains, trees, forests, kings, ministers, the wealthy, worldly gods, powerful lords of the earth, and so on, are the lower objects of refuge. Why is this so? This is because each one of them is still not free from their own form of fear. The supremely sublime objects of refuge are the Three Jewels. As Loppön Chenpo Padmasambhava said:

> No matter how excellent a worldly leader may seem,
> he will deceive you.
> The holy objects of refuge, the Three Jewels, are deceitless.

Thus it is said.

The main object of refuge is the pure aspect of the essential nature, which is from the beginning the stainless Dharmakaya; the pure aspect of freedom from temporary obscuration, the immeasurable appearances of the qualities of Dharmakaya, as the Sambhogakaya; and the manifestation of these Sambhogakaya appearances in the realms of sentient beings to guide them, the Nirmanakaya. These are the Three Kayas. Although these Three Kayas appear separately from the aspects of their qualities, they are actually indivisible as Svabhavikakaya,[72] or Vajrakaya, which is the fourth Kaya.

The quality of being free from stain is the wisdom of dharmadhatu.[73] The unobstructed appearance of all qualities of existence and enlightenment is mirrorlike wisdom.[74] No matter how diverse the wisdom manifestation of existence and enlightenment may appear to be, whatever arises, there is actually not even a subtle particle of goodness or negativity. Because the qualities of the nature of the basis and the way of appearing are the great nature of purity and evenness, it is the wisdom of equanimity.[75] The appearances of the oceanlike realms of the phenomena of existence and enlightenment are nonconceptual yet simultaneously and undistortedly known. This is the wisdom of discernment.[76] Buddha's simultaneous wish-fulfilling

72. Essence Kaya, which is the Three Kayas as indivisible.
73. chos dbyings ye shes.
74. me long ye shes.
75. mnyam nyid ye shes.
76. so sor rtog pa'i ye shes.

activity occurs effortlessly as whatever is needed to benefit sentient beings, pervading everywhere according to time and place without anything missing, and it is always self-accomplished. This is the wisdom of all-accomplishing activity.[77] These are the Four Kayas and the five wisdoms.

Also, according to the tradition of inner Vajrayana, the seven branches of union of Sambhogakaya are as follows. The certainty of the teacher is the lord of the five Buddha families, Vajradhara. The certainty of the retinue is that although there is an aspect of a retinue of peaceful and wrathful manifestations of the five Buddha families and the male and female Bodhisattvas who have attained the result of fully enlightened wisdom, the wisdom mind of the retinue is actually not separate from the wisdom mind of the teacher, Vajradhara. The certainty of Dharma is only the doctrine of the result of secret mantra Vajrayana. The certainty of time is the fourth time, which is the evenness of space. The certainty of place is the perfect pureland of Akanishtha, the Beneathless Pureland That Is Above All. Sambhogakaya, which has these five certainties, has inexhaustible qualities that are always in complete joy, in ever-enduring appearance as the male consort and great emptiness as the female consort of supreme aspects. Their constant indivisibility is union. Even every single pore of the enlightened body is completely filled with flawless great exaltation. This is not a corporeal body with faults; the nondual enlightened body of empty appearances occurs clearly and perfectly, while at the same time it is immaterial like a rainbow. Looking on all sentient beings, who are to be subdued, as the self-appearing manifestation of wisdom, is being always full of compassion. Because the enlightened activity of enlightened body and wisdom can never be exhausted, it is unceasing. As the occurrence of effortless enlightened activity that subdues beings in whatever way is necessary, it is unobstructed. These are the seven branches of union.[78]

Therefore, Sambhogakaya is the extremely pure form of Rupakaya. From its blessings, Nirmanakaya Buddhas self-occur, having the qualities of the five uncertainties. The five uncertainties are the uncertainty of the form of the teacher manifesting as an enlightened embodiment according to the pure and impure faculties of beings to be subdued; the uncertainty of the form of the retinue, who appear as various beings whose faculties and energy are uncertain; the uncertainty of the aspect of Dharma, which is the

77. bya grub ye shes.
78. kha sbyor yan lag bdun.

teachings on the many categories of the higher and lower vehicles according to what is suitable for the minds of beings to be subdued; the uncertainty of place, which depends on the right time arriving for beings to be subdued, and is the manifestation that comes in any place of the six realms; and the uncertainty of time, which appears as the past, present, future, or any time that corresponds to the capacity of beings to be subdued.

Furthermore, if one wonders what the difference is between the essence of the Three Kayas and their manifestation, it is as the Great Omniscient One, Longchenpa, said:

> So thus, the essence of Dharmakaya is stainless empty awareness. Its manifestation is the ocean of nonconceptual wisdom. The essence of Sambhogakaya is self-occurring, inconceivable natural light. Its manifestation is the immeasurable five Buddha families adorned with the thirty-two noble marks and eighty auspicious signs, which are signs of noble body and speech. The essence of Nirmanakaya is the basis of the wisdom of all-pervading compassion. Its manifestation is the revelation of the appearance of whatever is necessary to subdue beings.
>
> The essence of the Three Kayas is the same and indivisible. If one does not analyze the difference between the essence and the manifestation, then the fault is that, since Nirmanakaya and Sambhogakaya appear to the retinue, it would seem that Dharmakaya would also have to appear, although it never appears, because it is stainless, inconceivable emptiness. Or, since Dharmakaya is not appearing within form, it would seem that Nirmanakaya and Sambhogakaya would also not appear, which are always appearing. Therefore, it is important to discern the difference between the essence and manifestation, because the essence is oneness.

Thus it is said.

In this way, the unsurpassed refuge, which is the self-nature of the Four Kayas and five wisdoms, is Buddha. The appearance of actual Dharma is expressed as sounds, words, signs, and syllables with profound meaning in teachings. In order to understand these profound teachings, there are scriptures. Depending on the Dharma of teachings and scriptures,[79] the

79. lung gi chos.

wisdom of realization can arise in the mind of a practitioner, which is called the Dharma of realization.[80] So therefore, those who only rely on Dharma and develop virtue are called Sangha.[81] These are the three objects of refuge, the Three Jewels. So, as it says in the *Uttara Tantra:*

> Purifying and changing conditional phenomena
> Is not ultimate and still has to go with hope and doubt.
> So therefore, the two aspects of Dharma and Sangha
> Are not the ultimate, supreme refuge.
> That which is the absolute sublime,
> The sole essential refuge, is only Buddha.

The meaning of what is said about the view of the *Uttara Tantra* given here is that the absolute object of refuge is only the Dharmakaya Buddha, and not the Dharma and Sangha. This view belongs to the causal yana. In general, regarding the two aspects of Dharma, which are the Dharma of teachings and scriptures and the Dharma of realization just mentioned, the Dharma of teachings and scriptures is that of the Sangha that has not recognized wisdom mind but is accumulating virtue. The Dharma of realization is that of the sublime Sangha, who have recognized wisdom mind, the truth of dharmata, but are not yet always abiding in wisdom. Therefore, from the first to the tenth stages of the sublime Sangha, there is the residue of dualistic habit and cognitive obscurations, so the sublime Sangha can still be affected by dualistic phenomena. When Buddhahood is attained, there is nothing left of even the residue of habit. All form is Buddha, all sound is Dharma, and mind is undeluded wisdom. Whenever the truth of dharmata is recognized, the Dharma of realization is attained and one naturally passes beyond the Dharma of teachings and scriptures.

Until full enlightenment is reached, the entire Dharma of realization of the path of learning of the Hearers, Solitary Realizers, Bodhisattvas, and others in the sublime Sangha is to increase positive circumstances, so even the path itself is changing because it is still progressing and therefore considered impermanent. Because the Sangha has not fully purified the two obscurations, until the state of Buddhahood is reached it is necessary to rely on the path, but this is not the absolute state. Since it is not absolute,

80. rtogs pa'i chos.
81. dge 'dun, intention dedicated to virtue.

and since without depending on Buddha one is unable to abandon personal obscurations, there is still the element of destructibility and fear because full enlightenment has not yet been attained.

As previously quoted from the *Uttara Tantra,* these two aspects of Dharma and the Sangha entering the path are not considered in this case to be the ultimate objects of refuge. This does not mean that one is supposed to abandon Dharma and Sangha. This is analyzing the view of the causal Mahayana tradition that distinguishes fully enlightened Buddhahood, which is Dharmakaya, from the Sangha that is not yet fully enlightened and its realization. One has to be aware of how to analyze this view according to the teaching of the *Uttara Tantra* without misinterpreting it.

According to the tradition of unsurpassed secret mantra, both Dharma and Sangha are perfectly pure and inseparable from Buddha. This is because the objects of refuge who are the Three Jewels are the Three Roots. The essential nature of the body of the Three Jewels is the Lama, who is the Dharmakaya Buddha. The appearance of the qualities of that Buddha is the teaching of the sublime, stainless, holy Dharma, the Sambhogakaya Yidam. Thus, the perpetual dedication of the enlightened mind to stainless virtue is the Sangha or Dakini. These are the actual Three Jewels, the Three Roots. No matter how inconceivable the aspect of the appearance of their qualities, as wisdom deities who are peaceful, wrathful, male, female, or anything, all of them are the essence of the embodiment of all Buddhas as the Lama and the Lama's manifestation. This is the only way one can look at this; there is no way to distinguish Dharma and Sangha as lower according to the inner Vajrayana. Furthermore, the enlightened body of the Lama is the unsurpassed Sangha because it is the most sublime object through which to accumulate the two kinds of merit (merit and wisdom). The enlightened speech of the Lama is the holy Dharma because it is the cool nectar that dispels the heat of the suffering of karma and passions. The great Master Vimalamitra said:

> Having cleared the stain of duality and having measurelessly expanded nondual wisdom is Buddha.

Thus, as he said, the enlightened mind of the Lama is Buddha. All qualities of the Three Jewels are perfectly complete in the enlightened body, speech, and mind of the Lama.

Concerning what is called the Yidam, if one wonders what this really means, it is as follows. Wisdom deity is not to be understood as a separate, self-characterized aspect that is other than the Lama and Dakini. The Yidam has no objective material quality and is indivisible from Dharmakaya and fully enlightened Buddhahood.

According to practitioners and practice, one's own root Lama predicts, "This is your wisdom deity to accomplish enlightenment. You must practice this deity"; or, for any mandala, at the time of whatever empowerment is given by the root Lama, when one's flower is tossed in the mandala of the five Buddha families, in whichever Buddha family the flower lands, that is the deity of one's karmic connection. This deity brings the swiftest, most immediate signs of accomplishment when one practices. This deity is recognized as containing all other families of deities. One promises not to abandon this deity until enlightenment is reached, which is the reason for accomplishing the deity. That is the meaning of Yidam. It is not as though the Yidam is practiced because the Yidam is better than the Lama or Dakini. Whether a Lama is peaceful or wrathful, or whether a Dakini is peaceful or wrathful, whatever form of deity is predicted by the Lama or shown by the sign of where one's flower descends in the mandala is one's own deity to accomplish. That is called the Yidam. For example, if one accomplishes the practice of the Lama as Vajrasattva, Vajrasattva is also the Yidam. Likewise, if one accomplishes the Lama as Vajrakilaya, Vajrakilaya is also the Yidam. If one accomplishes the Dakini as Vajra Varahi, Vajra Varahi is also the Yidam. The Lama as the Wisdom Dakini Dechen Gyalmo is also the Yidam and the Dakini. This is how it is.

To clearly illuminate the pith, within the tradition of Mantrayana, when relying on the Three Roots as the synthesis of the Three Jewels, the meaning of the undistorted aspects of the qualities of Buddhas is revealed here. For example, that which is called the five Buddha families contains the inconceivable classes of all Buddhas synthesized into five families. Within each family, all the qualities of each of the other four families are perfectly complete and integrated. The distinction of the enlightened body, speech, mind, qualities, and activities of each family is called the Dharma of the result of twenty-five distinctions. Beyond that, there are hundreds, thousands, and millions of incalculable, inconceivable families and distinctions that are all praised as the appearance of all the aspects of enlightened qualities. In *The Prayer for Excellent Conduct,*[82] it says:

82. *bzang spyod smon lam.*

In one particle, there are immeasurable particles
with inconceivable Buddhas and purelands,
Where all Buddhas are abiding in the center of all
wisdom Bodhisattvas.
The Bodhisattvas are looking at how they can pass
beyond their activity to attain enlightenment.

Thus it is as said.

If nihilists say that there are millions of atoms within one cell, people believe it, but if they hear that there are millions of Buddhas in one particle, they do not believe it. The problem is that people do not believe in intangible qualities. Therefore, people can accept enormous numbers concerned with substance because of their reality attachment, while they deny enormous numbers of what is nonsubstantial.

Therefore, when the greatness of Buddha's secret, inconceivable qualities manifests as all aspects of Rupakaya's wisdom body and purelands as the Lama, Yidam, Khandro,[83] and so on, although they are said to have different names of wisdom deities, in essence there is nothing greater or lesser that can be distinguished about them; it would be like discriminating between hairs. Generally, according to the tradition of Mantrayana, if all the many deities' names that occur are synthesized, they are included in the two categories of worldly deities and wisdom deities who transcend the world. The meaning of the name "deity" is as said by Great Omniscient Rongzompa:

The immortal hero and the indestructibly firm support,
That which grants all needs and desires, the peaceful,
Abiding within form and accomplishing benefit—
Since these are qualities to be worshiped, praised,
and honored, this is called deity.

Thus, according to sublime teachings, whenever all these qualities arise, one has to recognize wisdom deity.

According to the teachings of Mahasandhi, nondualistic self-occurring wisdom having the two purities is contained in sole wisdom body and its

83. Skt. Dakini.

purelands, so any kind of aspect of all deities is manifesting from that state and is only the emanation of all Buddhas. There is no question that the Yidam is the sole essential Buddha. In the Kriya Tantra, that which is called the deity of dharmata and the deity of pure space are also completely pure. The reason is as follows, from *The Great Reminders of the View:*[84]

> It is known that the belief of the Kriya Tantra is the view of the deity as the pure nature of phenomena. This is accomplished through the strength of the view of the inseparability of the two truths. If the nature of phenomena is Buddha, it is unacceptable for conditional phenomena not to be Buddha. The essential nature of conditional phenomena is the pure nature of phenomena.

Thus it is said.

Therefore, the Lama is the embodiment of all Buddhas, the Three Jewels. Outwardly, the object of refuge is the Three Jewels; inwardly, it is the Three Roots; and secretly, it is the Three Kayas.

Outwardly, the Three Jewels are inconceivable. Inwardly, the Three Roots are inconceivable. Secretly, the Three Kayas are inconceivable. "Inconceivable" means that the inexpressible qualities of form, speech, and wisdom are immeasurable. So, whatever is said, whether outwardly, the Three Jewels, inwardly, the Three Roots, or secretly, the Three Kayas, all are the qualities of wisdom. The aspect of the qualities of each kaya being totally discerned is the Fully Enlightened Manifestation Kaya, or Abhisambodhikaya.[85] The aspect of the ultimate inseparability of the Kayas is Vajrakaya. However these Three Kayas, five Kayas, five Buddha families, five wisdoms, and so on manifest, they are all sublime objects of refuge.

Even if there is no capacity to understand the unobstructed, inconceivable wisdom qualities of the objects of refuge, the Three Jewels, new practitioners by having faith can focus on the objects of refuge, the Three Jewels, as objects of faith and devotion. In faithful times in India and Tibet, if something special was seen or heard, such as the form of the body of Buddha in clouds in the sky, or Dharma sounds such as bells or mantra, by having faith, the ones who perceived these could receive blessings. Any

84. *lta ba'i brjed byang chen mo.*
85. mngon par byang chub pa'i sku.

drawing of the image of Buddhas, such as frescoes and thangkas; any three-dimensional form or statue, such as those made of clay, copper, or bronze; forms such as those which are self-appearing in the shape of Buddha's body or sublime deities' form; the supports of holy Dharma, including all scriptures and syllables; and those ordinary people in the Sangha who are engaged on the path of Dharma—all these should be recognized as the actual Three Jewels, and refuge should be taken with respect.

The purpose of going for refuge is as follows. Those who have inferior capacities take refuge from fear of the lower realms, to achieve happiness in this life, and to take rebirth in the future as a god or human being. Those of intermediate capacities take refuge from fear of the suffering of cyclic existence and the wish to attain the personal goal of the state of peace and bliss. Those of superior capacities take refuge with the sole aspiration to achieve the state of Buddha that does not abide in either of the two extremes of remaining in samsara or the state of peace. In relation to the purpose of self, they attain the state of enlightenment without abiding in samsara, and in relation to the purpose of others, they do not abide only in enlightenment but vow to remain in samsara for the benefit of others.

According to the tradition of Mantrayana, refuge is taken until all impure phenomena transform into the perfectly pure, all-encompassing mandala of wisdom deities. Synthesized, it is as Vimalamitra said:

> Take refuge by remembering the fear of samsara and by
> remembering the qualities of enlightenment.

Thus, as it is said, the tradition of the Great Vehicle is not only to fear the miseries of the lower realms. By bringing together cyclic existence, enlightenment, and the path, all three, bring to mind whatever fears exist in all cyclic existence and the path of enlightenment. By remembering whatever is possible of the absolute supreme state beyond suffering, refuge is taken in the Three Jewels.

The vows of refuge are as follows. First, these vows must be taken from any fully qualified virtuous Lama. After that, during the six times, which are three times in the daytime and three times at night, or at least three times during the day without missing any, the meaning of refuge should be brought to mind, and one should try one's best to recite the corresponding words.

There are three prohibitions in the vows of refuge. Once having gone for refuge in the Buddha, who holds immeasurable qualities and abilities to place beings in the state of higher rebirth and liberation, one must no longer take refuge in worldly gods who lack the power to reveal the path leading to constant bliss. Once having gone for refuge in holy Dharma, which is the source of all benefit and happiness without exception, one should no longer hold the perverted views of mistaken religions that promote harmful doctrines. Not only that, one must always avoid harming sentient beings. Once having gone for refuge in the Sangha, one must no longer befriend or associate with those who hold views that are not in accord with Buddhist views, and especially those non-Buddhists holding views that are against Buddhist teachings. As it says in *The Sutra of Parinirvana:*

> Whoever takes refuge in the Buddha
> Is the perfectly pure Sangha.
> Never at any time
> Should they take refuge in worldly gods.
> Having taken refuge in holy Dharma,
> Be free from the mind that intends to harm.
> Having taken refuge in the Sangha,
> Do not befriend heretics.

Thus it is as said.

There are three trainings to accomplish in refuge. No matter what the quality of the aspect of the enlightened body of Buddha seems to be, whether good or bad, it should be recognized as a symbolic support for the precious gem who is Buddha and shown respect even if it is made of stone or some other ordinary substance. As said by Nagarjuna in *Harmonious Letter to a Friend:*

> Even if the enlightened form of Buddha is made of wood,
> Or whatever substance it is made from, it is always
> to be worshiped by those who are wise.

Thus it is said.

Likewise, it does not need to be mentioned that all the books and scriptures that represent the entire teaching of the holy Dharma in words and meaning are to be respected, even if they are an incomplete book or pages that contain the words and meaning of Dharma. They should never be disregarded, and they must be respected. From *The Ornament of the Hearing of Wisdom Mind:*[86]

> In the time of the five hundred degenerations,
> I will take form in the scripts of teachings.
> When you think that is who I am,
> That is the time to show respect.

Thus it is said by the Buddha.

By taking refuge in the Sangha, whatever appears as the Sangha, whether good or bad, must be recognized as the precious gem of the Sangha, and one should never show irreverence. From *The Sutra That Encourages Pure Intention,*[87] it says:

> Being full of self-righteousness is the root of all carelessness.
> Do not disparage even the simplest ordained practitioner.

So it is said.

Likewise, Mantrayana practitioners, no matter how they appear—as male novices, fully ordained males, female novices, fully ordained females, holders of precepts, holders of mantra who wear white clothes and long braided hair, or seemingly ordinary male and female householders—are called the Vidyadharas of the inner Sangha, so they are worthy of being shown respect and regard. In brief, as the Pandit of Ngari, Padma Wang-gi Gyalpo, said in *The Three Vows:*[88]

> However, those who have realized wisdom should be
> considered principal.

Thus, as said, through these teachings, become aware of the meaning and hold the objects of refuge.

The benefits of refuge are as follows. Once taking refuge, one joins the row of Buddhist practitioners, never falls to lower realms, is protected from whatever miseries are seen in cyclic existence, takes refuge as the support

86. *snyan gyi dgongs rgyan.*
87. *lhag bsam bskul ba'i mdo.*
88. *sdom gsum.*

for all other vows, and ultimately will achieve the state of Buddha. In this way, the benefits are immeasurable. As said:

> If a form could be made of the merit of taking refuge,
> Even the vessel of the three realms would be too small.

The passage continues:

> Those sentient beings who have refuge in the Buddha
> Cannot be slain by the power of even a million demons.
> Even if their morality declines and their minds become disturbed,
> With refuge, they will certainly be able to transcend.

These teachings are from *The Essence of the Sun Sutra*[89] and other sutras.

Offering prostrations is the antidote for pride, which is generally explained at the time of the seven-branch offering prayer. Although there are many traditions that teach the recitation of refuge verses while prostrating, here in this concise preliminary practice, although it is similar, there are only two lines of refuge verses. While performing one prostration and simultaneously reciting the verses, the action of body and speech are concurrent. This is the favorable way to arrange the practice. If one practices in this way, then while accumulating the five hundred thousand accumulations, one will be able to complete one hundred thousand repetitions of the refuge verses together with one hundred thousand prostrations. Also, if the verses of developing bodhichitta are included, then four lines will be recited while performing one prostration. When one hundred thousand prostrations are complete, one will therefore be able to simultaneously complete the recitation of the four-line verse that includes both refuge and bodhichitta.

At that time, the meaning of the practice is accomplished by the visualization of the field of refuge according to the tradition known as containing all objects of refuge within one jewel. In order to be most suitable for receiving blessings, this quotation is given by The Lord Father Great Tertön King of Dharma, Kyabje Düdjom Rinpoche, taught in *The Commentary on "The Profound Secret Heart Essence of the Dakini" Called The Lamp Illuminating the Path to Liberation*[90] as follows.

89. *nyi ma'i snying po.*
90. *khrid rim thar lam snang sgron.*

In a solitary place, be seated comfortably in a sitting posture, and with a relaxed mind practice the following visualization. Think that wherever the place of practice, it is a vast and perfectly arrayed pureland. The ground is extremely expansive and immeasurable, soft and resilient when pressed. There are rivers of nectar, forests of wish-granting trees, and many varieties of flowers. The earth is covered with saffron flowers and freshly sprouted grass, and adorned with many young trees. There are deer and all kinds of alert animals of all colors with beautiful fur, going and coming with peaceful, relaxed minds, gently grazing. In brief, all the characteristics of purelands are perfectly complete in this extremely exquisite and pleasing natural pureland. In the center of all of this is the stainless Lake Dhanakosha with swirling waters that have the eight pure qualities, filled with the pleasant sounds of many divine songbirds living there. The banks of the lake are piled with sand made of gold and precious jewels. In the center of the lake is a single lotus stalk made of jewels that has branches reaching out and up to fill the ten directions of space. The fully endowed bowing branches are laden with flowers and fruits. Linked together with a golden rope of silken flowers, they form a garland of bouquets. Lattices of precious jewels are delicately intertwined throughout with dangling gold and silver bells. By the slightest breeze, the natural sound of Dharma resonates.

In the heart center of the lotus is a jeweled throne supported by eight snow lions, which is very high and broad. On the center of this is a multicolored lotus of one thousand petals supporting a seat of the sun and moon. On this is the embodiment of all Buddhas of the three times, the nature of one's own most kind root Lama appearing as the Guru Who Subdues Phenomenal Existence with Splendor.[91] His color is most desirably radiant white with red. He is an extremely beautiful youthful eight years of age. With a magnificent presence, he smiles with a semiwrathful expression. His right hand holds a golden five-pointed vajra in the conquering mudra on his right knee. His left hand is in the mudra of equanimity, holding a skull filled with nectar that contains a

91. gu ru snang srid zil gnon.

> long-life vase. Garments layered one over another adorn his body, including secret white vajra garments, deep blue garments of Mantrayana, a red robe of ordination with golden patches, and a large power-colored (red) cloak. On his head, he wears a hat rimmed with upwardly folded flaps, with a white vulture feather as the crown ornament. In the cleft of his left arm, he holds a khatvanga (trident) that is the hidden sign of Mandarava.[92] His two legs are in the kingly pose as he abides in the expanse of gathering radiant transparent rainbow light rays. Visualize Guru Rinpoche sitting in front of us, his wisdom mind completely in happiness as he looks upon all beings with great compassion.

Thus visualize as said.

In the commentary, the root stalk of the lotus has four main branches growing out from it, so that including the central branch, there are five. In order to clearly visualize, a certain number is given according to the extensive teaching for the preliminary practices, in which each branch is a support for the more extensive visualization of the field of refuge above it. The reason that the branches of the four directions are not explained here is not to simplify the practice to make it easy or to falsify it and do it improperly, but as mentioned before, this visualization of the field of refuge is in the tradition of all precious objects of refuge contained in one jewel. Since one single Lama Guru Rinpoche perfectly contains all objects of refuge, one will be able to practice easily and receive blessings more swiftly. Therefore, refuge is simplified in this way.

As mentioned earlier, whether the objects of refuge are the Three Jewels, the Three Roots, or the Three Kayas, according to the detailed description that was given, if the meaning has been internalized, then it is understood that all aspects of the qualities of Rupakaya are contained as one taste in the nature of Dharmakaya. The single quality of the great soleness of Dharmakaya arises as the inconceivable aspects of Rupakaya. When the truth of this is recognized from the depth of one's heart, it is as the great accomplished masters of the past have expressed:

> By the practice of one deity with pure faith, one hundred deities are naturally accomplished.

92. lha lcam.

Thus, by holding the meaning of this in the mind, one can avoid the pain of contradiction. While visualizing, imagine that one's father of this lifetime is on one's right and one's mother of this lifetime is on one's left, and behind oneself are one's relatives. Surrounding all of them are enemies, friends, and all other sentient beings who are equal to limitless sky. Imagine that one is leading the chant, which is said together with all beings. With devotion expressed by the body, bring one's palms together into the shape of a lotus bud and touch one's three places. At the same time, express devotion through the voice by melodiously reciting the verses of refuge, bringing to mind the meaning of the explanation as given before. With great faith, placing all one's trust in the Guru who is all-knowing, refuge is taken with yearning devotion until absolute enlightenment is attained.

From this moment until attaining absolute enlightenment, in the unsurpassed tradition of the Great Vehicle, until I attain the complete state of Buddha, **in** you, the source of all Buddhas, my supremely kind root **Lama** who is the essence of **the Three Jewels, I take refuge** from my heart. **From this moment until attaining absolute enlightenment, I take refuge in the Lama, who is the Three Jewels.**

Thus, one accumulates the practice of refuge. After the session, from the heart of the object of refuge, Guru Rinpoche, inconceivable light rays radiate and illuminate oneself and all sentient beings. All obscurations are completely purified without a trace remaining. The bodies of all sentient beings including oneself become a sphere of light and dissolve into Guru Rinpoche. Then Guru Rinpoche dissolves into a sphere, and the sphere dissolves in stainless space like a rainbow. In the great exaltation of the indivisibility of empty, light self-awareness, abide in equanimity, free from grasping. This is the refuge of the result because it is the nature of one's own mind, the essence of Buddha, pure from the beginning. The blessings of the Lama cause these qualities to manifest, and the temporary stain of delusion is self-purified. All appearances become only the Lama and the manifestation of the Lama, which is male and female wisdom deities whose nature is the stainless great exaltation of enlightened forms and purelands. All of this does not manifest from root and contributing circumstances. As the great, uncompounded nature, free from abandoning and obtaining, it is Buddha. As its natural qualities of unchangeable, stainless phenomena, it is Dharma. Always abiding indivisibly in all flawless virtue of unsurpassed qualities, it is Sangha. As it says in *Accomplished Wisdom:*[93]

93. *ye shes grub pa.*

Free from obtaining, pure from the beginning, mind is Buddha.
Abiding in that state unchangeably is stainless Dharma.
The simultaneous perfect accomplishment of all virtues is Sangha.
Since this is the nature of one's own mind, this speech is supreme.

Thus it is said.

Developing Bodhichitta

Second, developing the enlightened mind is as follows.

From now until samsara becomes empty, I will strive for the benefit and happiness of sentient beings, who have all been my mother. Thus, the essence of bodhichitta is as said in *The Ornament of Manifest Realization:*[94]

Bodhichitta is to fulfill the aim of others
By wishing for the state of perfect enlightenment.

Thus it is said. The reason the cultivation of this supreme bodhichitta is so important is as Buddha said:

For those who wish to attain Buddhahood,
  do not study many Dharmas.
Only learn one.
What is that? It is great compassion.
For those who have great compassion, it will be like
  having all holy teachings of Buddha in their hands.

Also, the great Bodhisattva Shantideva said:

Like the supreme substance of alchemists,
The mind of bodhichitta transforms the impure form
  of human flesh
Into the precious, priceless body of Buddha.
That which is called the mind of bodhichitta must
  be held very firmly.

94. *mngon rtogs rgyan.*

Thus it is said. To cultivate bodhichitta for the purpose of self and all sentient beings is the root teaching of Mahayana.

Also, if one thinks of and measures the general phenomena of sentient beings, cyclic existence has no beginning. If one thinks of and measures the phenomena of an individual practitioner on the path, the result of the path can be attained in the state of Buddhahood, so therefore there is an end to cyclic existence, it is said. Teachings like these, which emphasize either relative or absolute truth, are given according to the faculties of beings to be subdued. The meaning is that it is necessary to know that personal and general phenomena appear interdependently and are not individually established as true. In a simple way, until dualistic appearances are purified in stainless, nondualistic wisdom, one's own phenomena of cyclic existence will endure, and from that, the externally manifesting objective appearances of sentient beings in cyclic existence will also endure. No matter how one categorizes one's own phenomena and the phenomena of other beings, however, the essential nature of all sentient beings is Buddha, pure from the beginning. So therefore, by purifying the temporary stain of delusion, the natural, perfectly pure Buddha is accomplished. As said:

> When all ephemeral stains are cleared, that is Buddha.

Thus it is said.

Also, Great Omniscient Longchenpa said:

> From the original Buddha, again Buddha manifests.

Thus he said. To synthesize, until one's own phenomena of cyclic existence are completely emptied, the phenomena of other sentient beings will endure. However much self-form of the habit of sentient beings exists, that much bodhichitta is focused toward them. By considering all beings, **from now until samsara,** which although non-existent continues as the activity of deluded appearances, **becomes empty**, I will place all sentient beings without a single exception in the state of Buddha. **I will strive** only **for the benefit and happiness of all sentient beings, who have all been my mother** during innumerable rebirths in the realms of existence. Thinking like this, it is necessary to develop bodhichitta.

Also, the phenomena of other sentient beings occur through the increasing strength of the habit of one's own mind. This can easily be proven by one's own reasoning. If one did not possess a mind, then who would know the outer container of the universe and inner essence of beings, including cyclic existence and enlightenment? Earth, stones, and other inanimate objects cannot know one another, due to not having minds. Therefore, that is why in the description of the good and bad appearances of self and others, no matter how they are described, one must know they are actually only the magic of one's own phenomena. In sublime teachings, it is said:

> There is no question that mind is Buddha.
> Even all sentient beings are one's own mind.
> The teachings by Buddha are one's own mind.
> Therefore, since the essential nature is equal,
> The ultimate meaning of the exalted path is not other than this.

Thus it is said.

While practicing on the path, when all delusion of one's own phenomena including habit is purified, the phenomena of others of the habit of samsara are purified at the same time. It is impossible to consider that even a particle could be left behind. Loppön Chog-kyi Langpo[95] said:

> Except for conception,
> That which is called samsara has never existed.
> If there is freedom from conception,
> Then you will always abide in enlightenment.

Also, when the mind and phenomena of the self-delusion of samsara become empty in the state of Samantabhadra, even if one searches for the name of a subtle particle of what is called the phenomena of other sentient beings, it is impossible to find it. This is because it is the perfectly pristine truth of dharmata. So therefore:

> May all parent sentient beings of the six realms, without exception,
> Simultaneously arrive at the state of original purity.

Thus, as the prayer says, this is the meaning.

If one were to wonder what the difference is between accomplishing the

95. slob dpon phyogs kyi glang po; Skt. Dignaga.

aims of all beings in the state of Buddha and accomplishing the aims of all beings on the stage of the path of practicing, it is as follows. The impure state is having not yet completely purified all previous residual habit, and the pure state is always increasing the qualities of purification and realization that lead to the state of Buddha. While one is a Bodhisattva, these impure and pure appearances both occur according to accumulation and realization. When the irreversible meaning of the wisdom of the nature of emptiness is realized, then at that time the focus is toward impure sentient beings who have not yet realized this. It is as said:

> Until the end of space is reached,
> Sentient beings also without exception will endure.
> Likewise, their karma and passions will endure to the end.
> That much, may my aspiration prayers endure to the end.

Thus it is said.

> Until the sickness of the passions from which all sentient beings suffer is cured, the illness of the compassion of all Bodhisattvas cannot be cured.

As it is said, in order to accomplish the purpose of immeasurable sentient beings, one must focus on them while accomplishing the oceanlike two accumulations of merit and wisdom, ripening oceanlike sentient beings to the fruit of enlightenment, practicing oceanlike purelands, and so on.

The way of accomplishing the purpose of beings in the extremely pure state of Buddha is as follows. As it was mentioned earlier, before all Buddhas were enlightened, they took birth as Bodhisattvas with a combination of impure and pure appearances while on the path of practicing bodhichitta and developing enlightenment. Through the strength of their immeasurable prayers and beings' karma and pure aspirations, when the auspicious connection between root and contributing circumstances gathers, without aim or intention, the needs of beings are fulfilled. This is like the example of a wish-fulfilling jewel or a wish-granting tree, which benefits without intention.

Within all of the tantric categories of the Old Tradition[96] of upadesha, it

96. rnying ma; Nyingma.

is said that from the self-nature of the Three Kayas of Buddha, the nature of phenomena is the qualities of the unobstructed compassion of Nirmanakaya. This does not depend on previous prayers of Bodhisattvas and beings' karma and pure aspirations when an auspicious connection between root and contributing circumstances gathers. By the essential nature as it is, the purpose of beings is effortlessly and spontaneously accomplished. From *The Secret Essence:*[97]

> Unobstructed compassion appears
> For beings of the six realms within time and place
> without exception.

Thus it is said.

The categories of bodhichitta according to the strength of capacities are as follows. To have the wish first to achieve liberation for oneself and then to benefit all parent sentient beings is the bodhichitta that is like a king. To strive diligently to bring oneself and all parent sentient beings to the state of liberation together, like bringing all the passengers on a ship along with oneself together across the sea, is the bodhichitta that is like a sea captain. To cherish others more than oneself, wishing first to liberate all beings from the suffering of cyclic existence, and then to attain the state of liberation oneself, like a shepherd who protects animals such as cattle and sheep from the fear of wild predators by taking care of the needs of the herd before considering himself, is the unsurpassed bodhichitta that is like a shepherd. In this way, embracing any of these three attitudes according to the strength of one's mind is as said:

> Skillful in giving the vow-bestowing ceremony,
> And personally upholding whatever vow is being conferred,
> The preceptor who gives the vows must have compassion
> and patience.
> The supreme noble Lama who has these qualities should
> be recognized.

Thus, as it says in *The Lamp of the Path,*[98] when one finds a virtuous spiritual guide who is in accord with tradition, one should then receive the vows

97. *gsang snying;* Skt. *Guhyagarbha Tantra.*
98. *lam sgron.*

of bodhichitta from this teacher. In case one is unable to find such a qualified spiritual teacher, then in the space in front of oneself, visualize that Buddhas and Bodhisattvas are actually present. Receive the vows in their presence with strong fervent devotion, or receive the vows of bodhichitta in the presence of a holy object of refuge, such as a statue. The meaning is that from beginningless past lives until now, one has been wandering in cyclic existence taking rebirth depending on parents. Concerning parents:

> The magpie chick who plucks out its mother's feathers thinks that this repays her kindness.

With some exceptions, such as this example and that of the class of certain carnivorous animals who harm their offspring by devouring them, almost all other parents have only love for their children. Therefore, from the depth of one's heart, recognize all sentient beings as one's own parents, remember their kindness, appreciate their kindness, and return their kindness. Through this, be loving toward all sentient beings, let compassion blossom for all sentient beings who are suffering, meditate on the joy that it brings when sentient beings have happiness and rejoice in it, and sustain equanimity for all sentient beings with great loving-kindness, free from the bias of friends and enemies. Meditate on these four boundless wishes.[99]

Also, for all these sentient beings, giving Dharma, material objects, protection from fear, and so on, is the practice of generosity. Disciplining one's body, speech, and mind by abstaining from all negative actions, accumulating all virtue, accomplishing the benefit of sentient beings as much as one can, and so on, is preserving morality. While accomplishing the benefit of others, not letting oneself be overpowered by contributing circumstances is the patience of being unaffected by negativity. Being able to contain the meaning of the general teachings of Mahayana and especially the teachings of Mahamudra,[100] Mahasandhi,[101] and other profound teachings in one's own mind is the patience for Dharma. Not considering oneself where the benefit of sentient beings is concerned, and being patient in clearing their suffering without leaving it as unimportant, is the patience of bearing the burden. Being able to endure difficulties in accomplishing the benefit of sentient beings is armorlike diligence. For the benefit of others,

99. The four boundless wishes are equanimity, compassion, loving-kindness, and joy.
100. The Great Gesture.
101. The Great Perfection.

joyfully purifying one's own passions and practicing virtue is called the diligence of joining. Even if some small virtue is accrued, thinking that it is enough is being overpowered by laziness; or thinking, "Just look at this virtue of mine that has been accomplished," is boasting to others. Without letting oneself be overpowered by pride, and so on, diligently cultivating virtue that is always increasing until the state of Buddha is achieved is called the diligence of never thinking one's virtue is enough.

Concerning samadhi,[102] although there are many descriptions such as worldly and transcending samadhi, the meaning can be synthesized into either tranquil stillness[103] and true seeing,[104] or abiding in evenness[105] and after-evenness.[106]

In the practice of tranquil stillness, it is necessary to rely on the nine methods of sustaining the mind. In front of oneself, one may place as a support for focusing a twig or stone, or as a pure support for focusing an image of the Buddha in the form of a non-elaborate drawing or statue. Then, one leaves the mind on that.

When distracted outwardly through the six senses toward the six objects of form, sound, smell, taste, touch, and phenomena, bringing the mind back when it goes outward so it is not distracted is the method of placement. Whenever the mind is distracted again, without regret, to catch it and again put the mind inward is the method of bringing the mind back to placement again. If one is distracted again, to again place the mind in the state to which one brings it back is the method of continuous placement. Without constriction and with mindfulness, to place the mind again and again back in the state of insubstantiality is the method of close placement. Thinking of the quality of samadhi and meditating in order to reduce the gross mind are the method of subduing. When trying to make the mind tranquil, seeing that distraction is false and being repulsed by it causes the mind to become unhappy; purifying this unhappiness is the method of pacifying. With refinement, not leaving distraction is the method of extremely pacifying. If distracted in samadhi, entering in samadhi unceasingly without constriction is the method of one-pointedly pacifying. Whatever happiness, unhappiness, excitement, depletion, attachment, and

102. bsam gtan.
103. zhi gnas (shi-ne); Skt. shamatha.
104. lhag mthong (lhakthong); Skt. vipashyana.
105. mnyam bzhag.
106. rjes thob.

aversion occur, in order to reduce all of these, one has to abide in evenness, which is the method of abiding in equanimity. Tranquil stillness is abiding in oneness, so it cleans the mind. The nine errors of practicing tranquil stillness are purified by these nine methods.

From the power of these nine methods, the senses are naturally pacified. The organ of the eyes and its corresponding consciousness together focus on objective form and become attached to the attractive and averse to the unattractive. The organ of the ears and its consciousness together focus on objective sound and become attached to pleasant sounds and averse to unpleasant sounds. The organ of the nose and its consciousness together focus on objective smells and become attached to fragrant smells and averse to foul smells. The organ of the tongue and its consciousness together focus on objective tastes and become attached to delicious tastes and averse to repulsive tastes. The organ of the body and its consciousness together focus on objective touch and become attached to the sensation of soft objects and averse to the sensation of rough objects. The organ of mental activity and its consciousness together focus on objective phenomena and become attached to any kind of soothing phenomena and averse to disturbing phenomena.

When the mind becomes completely distracted outwardly by the pursuit of the appearances of the six sense gatherings, passions cause the karma of the happiness and suffering of existence to be unceasingly accumulated. By the power of samadhi, all passions are naturally pacified. This is like rough, rushing water descending from steep mountains that becomes calmer as it approaches the evenness of a valley's streams, until gradually even its rippling waves become less and less. If the bliss of the body and mind becomes extremely refined, it is the accomplishment of the state of tranquil stillness.

The antidote for the five faults that obscure samadhi is reliance on the eight recognitions. Also, investigating to determine whether the mind actually exists within the five skandhas materially or whether the mind exists in an immaterial way is the analytical meditation[107] of scholars. Not investigating or analyzing to determine whether the mind is established as actually existing within the five skandhas materially or whether the mind exists in an immaterial way, but instead allowing the mind to abide naturally is the carefree meditation of leaving the mind as it is.[108] Whichever practice

107. dpyad bsgom.
108. 'jog bsgom.

one relies on, whether the practice of scholars or kusulu,[109] it is necessary for the qualities of true seeing to be enlivened by seeing the naked empty awareness of mind.

The five faults are as follows. Concerning the speech of the Buddha or the instructions of the Lama, and so on, not considering the meaning so that one does not follow it is laziness. Even if one pays attention to the meaning, not relying on continuous mindfulness is forgetfulness. Becoming lost from time to time in unclearness, fogginess, and not being pristine, and then in extreme elation, overly distracted toward objects and wild so that the mind cannot abide in samadhi, is dullness and elation. Being distracted becomes an obstacle for uniting tranquil stillness and true seeing, which is not being focused. When the mind is abiding in stillness, not staying in that state with relaxation but focusing on that state excessively and again becoming tense is constriction. These are the five stains, or faults.

By the four antidotes of faith, intention, diligence, and refined practice, laziness is purified. By being mindful, forgetfulness is purified. By being alert, dullness and elation are purified. When not establishing the mind's focus, establishing it causes confidence. Being in equanimity is the antidote for mental constriction. Then, in equanimity, eventually, the appearances of the objects of the sense organs cease, which is similar to the formless god realm of Limitless Space.[110] When, in equanimity, from the perspective of cognition there is clarity, and from the perspective of appearances there is cessation, this is similar to the realm of Limitless Consciousness.[111] Similar to the state of deep sleep, all feelings cease, which is called Leaving Nothing.[112] Although there is a slight subtle feeling of bliss, it is realized that nothing at all appears, which is called Indeterminate.[113] When there is liberation from the obscuration of the samadhi of the four edges of the formless sense sources, this is the quality of abiding in evenness and true seeing, or freedom from the characteristics of the five skandhas,[114] so it is reaching actual pure truth.

As it says in *The Vajra Essence:*[115]

109. Wandering practitioner; sometimes spelled *kusali.*
110. This is the first of the four edges of the formless sense sources.
111. This is the second of the four edges of the formless sense sources.
112. This is the third of the four edges of the formless sense sources.
113. This is the fourth of the four edges of the formless sense sources.
114. The five skandhas, or aggregates, of form, feeling, perception, intention, and consciousness.
115. *rdo rje snying po.*

> The experience of the union of tranquil stillness and true seeing is clear and pristine, radiating but nonconceptual. These four are called abiding in evenness having the four characteristics. Since this is free from the five skandhas, not establishing the essential nature of shape and color is freedom from the skandha of form; not having attachment to all kinds of experiences is freedom from the skandha of feeling; being free from the aim of distinctions is freedom from the skandha of perception; having no mental motivation is freedom from the skandha of intention; and not grasping at objective appearances is freedom from the skandha of consciousness.

Thus it is said.

In this way, if one abides correctly in equanimity that is free from the five skandhas, there is freedom from the mind of the three realms. When sustaining in awareness while not distracted with desire, there is freedom from the mind of the god realm of desire. When sustaining in clarity while not grasping at form, there is freedom from the mind of the god realm of form. When sustaining in conceptionlessness while appearances of objects are unobscured, there is freedom from the mind of the god realm of formlessness. This is said by all sublime scholars and accomplished practitioners of the past.

Furthermore, in order to develop the qualities of tranquil stillness and true seeing, faults or obscurations are identified to purify them and qualities are recognized to find profound confidence. As it is said, first, of the six faults of samadhi, there are three faults that make tranquil stillness unable to develop. One fault is that when the mind is abiding, if it is disturbed by various kinds of collecting, it will become distracted. Like a butter lamp placed outside in the wind, it will flicker and be unclear. Another fault is that if one prevents one's own perpetual collecting, then even mind itself will be blocked, causing cessation. It is like when the butter lamp's own air is blocked and its light is blocked or dies out. One can therefore prevent other useless thoughts, but do not prevent collecting of the methods of meditation. Another fault is that when one is bound by constricted thoughts, because they are only conceptual, it is impossible to enter the inconceivable object of samadhi. This is when subsequent thoughts fall immediately on the previous thoughts like leaking drops of water, so that the next drop lands wherever the previous drops have already fallen. Therefore, leave mindfulness free.

The three faults of true seeing are as follows. One of these faults is being overcome by grasping attachment, which causes separation from realizing selflessness. Due to this power of grasping attachment, whatever appears as the object of samadhi obscures liberation. Another fault is called decay, which comes from thinking only of existence and non-existence, due to ignorance of the understanding that all phenomena come from interdependence. From this, whatever comes to mind always falls to the extreme of existence or non-existence, so therefore wisdom decays and is obscured. Another fault is circling in delusion because of having less knowledge, so that one does not know how to enter samadhi due to little hearing and contemplating. Like a bird bewildered in darkness, the mind is obscured by circling in delusion.

When these faults obstruct the arising of the qualities of tranquil stillness and true seeing, they are called the six faults of samadhi.

Also, there are nine obscurations of the path. Immovable samadhi, the dissolution of the path, and clarity are the three ways that correct effort is obscured. Thus, in immovable samadhi, even though there is no movement, one does not give up one's previous habit of meditation, so therefore one does not make the effort to find a new, appropriate path. This is like a baby bird who does not leave the nest. Likewise, in the dissolution of the path, because the path is obscured, there will be no attempt to make any more effort, like an arrow shot at a fallen target. Even though there is extreme clarity, it causes obscuration because one is so satisfied by it that no effort is made. This is like the intellect extremely holding on to the sense organs that perceive the object.

Wishing that the mind would develop more knowledge, wishing to achieve clairvoyance, and wishing to develop obvious miraculous abilities are the three ways in which correct samadhi is obscured. It is like when a wealthy family desires butter and relies on many young cows; if the family becomes attached to enjoying milk and yogurt, this obscures the essence of butter.

Thinking there is a better, more unsurpassed teaching that one hopes to receive, thinking that one's own view is superior, and looking down on the views of others are the three ways in which correct mindfulness is obscured.

Correct mindfulness is as follows. If one still has these obscurations, they must be abandoned, so that the absolute meaning of the sutras and the profound instructions by voice received from one's holy spiritual guides are not forgotten. As an example, if a king's or minister's young son becomes spoiled by being arrogant, then he will not retain in his mind all the advice he receives. The natural obscurity that results from the ten modes of conduct is like flat boards stacked on top of one another so that each obscures the surface of the next. Rather than that, because the purpose of the practice of samadhi is so important, it should not be exchanged for minor purposes that are less important, such as intellectual writing and other ordinary conduct. It is said that the meaning of all this is that by purifying all the faults and obscurations of samadhi, one will enter the path to liberation. Thus it is said in sublime teachings.

When experience of enlightened mind becomes profound and one attains confidence, the sign of having power over the mind is as said in *The Meditation of the Enlightened Mind:*[116]

> However much the mind is moving, that much does it become a subtle object of the demons' path. Not abiding in the conditional direction of movement, not abiding in nonmovement, and also not abiding in abiding, that path of the middle, with no certain phenomena, is called the enlightened mind. Thus the Sugata said.

Thus it is said.

The middle path is often misinterpreted. Some people who know that it is said that one should not fall to either the eternalist or nihilist extremes make up the idea that there is just a middle. This idea goes with conceptualization, not wisdom. The middle path is about wisdom. The Western version of the middle path of the Madhyamika is that it is "non-aligned," as though it did not belong with one side or another in this war or that war, but just stayed alone being quiet. The actual middle path of the Madhyamika is insubstantial, so there are not two extremes. If the middle path is beyond the two extremes, the result will be Dharmakaya. That is why there is no certain location between anything, because there is no substantiality of eternalist or nihilist phenomena.

From *The Sutra Requested by Ödsung:*[117]

> If one says existence, it is the eternalist extreme.
> If one says non-existence, it is the nihilist extreme.
> Whoever is wise does not remain even in the middle.

116. *byang chub kyi sems bsgom pa.*
117. *'od srung gi zhus pa'i mdo. Ödsung* is *Kashyapa* in Sanskrit.

Like this, whatever phenomena or conceptualization arise, do not stop them. Just let them come, self-occurring. Without following them, they become naturally pristine, or peaceful. When one gains confidence in abiding in the great, uncontrived, effortless nature of evenness for a long time, whatever phenomena arise, one will not cling or be attached to them the same as before. Whatever outer or inner phenomena occur, including those of the eight consciousnesses—which are the five sense consciousnesses of the eyes, ears, nose, tongue, and body, the consciousness of mind,[118] the mind of the passions,[119] and the consciousness of the basis—they become lighter, so one is not going to materialize them. For example, even if one dreams, clinging and attachment to the dream have ceased.

Likewise, even more so, if wisdom and samadhi are functioning, not only will grasping at appearances as real become more subtle, but as conceptions arise, they will continue to become more subtle. For example, if sleep becomes so light while dreaming that one almost awakens, not only does attachment cease but even the nature of the dream appearances themselves becomes subtle. Then, if there is total mastery of wisdom and samadhi, whether one considers the experience of the collecting of mental movement, the experience of nonmovement, or that there is something to experience beyond both of these, since there is nothing to experience, this is called the middle path of no appearance. At that time, there is the cessation of experiencing. There is even freedom from both the perception and feeling that there is an experience. That which is free from the thought of a particular recognizable meaning and which cannot possibly be given a designated identity is called the middle path of no appearance.

This is said in *The Lamp That Illuminates the Darkness of Limitations*[120] as follows:

> If it appears to one's mind
> That one has the experience of the profoundly nonconceptual,
> Since this nonconception is experienced intellectually,
> It is not actually nonconceptual.

118. yid shes.
119. nyon yid.
120. *mtha'i mun sel sgron ma.*

Thus it is as said. Therefore, even showing the level of experience of the mind, when the movement of the appearance of conception ceases, that itself is a level. When the cessation of attachment to conceptual appearances is known, it is the attainment of the confidence of enlightened mind. Thus it is also said.

Furthermore, at the time of the meditation of tranquil stillness and true seeing, although this meditation is not the basic nature of clarity and emptiness just as it is, it is the arising of an aspect of experience that is similar, like the way the form of the sky appears in water. This is called an example demonstrating clear light. The essential nature of wisdom is free from the coverings of experience, like stainless sky. When this is realized, it is called absolute clear light.

By realizing the basic nature of the great bliss of the clear light of empty awareness and by continuously sustaining it, when one actually accomplishes the stages of the path, the consciousness of the five senses will dissolve into mind. Mind will dissolve into the consciousness of alaya. When alaya dissolves into the dharmata of empty clear light, even though there is no consciousness, because consciousness is purified from the root, self-awareness wisdom light will arise like stainless sky. Thus it is also said. For example, when gold mixed with earth, stone, sand, and so on, is melted down and refined, the power of the ordinary stain or nature of the elements of earth and stone is reduced more and more, like the gross energy of obscurations, and the quality of the element gold is purified more and more. Eventually the time will come when even the object of purification, the gold itself, will be purified and there will be nothing left.

Similarly, if one wonders about the difference between the emptiness of after-evenness and the emptiness of abiding in evenness, consider the following example. Through the circumstance of the sky appearing as a reflection in water, the water becomes the contributing circumstance for the sky being reflected. Therefore, until the water dries up, the reflection of the sky in water cannot join with the actual sky. Likewise, until all habits of dualistic mind are fully cleansed, the perfect manifestation of all appearances as nondual absolute wisdom is not apparent. The power of nondualistic wisdom mind at the time of abiding in evenness, however, permeates the state after attaining evenness. Since this is approaching actual emptiness, it is called the example of wisdom. Absolute wisdom is when there is nothing left of the reflection of the sky in the water and this reflection of the sky has joined the actual sky as oneness. Or, like the sky within a vessel, when the vessel is broken, the vessel's sky becomes the vast sky as indivisible oneness. This is extremely undeluded perfectly pure space. Or, with nothing that is between, with no edge or limitation, all is the great, all-pervasive soleness.

Until confidence is attained in the wisdom of indivisible evenness and after-evenness, do not allow the mind to be deluded, and maintain mindful alertness without constricted thoughts. It is necessary to uproot all coarse and subtle underlying conceptions. It is said that underlying conceptions are like puddles of water covered by grass and chaff. The surface of a puddle of water may be completely covered so that the movement of the water cannot be seen from outside, although it is still naturally moving inside. Likewise, the movement of very subtle conceptions is the basis that supports habit. As another example, when there is a pile of ashes as the result of burning firewood, in the embers lying below the ashes there is heat that, although unseen, is ready to burst into flame. Because the embers are dormant, whenever there is the condition of more firewood being placed on the ashes, the fire will once again ignite. Likewise, depending on underlying dormant subtle thoughts, coarse karma and passions increase. Therefore, in order to cut habit at the root, it is necessary to discern this very clear awareness and then sustain it. According to different teachings, there are various explanations about the way to recognize habit. Although there may be slight differences, the essential point is that there is no habit that is not included in the very subtle dormant mind and the very coarse obvious mind.

For example, the shadow of a seagull flying above the ocean can be seen on the ocean by a crocodile, who tries to chase it, but the seagull does not see the crocodile chasing after its shadow at all. According to Sutra, this is explained as lying dormant. According to Abhidharma, this is explained as subtle mind causing gross passions to increase. Likewise, while meditating on the path, conceptions lie dormant at times, and there is an undercurrent of the movement of subtle conceptions. If the seagull lands on the water together with its shadow, it will become clear to the seagull that the crocodile is chasing it. This is called becoming fully apparent or conspicuous. Just as it is said, when subtle, dormant conceptions meet with contributing circumstances, they become coarse thoughts, and once again the coarse and subtle habits of karma and passions are unceasingly accumulated, whether they are dormant or subtle habits. Therefore, it is only necessary to predominantly rely on sustaining the nature of present awareness with uncontrived, nongrasping, watchful mindfulness, in order to uproot the undercurrent of conceptions. This is the way to completely liberate all cyclic existence.

Also, from distinguishing between past, present, and future, do not think what is called present awareness is another awareness contrived by the intellect. Without retracing the past and without anticipating the future, it is necessary to sustain awareness of the nature of great liberation from limitation. When it is sometimes mentioned that the fourth aspect of time is free from all three times,[121] do not think that the fourth aspect is another actual time that is other than the distinction of the three times. Recognize that it is only the evenness time of original purity, absolutely beyond the limitation of eternalism or nihilism, free from thought or expression. When there is no movement whatsoever or when deluded habit is completely exhausted, this is the enlightened mind of Buddha. Until one has achieved stability, not allowing delusion, it is necessary to sustain the nature of awareness. Do not become discouraged, lazy, or confined by constriction, thinking that it is impossible to abide in the freshness of this present awareness for very long. Instead, it is necessary to sustain the nature of awareness with diligent endurance.

Even though there are many categories of mindfulness, if during meditation one understands the meaning of the mindfulness of focusing on one point[122] and the mindfulness of dharmata,[123] it is beneficial to the development of meditation practice. The characteristic of the mindfulness of focusing on one point is an objectification of dharmadhatu,[124] or sustaining the state of indivisible awareness and emptiness; that mind is called the clear subjective mind that does not allow delusion. Also, that which is called watchful mindfulness[125] recognizes distraction when it occurs and by sustaining mindfulness leaves the mind uncontrived. At the time of leaving the mind uncontrived with mindfulness, if clinging occurs, there will be pressure and tension. Rather than that, it is necessary to sustain a level of leaving the mind uncontrived that is relaxed and free from clinging, not overly strained or unrestrained.

Once, the Buddha asked Ananda to give meditation instructions to a monk named Droshinkye,[126] but Droshinkye was unable to make any progress because his meditation was either too forced or too loose. When he

121. bzhi cha gsum bral.
122. 'du byed kyi dran pa.
123. chos nyid kyi dran pa.
124. Although dharmadhatu is stainless, it can be experienced as an object by practitioners.
125. dran pa'i so tshugs pa.
126. gro bzhin skyes; Skt. Shrona.

told this to the Buddha, the Buddha asked him, "Droshinkye, when you were a householder, were you skilled in playing the vina?"

He replied, "Yes, Buddha, I was expert at that."

"Well, then," said the Buddha, "did the sound of your vina come from playing with the strings tuned too tightly?"

He replied, "No, Buddha, it did not."

"Well, then, did it come from playing with the strings tuned too loosely?"

He replied, "No, Buddha, it also did not."

The Buddha said, "Well, then, from where did the melodious sound come?"

Droshinkye answered, "It came from playing the vina with the strings neither too tight nor too loose."

The Buddha replied, "Well, then, it is necessary for you to practice meditation without being too tight or too loose."

Droshinkye understood, and he meditated in that way. Thus, he saw the truth of the pure nature of his mind.

Also, from Machik Labdrön:

> Tighten by tightening, loosen by loosening.
> Then there is the essential view.

Thus it is as said.

In mindfulness of dharmata, characteristics do not exist. The object that is viewed and the viewer, the object of distraction and the one who is distracted, the object of meditation and the meditator, and so on—the characteristics of dualistic phenomena—do not exist in any way at all.

It must be understood that mindfulness of dharmata is only perfectly pure. It is said in *The Speech of Mindfulness, an Ocean of Qualities:*[127]

> Here, when there is complete profound awareness, the object of distraction is dharmata. Regarding awareness of dharmata and appearances of dharmata, of these two, here, the first, awareness of dharmata, follows.
>
> Conditional mind does not remain in delusion, so the object of distraction has gone in dharmata.

127. *dran pa'i gtam yon tan rgya mtsho.*

The pure nature does not abide in nihilism, so the object of distraction has gone in dharmata.
There is no abiding in either existence or non-existence, so the object of distraction has gone in dharmata.
There is no abiding as one or many, so the object of distraction has gone in dharmata.
The view of philosophical doctrines is exhausted, so the object of distraction has gone in dharmata.
The partiality of view and meditation is purified, so the object of distraction has gone in dharmata.
All that is the basis of delusion is free, so the object of distraction has gone in dharmata.
The great continuity is abiding as awareness, so the object of distraction has gone in dharmata.
The supposition of mind is purified, so the object of distraction has gone in dharmata.
There is no basis or root of distraction, so the object of distraction has gone in dharmata.
There is pervasive evenness like sky, so the object of distraction has gone in dharmata.
There is no distinction of day or night, so the object of distraction has gone in dharmata.
Meditation and nonmeditation are purified, so the object of distraction has gone in dharmata.
All knowledge has no self-existence, so the object of distraction has gone in dharmata.

In that way, by the wisdom of the exhaustion of dharmata, beyond example and speech, there is even no place to be enlightened, so there is no expectation toward Buddhas. Because there is no place to wander in samsara, the doubt of being reborn as a sentient being is abandoned. By not seeing any more than a partial view, when one again tries to find the view and meditation, it is too much additional work. An indecisive mind that is trapped in intellectual understanding does not enter the stages and paths. There is no progress from realization, because beginningless awareness has been reached just as it is. Since the result is perfected in the cause, there are no faults or qualities. Cause and

> result and high and low have become extremely even, so happiness and suffering are finished in dharmata. There is nothing born, so there is no cessation; there is only great sole oneness.

Thus, as said, until confidence is achieved, it is necessary to depend on the mindfulness of focusing on one point. But sometimes, if mindfulness cannot be sustained and the mind is moving, it is not at all necessary to become discouraged and so on, and give up meditation. For those who are new practitioners with little experience, it is necessary to remember that from beginningless time, we have had the strong habit of delusion that moves the mind. Without question, it is said, even all Bodhisattvas abiding on the stages of the path experience movement while resting in the equanimity of samadhi.

As it says in *The Sutra Requested by Ocean of Knowledge:*[128]

> You, Ocean of Knowledge, listen to me. If you look at the great ocean from a distance, it appears to be extremely unmoving, yet if you approach it and look closely, it is found not to be still.

Likewise, what appears to be the perfectly unmoving samadhi of Bodhisattvas is not unmoving for the appearances of Buddhas with wisdom eyes. And similarly, concerning tranquil stillness and true seeing, it is as said in *The Sutra of Parinirvana:*

> All Hearers place more emphasis on tranquil stillness and less on true seeing, so therefore they cannot see the nature of Buddhas. All Bodhisattvas put less emphasis on tranquil stillness and more on true seeing, so therefore they cannot completely see the nature of Buddhas. All Buddhas unite tranquil stillness and true seeing indivisibly, so therefore they see completely.

Thus it is said. So, if those of us who are new meditators with little experience cannot abide in unwavering equanimity, then rather than becoming discouraged, it is necessary to uplift the mind by placing it in mindfulness.

Also, it is said:

128. *blo gros rgya mtshos zhus pa'i mdo.*

One must catch the covetous monkey.
One must bind the thieving cat.
One must destroy the stacks of empty houses.
One must block any gaps or windows.
One must open the king's treasury.
The one who does this is always Buddha.

Even if we purposely ask a monkey to do something, it does not do it, and even if we ask a monkey not to do something, it keeps doing it. The meaning of catching the monkey of mind is to put this monkeylike consciousness in the vessel of alertness and mindfulness. It must be bound in order for it not to move somewhere else.

When the mind of the passions, which has extremely subtle movement, turns to alaya, then from that, by its self-conceit, the view of consciousness adjusts to the naturally disintegrating skandhas, and everything is blessed into falseness. So therefore, if all phenomena are not bound by the cord of wisdom, there will be no opportunity for liberation. The meaning of binding the thieving cat is that the mind of the passions and the consciousness of mind must be tied by selfless wisdom.

The meaning of the destruction of the stacks of empty houses is the destruction of the empty town of the skandhas and senses. When there is no independent possessor, it is an empty town. Since an essence of a self-owner does not exist, even the empty town does not exist, so it must be realized that it is like stainless sky. This is also sustaining in true seeing.

The meaning of blocking all gaps and windows refers to the distraction toward the objects of the five senses that is drawn into mindfulness.

The meaning of opening the king's treasury is that there must be incisive experience of the characteristics of the consciousness of alaya. For example, in a king's treasury, there are precious jewels and so on, and priceless wealth. There may also be base substances, such as poison. Similarly, the consciousness of alaya is tainted by stains and also is the treasury of all phenomena that are stainless. It is said to be the dwelling place of all knowledge. Therefore, the consciousness of alaya should be transformed into wisdom, and alaya should be transformed into Dharmakaya, which is only pure.

At the time of meditation, it may seem that more conceptions are arising than before one meditated, but more conceptions are not actually arising. Previously, because the mind of the six sense consciousnesses was continuously distracted between objects, one did not even notice when one was deluded or where one was deluded. Therefore, it seemed as though there were fewer conceptions. Now, while meditating, as a sign that the mind is spying on itself, it seems as though there are more conceptions than before. At this time, the first sign that sublime meditation is developing is called the experience of movement, which is like a waterfall hurriedly cascading down a steep ravine. Therefore, when conceptions seem to increase and become more intense, do not think one does not have the karma to practice, and do not let oneself become overpowered by discouragement, sadness, laziness, or rigidity, using too much constriction in order to stop conceptions, for this will only become an obstacle causing excessive vital energy in the heart. Instead, by allowing the mind to be naturally at ease without restrictions, it is necessary for the mind to spy on the mind with open, relaxed mindfulness.

All new meditators should practice in shorter, more frequent sessions. At the time of concluding the practice session, the mind should remain undisturbed by conceptions. If one is able to abide peacefully without being disturbed by conceptions, it is important to leave the mind in that state for a while. The reason is that if the time between sessions is filled with disturbed conceptions, when the time comes to practice meditation again, the mind will continue to connect with previous disturbed conceptions. There is then the danger that the mind will not be allowed to abide peacefully. Therefore, during the time in between sessions, if the mind is left in clarity, when the time comes to practice meditation again, the mind will continue to join with this previous clarity, and from that, gradually, abiding in the state of meditation will become longer. Similarly, when getting up from meditation, one should not just suddenly get up, but slowly get up and slowly walk, preserving mindfulness.

In order for mindfulness to continue to be open, free, and firm, instead of engaging in momentary random conversations, speak peacefully and pleasingly. In that way, the continuity of uninterrupted mindfulness and alertness will finally be beneficial for abiding in evenness and after-evenness to become inseparable. By introducing various methods, and by diligently leaving the mind in tranquillity, there will later be times when the mind stays and times when the mind moves. At these times, when the mind moves it is not displeased, and when the mind stays in stillness it is not pleased, so the displeasure and pleasure of the waves of aversion and attachment are gradually reduced. At this time, when abiding becomes continuous, this is called the intermediate experience, which is like a gently flowing river. By continuing to meditate in that nature, the movement of all coarse and subtle conceptions will decrease, and the mind will be able to abide without interruption for a long time. That is a sign of the final stage of abiding, which is said to be like an ocean undisturbed by wind.

Also, at the time of meditating, it is a great flaw if the aspects of bliss, clarity, and nonconceptuality become uneven. If the experience of bliss predominates, this is called experience with the materialization of bliss. Self-characterized desire is like firewood being added to a raging fire. If a fully ordained practitioner yearns for a desirable object, becoming attached, this causes discipline to diminish. A beginning Mantrayana practitioner who lacks the wisdom of the view concerning desirable objects may engage in reckless, wild conduct. Through grasping with attachment at the experience of bliss, attachment will escalate, becoming the cause for continuing samsara.

If the experience of bliss is less and the experience of nonconceptualization predominates, tranquil stillness may soar up or fall down into inertness, thus causing one to become overpowered by unclearness and fogginess, or fall to the even nothingness of cessation without mindfulness, so liberation will not be attained. When both clarity and nonconceptualization are even but bliss is less, there will be no joy in practice, and consequently no aspiration to meditate. If the aspect of abiding lessens, then overwhelmed by wild, turbulent conceptions, the mind will not be settled. If both bliss and nonconceptualization are equal but clarity is less, awareness will become dormant, so that without being able to discern between pure and impure meditation, the mind cannot become pristine. Even if there are the two aspects of bliss and clarity, without the experience of nonconceptualization, one will fall to the direction of materializing. Without the ability to focus in meditation, temporarily there will be restlessness and all activities will come under the power of the ordinary so that the time for the ultimate attainment of liberation will not occur.

In order to apply the methods for reversing the three faults mentioned above, it is necessary to be diligent in evenly sustaining the three aspects of bliss, clarity, and nonconceptualization. What is that? It is abiding that is free from both abiding and not abiding; clarity that is free from both clarity and the absence of clarity; bliss that is free from both bliss and the absence of bliss; and emptiness that is free from both emptiness and non-emptiness. This is a sign of the original, uncontrived, spontaneously present nature. Since this is the unconditioned nature of the clear light awareness of dharmata, this is said by all great sublime beings whose realization has become profound. It is therefore necessary to achieve stability.

Although one may have encountered the nature of awareness, one may be unable to sustain that state of awareness without movement. Or, if conceptions cannot be purified so there is no distinction of arising and liberation:

> Although meditation may be understood, one does not
> know how to be liberated,
> So it is said that there is no difference between this
> and the samadhi of worldly gods.

Thus, as upadesha teachings have said, this is only a worldly samadhi with faults, and not close to flawless samadhi.

From the Great Omniscient One:

> Even if one recognizes one's own stainless mind, if one does not
> become accustomed to it,
> One is kidnapped by the enemy, conception, like a child in battle.

After sustaining meditation in the uncontrived nature, then by eventually recognizing the arising of conceptions, they are liberated, like meeting again with someone known before. Even if conceptions arise, they are not the same as before, so therefore it is not necessary to depend on other antidotes. Self-liberating conceptions is like a snake's knot untying itself. Liberating conceptions in the state of no benefit or harm is just like a thief who goes into an empty house to steal, but there is nothing for the thief to take; nothing can be lost from an empty house, because it is empty. These three ways of liberating gradually occur. Not only that, if one remains unable to abide in the unconditioned nature just as it is, and therefore develops attachment for mere intellectual understanding and experience, one should know that this attachment opens the door to demons, as stated in previous quotations. It is necessary to recognize this. As it says in *The Sutra Revealing the Inconceivable State of Buddha:*[129]

> That which is called achievement is essentially movement.
> That which is called actual realization is essentially the
> prideful mind.
> Whenever there is movement and a prideful mind, that is
> the activity of demons.

129. *sangs rgyas kyi yul bsam gyis mi khyab pa bstan pa'i mdo.*

The one with exceptional pride will claim to be the one
with achievement.
Claiming that one is actually realized becomes a conception.

In *The Sutra Revealed by Stainless Renown,*[130] it says:

If you think you have attained the Arhat state and have
a prideful mind, thinking,
"I have rejected all of my passions," then you have not
become Arhats.

Also, from the Mahasandhi teaching, *The Meditation of the Enlightened Mind:*

No matter what virtue it is, if it is not dedicated in Kuntuzangmo,[131]
great stainless wisdom emptiness,
Even if it is the activity of Kuntuzangpo, great phenomena,
it will be the activity of demons and it will end.
If activity is pervaded by stainless emptiness, Kuntuzangmo,
even the activity of demons becomes enlightened activity.

Thus it is said. Also, Glorious Saraha said:

Whatever there is attachment to must also be given up.

Thus it is said. By depending on correct mindfulness as a branch of enlightenment, if one is able to relax and abide within the great equanimity of indivisible emptiness and awareness, that is what is to be constantly sustained. If perhaps fogginess occurs, it is as said in *The King of Samadhi Sutra:*[132]

Stainless, golden-colored body,
Always exquisite Lord of the Universe,
Whoever beholds this
Is in the samadhi of Bodhisattvas.

It also says in *The Secret Essence:*

130. *dri ma med par grags pas bstan pa'i mdo.*
131. Skt. Samantabhadri.
132. *mdo ting nge 'dzin gyi rgyal po.*

In the center of stainless sky space, on a sun and moon,
See the wisdom king Kuntuzangpo and his wisdom consort Kuntuzangmo in union.
All mandalas of the Victorious Ones,
Perfectly contained without exception, will be accomplished.

Thus, as said, in the space in front of oneself, visualize the source of manifesting and drawing back of all the Victorious Ones, Kuntuzangpo and Kuntuzangmo, in the flawless exaltation body of union without ornaments, as the supreme enlightened form of light, luminously radiant. With unrestrained awareness, relax.

At times when the mind becomes wild, apply antidotes such as thinking about impermanence and the faults of samsara, as well as gazing downward and sustaining the mind in relaxation. At times of abiding in emptiness, if there is nothing that can be found to be seen, do not be afraid or doubtful, thinking that one has fallen to the negation of nihilism. If mindfulness is maintained with emptiness, then there will be no deviation from unwavering great emptiness, the space of phenomena. The *Prajnaparamita* says:

By not seeing any phenomena, this is the prajnaparamita.

Thus, seeing the meaning of the wisdom of Buddhas that transcends the limitation of eternalism and nihilism is as said:

Do not look for a form or characteristic of Buddha.
Also, do not analyze Buddha by caste, nature, or language.
This will not become nihilist.
Also, Buddha is not differentiated by mind and the consciousness of mind.
Whatever is dharmata, that is Buddha.

Thus it is said.

It is impossible for direction, time, or any conceptual designations to defile the nature of phenomena. Since the four demons[133] are annihilated

133. The demon of the passions causes all kinds of passions, including the passions of the three or five categories. Being very attached to desirable qualities causes the demon of the son of the gods, which causes beings to suffer by being lured. Although desirable qualities may sound pleasant, it is obvious that all sentient beings are suffering from attachment to desirable qualities,

from the beginning, and the six supreme qualities[134] are effortlessly perfected from the beginning, one must understand that this alone is the perfectly pure nature of mind. Why is this so? "Whatever is dharmata, that is Buddha." Thus it was said. Whether the emptiness of mind arises, whether the clarity of mind arises, or whether clarity and emptiness arise inseparably, whatever seems to be arising, dharmata is unchangeable. In the *Prajnaparamita,* it says:

> There is no decreasing or increasing.

Thus it is said. Concerning the meaning of dharmata, do not think that dharmata is only supposed to be Buddha and not the minds of sentient beings. One is not supposed to have the conception that Buddha is an object and sentient beings are the holders of objects. There are never two things in dharmata, so it is indestructible. Objects and holders of objects do not exist within one's sole mind. One's sole mind is dharmata, so totally believe in that, and uplift and inspire one's awareness.

In *The Sutra of the Adornment of Stalks,* it says:

> Oneself and all Buddhas
> Abide as naturally the same.
> Not remaining anywhere, not accepting anything,
> Is becoming Sugata.
> Form, feeling, perception,
> Consciousness, and intention,
> These countless Tathagatas
> Will become great Buddha.

Thus it is said. Therefore, knowing that dharmata is pure from the beginning, if the meaning of the impossibility of the basis of delusion is

---

which is the demon of the skandhas. Since there are skandhas, there will be death and diminishment, which is the demon of death. From the beginning, these four demons are annihilated by Buddha. Buddhas have no passions, so passions are annihilated; therefore, they cannot be lured by the son of the gods, so there are no five skandhas, because the passions and the lure of attachment are purified. If there are no skandhas, there is no death, so from the beginning, death is annihilated.

134. The Buddhas hold the six supreme qualities, which are glory, renown, perfect power, flawless noble body, wisdom, and effortless diligence.

correctly understood, then since there is no need to purify delusion, which is self-purified, it is therefore unnecessary to reject it and apply antidotes. If one is able to abide in this way in evenness, all qualities that are developed on the stages and paths of the six paramitas of the Mahayana will be effortlessly, spontaneously present and perfectly complete.

If one wonders how this occurs, having no attachment at all to any substantial or insubstantial phenomena is the perfection of generosity. Having no conception of purity or impurity is the perfection of morality. Having no object that disturbs and no self that can be found to be patient is the perfection of patience. Since the result of Buddha is found by oneself, there is no need for the effort of expecting anything from somewhere else; therefore, this is the perfection of diligence. Not thinking that there is or is not any particular direction is the perfection of samadhi. In the uncontrived nature of the great wisdom of the purity and equality of samsara and enlightenment, being unable to find any other conceptual phenomena that can be known or objectified is the perfection of wisdom. From *The Sutra Requested by the Special One:*[135]

> Not grasping is generosity;
> Not remaining is morality;
> Not guarding is patience;
> Not trying is diligence;
> Not thinking is samadhi;
> Not aiming is wisdom.

Thus it is said.

Also, if one wishes to know how the ten perfections connect to the ten stages of the path during the state of after-evenness, this will be explained later.

According to the tradition of secret mantra, in the uncontrived pure essential nature of phenomena, without visualizing wisdom deities, they manifest as spontaneously present appearance and emptiness, the profound naturally perfected developing stage that does not need to be developed. It is said:

> For those abiding in unconditioned mind,
> Deities and mantra purely abide.

135. *khyad par gyis zhus pa'i mdo.*

Thus it is said. So therefore, if one abides in the state of great sole awareness mind, then there is no self. Since there is no self, there is no grasping to possess anything. Since there is no self, then there is no basis of deluded mind. Since there is no basis of deluded mind, then there are no deluded phenomena. Since there are no deluded phenomena, that is the sound of Buddha.

Well, then, what is that which is called an ordinary individual? The term *gang zag* means ordinary individual. Literally, *gang* means a mind filled with passions, and *zag* means to fall into samsara, which is caused by the creation of karma from the passions. This is the view that there is an existing self. But with passions as the root of what is being called an ordinary individual, it is not necessary to think that this always refers to the cause of negatively falling into samsara. It is uncertain. It depends on the context. For example, Hearers still depend on the condition of being an ordinary individual, because without this condition they cannot find any substantial conceptions of passions to abandon. If there are no conceptions of passions, it is impossible for flawless wisdom to occur. The path of Bodhisattvas is the recognition that all appearances, like magic, are unreal, and passions are transformed into dharmata while activity is directed toward the benefit of others. Depending on passions, an ordinary individual attains the transformation of these passions into qualities. It is said in *The Sutra Revealed by Stainless Renown:*

> Passions are the heirs of Buddhas.

Thus it says. Especially, in all of the tantric categories of unsurpassed secret mantra, the hidden meaning of this is found in these branches of samaya. The transformation of desire is attachment to sentient beings with compassion. All reverse views are destroyed by the wisdom of natural awareness, which is the transformation of the passion of anger. When it is realized that all phenomena are even, there is nothing to reject or accept, so this is the transformation of ignorance. When the view of evenness is realized, there is nowhere to fall down, so it is the transformation of pride. When it is realized that dualistic conception cannot fit in the expanse of evenness, it is the transformation of jealousy, and so on. It is said that all those who realize this have the wisdom of knowing the order of the connection between the five passions and the samaya of the five wisdoms.

Also, if one wonders who sublime beings are, sublime beings are those for whom conceptions of either having passions or not having passions do not exist. This is because there is no "I," so there is no aggressiveness to grasp, so they are beyond all conception in completely uncompounded great inconceivability. Buddha said that sublime beings are uncompounded, and that is the way they are discerned.

Following that, the speech of Buddha can be contained in eighty-four thousand categories. The commentaries by Buddha's learned disciples are called shastra.[136] According to Mantrayana, there is the speech of the victorious Buddha Vajradhara and commentaries that are the upadesha of the ocean of Vidyadharas and Mahasiddhas.

To synthesize the essential meaning of all this upadesha: the purpose of these teachings is to completely exhaust karma and habits so that the state of Dharmakaya Buddha can fully expand and manifest absolute pure phenomena. The supreme and only way to practice with these teachings is to exhaust dualistic appearances. It is therefore necessary predominantly to abide in evenness, sustaining the uncompounded awareness of unending dharmata. When this evenness cannot be maintained due to the unevenness of the mind's previous habit of movement, then be diligent in accumulation and purification, and so on, during all other activities, such as eating, sleeping, going, sitting, and so on by maintaining the view that everything is dreamlike or magical, without substantial characteristics. Then, again rest in even awareness, as it is important to join the states of abiding in evenness and after-evenness. The reason for this is to avoid the deviation of falling to the extreme of nihilism during the appearances of after-evenness and while accumulating virtue. By accumulating and perfecting virtue, ultimately both Rupakayas will be accomplished. While accumulating the virtue of evenness, which is the state without appearances, without falling to the extreme of eternalism, the accumulation of wisdom virtue is perfected, which ultimately leads to attaining the state of Dharmakaya. All of this must be realized and then practiced. It is not enough merely to understand it.

> Understanding is like a patch that can fall off when
> circumstances arise.

It is thus very difficult to establish practice when unable to face circumstances. If one is attached to the experience of ordinary mind, then one is not going to be liberated from samadhi. If practice wavers, sometimes

136. bstan bcos, enlightened commentary.

increasing and at other times decreasing, this is a sign of only having experience, just like mist that is going to vanish. So therefore:

> Realization never changes, like stainless sky.

Thus, if one abides unwaveringly in the correct realization of the meaning of the unconditioned nature, then the suffering of samsara, including cause, result, and even the names of the five skandhas, will be completely purified without a single exception.

Instead of being attached to the taste of the experience of realization, the way to increase the qualities of wisdom is therefore as said:

> There is never any time when the profound meaning
> of the nonconceptual can be shown to others.

If one thinks one can show realization to others, that is also just another conception since it is an experience, so it is not called seeing the nature of truth.

Because the nature of truth is the definitive nature of all phenomena, there is no potential to show personal experiences of it to others. For example, the experience of the taste of salt is known to most humans and animals. Even if one tries, however, to explain the taste of salt to someone who has never experienced it by saying, "The taste of salt is like this," there will still be no way to demonstrate the actual experience of tasting the salt. Similarly, if one has experienced the taste of samadhi but cannot show this experience to others, the fact that one cannot show the experience does not count as anything profound. It is just another conception. Moreover, in other teachings it is said that the path of actual bliss must be free from feeling. The unsurpassed state of full enlightenment is also free from feeling and the activity of dualistic mind. It says in *The Sutra Revealed by Stainless Renown:*

> Buddha, you have completely annihilated hordes of demons
> And discovered the supreme awakening of deathless exaltation.
> In this state, there is no mind to know this feeling, and there
> is no mental activity.

Thus it was said at the time when Buddha attained enlightenment.

By materializing, the immaterial state cannot be seen. Through faith, belief, praying to Buddhas, and receiving blessings, meditators can see wisdom itself by self-awareness, which is not the same as seeing a material concept. As it is said: the mother of all immeasurable Buddhas is unborn Dharmakaya. When the wisdom of awareness mind is realized, that is called seeing truth, or sublime wisdom, which cannot be apprehended as a concept or a material reality.

To synthesize: seeing truth is seeing that the obvious movement of appearances and their conceptions cease. When all dormant subtle habit is cleansed, enlightenment is attained. Whenever seeing truth, it is actually just a term for not seeing anything, which is seeing stainless dharmata. As said in *The Sutra Revealed by Stainless Renown:*

> Since those who see truth are not seeing truth itself, how can they even see untruth?

Thus it is said. Also, in *The Collection of Verses,*[137] it says:

> If sentient beings say that they can see the sky,
> It must be examined how they see empty sky.
> Buddha introduced that whatever phenomena are
> seen, they are seen like that.

Thus, as this teaching says, so it is.

From *The Jewel Rosary:*

> That which is extremely meaningful
> Is one word that must be repeated twice.

Thus, as this says, to once again synthesize the meaning of abiding in evenness, it is self-occurring awareness unaffected by duality, like the nature of sky free from being born, free from ceasing, and free from abiding. It is unwavering within the uncontrived nature of the great sole inconceivable sphere. In the state of after-evenness, when the mind moves from the state of abiding in evenness, one should not become deluded by the appearances of the six gatherings of the senses in the way that ordinary worldly

137. *sdud pa tshigs su bcad pa.*

individuals do who hold on to appearances as substantial and existing independently. Everything that arises, although appearing, has no true inherent existence. So, abiding within the view of the magical nature of appearances, as explained previously, and considering the purpose of magic-like sentient beings, diligence should be applied to the practices that accumulate merit and purify obscurations.

As it says in all Mahayana scriptures, all phenomena are like magic. How is the characteristic of magic to be understood? The characteristic of magic is that although it appears, the way it appears is naturally not true. For example, whatever magic a magician wants to perform, using sticks, pebbles, cloth, and so on, if an incantation is used on an object, it then transforms into the appearances of various magical deceptions, such as a man, a woman, a house, a horse, an elephant, and so on. It only appears from the temporary gathering of the interdependence of cause and result. At the beginning, it never arose out of a self-established cause. In the interim, while the magical appearance is being perceived, in order to be considered magical, it is established as having no true inherent characteristics. Finally, at the end, when the magic dissolves, just as the magic never existed from the very beginning, although it appeared, there is really nothing at all that is dissolving. Therefore, it is the characteristic of magic that no characteristics at all can be established.

Likewise, all deluded appearances of the samsaric phenomena of all sentient beings do not exist but are grasped as truly existing. They are all fabrications about what are only magical phenomena. Then, the magic created by a magician appears momentarily, whereas the appearances of all sentient beings last a long time. Since magic does not have a mind, whereas all sentient beings possess not only minds but also an abundance of mental events, one might think that this means they are not the same. That also is not so. Since time is a distinction made by dualistic mind, then during the time that the magician and spectators are engaged in the activity of a magical display, depending on the display of magic, the appearance of time does not cease. Therefore, the distinctions of whether or not there is a mind, or whether the duration of time was short or long, cannot be decided on. All sentient beings, however, by holding on to magical appearances as truly existing, drift after deluded appearances. How does that occur? It is as said in *Entering the Way of the Great Vehicle:*[138]

138. *theg pa chen po'i tshul la 'jug pa.*

> Well, then, if one asks by whom, where, and for how long there have been deluded appearances, in general terms, who is deluded? It is the sentient beings of the six realms who are deluded. Where are they deluded? They are deluded in the three realms of existence. From what time are they deluded? They have been deluded since beginningless time.

This is a general response. Actually, it is not like this. To explain how it really is: the nature of the appearances of objects, time, and ordinary individuals is delusion. For example, if something meaningless becomes very important in a dream, the distinctions of appearances are from the view of the phenomena of objects, time, and ordinary individuals, who then have the phenomena of experiencing happiness and suffering. Therefore, if oneself and others are staying in a place that is pleasing or displeasing, then while engaged in the experience of happiness or suffering, whether it seems that one stays there for a long time or a short time, the nature of the appearance is that just when it is appearing, there is no objective reality. There is even no individual, there is even no time, and there is even no happiness or suffering. Even though they are non-existent, they appear to exist. Likewise, for all beings under the power of the sleep of ignorance, who do not recognize this, existence has appeared to them from beginningless time. The nature of deluded mind is that, within one moment of being in the basis of mind, it perceives the entire world without limit. Also, sometimes it seems like a reflection appears inside a mirror, and sometimes on the surface of a mirror. Whichever way it is perceived, there is no inside of a mirror, and the reflection has no particular independent place. Likewise, the mind has no particular independent place, so there is no small or vast place in existence that is independent or certain.

Also, about time: in dreams, even if a dream does not last an hour, its duration can seem like more than an eon within one moment; but if the dream seems to last more than an eon, that does not mean it is truly lasting for an eon. Bodhisattvas can bless seven days to become the duration of a great eon of time. The seven days are only the appearance of the mind, and the great eon is also only the appearance of the mind. A longer duration of time is not shortened. At the time that seven days were blessed to become an incalculable eon, a shorter time was not extended to become longer. Likewise, all those who believe in the existence of time from the time of beginningless existence are only deluded by the mind's conceptions of time. Thus it is as said by Omniscient Rongzompa, Dharmabhadra.

Sentient beings, however, are not experienced in the magical nature of appearances, so they hold on to and establish deluded appearances as true, and so they experience suffering. Sublime beings know that magic is magic, so whatever occurs is not restricted by fixation, and this causes liberation and not delusion. Buddhas have completely purified all dualistic phenomena, as well as distinctions of truth, falseness, magic, not-magic, and so on. Because all conceptual obscurations without exception are fully purified from the beginning, they abide in the unwavering state forever, in the wisdom of the nature of equality that is undeluded.

Buddhas do not have even a subtle particle of dualistic phenomena, but the qualities of the unobstructed aspect of their omniscience are like rays from the sun, unceasingly and effortlessly arising. This is called the manifestation of wisdom magic. In this way, all Buddhas have fulfilled the truth of the purity of dharmata's unceasing compassion and have the power to manifest wisdom magic. The magic of ordinary magicians and also the magic power of the samadhi of worldly sages cannot compare to Buddha's miracles of wisdom magic.

There was once a magician named Noble Magician who wondered whether or not Buddha was omniscient. In order to test this, he invited Buddha along with his entire retinue of monks to a festivity at which he offered a deceptive noon meal. To trick Buddha, he made many different substances appear in a show of magic, including an immeasurable palace and a great variety of delicious foods. Aware that the magician's intention was negative, the omniscient Buddha departed without hesitation for the magician's residence. At the entrance, Noble Magician had created many magical lotuses for Buddha to walk upon, wanting him to step upon the lotuses and then fall down as the lotuses disappeared. Buddha made these lotuses firm, graciously stepping as steadily as usual on them, and entered the magician's palace with his retinue. Seeing this, Noble Magician had goose bumps. As Buddha began to accept the offering meal, Noble Magician wanted to make it vanish, but Buddha blessed all of the substances that Noble Magician had magically displayed so they would stay as they were. Then, Buddha and his retinue completed all of the noon meal in front of Noble Magician and his entourage according to their obvious reality phenomena. Extremely astonished, Noble Magician and his entourage had unbearable goose bumps, shriveling their splendid power. Having finished the meal, Buddha offered this prayer:

Whoever has received it, whoever has given it, and whatever substances have been offered, this generosity
Is all nonmaterial. Therefore, by the nature of the generosity of the state of immaterial evenness,
I dedicate this to you, Noble Magician. May you receive it completely.

Thus, the Buddha made this prayer of dedication, and Noble Magician perfected the two accumulations through this manifestation of magical wisdom. Later, Noble Magician became one of the precious disciples of the Buddha, and at his request, *The Sutra Requested by the Noble One*[139] was given.

Now that the characteristics of magic have been briefly explained, it is explained how to purify and accumulate within magic-like phenomena in the state of after-evenness, from the first stage up to the tenth stage of the prajnaparamita. There is no difference from the first stage up to the tenth stage in the wisdom of abiding in evenness, because the wisdom of conceptionless emptiness has no difference. In the ten stages of after-evenness, however, there are differences.

In the first stage, from having seen the actual meaning of the truth of Dharmata that transcends the world, like a poor person who has found a wish-fulfilling jewel, comes the power to fulfill the vast purpose of self and others. One is thus satisfied and extremely joyful. This stage is called Extreme Joyfulness, which predominantly emphasizes the practice of the perfection of generosity.

In the second stage, with freedom from the stain of losing morality comes the perfect purity of the three moralities.[140] This stage is called Stainlessness, which predominantly emphasizes the practice of the perfection of morality.

In the third stage, with no regard for one's body or life, by cleansing the continuity of mind through hearing and contemplation, the profound meaning of truth is fully understood, and so the strength of patience arises, radiantly dispelling the darkness of ignorance in self and others. This stage is called Radiance, which predominantly emphasizes the practice of the perfection of patience.

In the fourth stage, by meditating on the profound meaning of dharmata,

139. *bzang pos zhus pa'i mdo.*
140. The three moralities are abstaining from immoral behavior, accumulating virtue, and accomplishing benefit for other sentient beings.

there is actual deep joy, and through that meditation, wisdom blazes like the fire at the end of time, burning the habit of duality. This stage is called Shining Light, which predominantly emphasizes the practice of the perfection of diligence.

In the fifth stage, according to the karma and action of self and others, by sustaining samadhi that is neither dull nor elated, that which is difficult to arise increases, and that which is difficult to clear away is purified. This stage is called Purified Difficulties, which predominantly emphasizes the practice of the perfection of samadhi.

In the sixth stage, the meaning of all the phenomena of samsara and enlightenment is incisively known as unborn, unceasing, and so on. This stage is called Undistorted Apparentness, which predominantly emphasizes the practice of the perfection of knowledge.

In the seventh stage, having vast skillful means is a far distance from the Hinayana, the Lesser Vehicle, which is abiding in peace oneself but not having great compassion and great methods to guide other beings. This stage is called A Far Distance Away from the Hinayana, which predominantly emphasizes the practice of the perfection of method.

In the eighth stage, by the power of previous great prayers, without falling to the lower path of the Hinayana, characteristicless wisdom is not influenced by the circumstance of characteristics. This stage is called The Unwavering, which predominantly emphasizes the practice of the perfection of aspiration.

In the ninth stage, there is knowledge of the perfectly pure discernment of Dharma, knowledge of the perfectly pure discernment of meaning, knowledge of the perfectly pure discernment of the certainty of words, and knowledge of the perfectly pure discernment of confidence; so whatever questions others ask are answered at the same time they are asked. Having achieved the power of these four perfectly pure discernments,[141] one cannot be suppressed by others. This stage is called Sublime Intelligence, which predominantly emphasizes the practice of the perfection of strength.

In the tenth stage, like clouds gathering in space, rain falling from the clouds to the earth, and crops ripening to fulfill the needs of beings, from within the sky of wisdom, from the gathering clouds of impartial compassion without aiming toward particular beings, the rain of the various Dharma vehicles descends to fulfill the needs of sentient beings. This stage

141. so so yang dag rig pa bzhi.

is called Clouds of Dharma, which predominantly emphasizes the practice of the perfection of wisdom.

Likewise, the qualities that develop from the first to the tenth stage are, as said in *Phal po che:*[142]

> One hundred forms of samadhi,
> Seeing one hundred Buddhas,
> Going to one hundred purelands,
> Leading one hundred beings to enlightenment,
> Opening one hundred gates of Dharma,
> Entering one hundred eons of time,
> Revealing one hundred forms,
> One hundred heirs of the Victorious Ones
> Will reveal these groups of one hundred.
> There is no prayer more powerful than this.

Thus, as said, at the first stage, there are one hundred times twelve qualities. At the second stage, there are one thousand times twelve qualities. At the third stage, there are one hundred thousand times twelve qualities. At the fourth stage, there are twelve hundred times ten million qualities. At the fifth stage, there are twelve thousand times ten million qualities. At the sixth stage, there are one hundred twenty thousand times ten million qualities. At the seventh stage, there are twelve hundred thousand times ten million qualities. At the eighth stage, there are qualities equal to the particles of the great thousandfold universe times one hundred thousand. At the ninth stage, there are qualities equal to the particles of the great thousandfold universe times one million. At the tenth stage, there are qualities equal to infinity. It is said that the faces of Buddhas are seen, Dharma is heard, purelands move, there is illumination by light, and there is the ability to go to all purelands, to ripen sentient beings to the fruit of enlightenment, to open the door of Dharma, to abide in the equanimity of samadhi, to show one instant as many eons and many eons as one instant, to see whatever existed in the past and whatever will exist in the future, to emanate from one's own body many manifestations of Buddhas' bodies, to emanate many surrounding retinues from the manifestation of each Buddha's body, and to manifest instantaneously without distinguishing between what is before and what is after.

142. Skt. *Avatamsaka Sutra.*

Since there are no differences in the state of abiding in the evenness of wisdom emptiness from the first stage up to the tenth stage, why are there differences during the corresponding stages in the state of after-evenness? From attaining stability in evenness for a longer duration, the power of abiding in after-evenness gradually increases. For example, if the sun shines on a pool of water for ten successive days, the water will gradually evaporate from the combination of heat and moisture. Finally, on the tenth day, the water will be completely dried up, but from the first to the tenth day, there will have been no difference in the way the sun was shining. The length of time that the sun and moisture are together, whether short or long, causes the water to completely dry up by the final day. It is like that.

Likewise, there is no description of the ten stages for Hearers and Solitary Realizers, because by only realizing the selflessness of the self and striving to accomplish the aim of personal peace, they therefore lack the capability to guide other beings with compassion. All Bodhisattvas abide in the equanimity of actual realization of the truth of dharmata, which is the emptiness of the two aspects of selflessness. Their after-evenness has loving-kindness and compassion for sentient beings, and they offer immeasurable, vast prayers for the benefit of others. This is exalted sublime activity that fulfills the purpose of others.

The eleventh stage, All-Pervasive Light, is the stage that contains the result. This is like the sun shining in the great stainless sky, so that the appearance of light pervades everywhere. Having completely purified the two obscurations through the selflessness of the self and the selflessness of phenomena, and all residue of habit, there is full perfection of the four enlightened bodies, the five wisdoms, preservation,[143] intrepid wisdom[144] (which is dauntless courage based on wisdom awareness), strength, fearlessness, and so on, including every aspect of the Dharma of Buddha. Buddha is like the great sun and the appearance of the light of compassionate wisdom, which unobstructedly shines upon and completely permeates all sentient beings. Since this dispels the root of the darkness of ignorance to benefit all beings, this is the stage called All-Pervasive Light, the stage of fully enlightened Buddha.

143. gzungs. Generally, gzungs is the preservation of any kind of knowledge. Since ordinary beings have dualistic habit, there is always a gap between the knower and knowledge, which is why ordinary beings are forgetful. In the state of Buddha, there is no different knowledge to hold because knowledge is the knower and the knower is knowledge, forever. That is why enlightenment is called the body of indivisible knower and knowledge.

144. spobs pa.

In the swift, profound path of the Vajrayana tradition, by depending on the completion stage with and without characteristics, if an individual is a practitioner of Mantrayana and has first recognized the point of view, then it is as said:[145]

> Buddha, even though your nature is naturally free from
> attachment and aversion,
> You manifest desirable qualities for those who have desire,
> And you manifest wrath for those who are wrathful.
> By skillful means, you always guide beings. I bow to you.

Thus, as this shows, all Buddhas, who are free from duality and abiding in the dustless space of dharmadhatu, can be synthesized according to Mantrayana tradition into the peaceful and wrathful enlightened bodies and purelands. All of these enlightened bodies and purelands appear according to the minds of all sentient beings, the objects to subdue. Thus, by directly knowing the peaceful and wrathful mandala of the Three Kayas that abides in one's own mind, from experience, it is necessary to open this mandala until it is fully apparent. As it says in *The Ocean:*[146]

> The truth of Buddha is fully perfected from the beginning,
> And since this abides within all who possess a body,
> This spontaneously present mandala of the Victorious Ones
> Resides in the heart of all who have bodies.
> Holding boundless aspects of peacefulness and wrathfulness,
> If this precious nature is not forsaken in this life,
> By the power of practice it is made clearly apparent.

Thus, in the heart of all sentient beings dwells the mandala of the forty-two peaceful wisdom deities, and, as the natural manifestation of the forty-two peaceful wisdom deities, in the brain within the skull is the mandala of the fifty-eight wrathful deities, which are the origin of inconceivable peaceful and wrathful deities. Their essence is immaterial and naturally appears as the five lights that rely on the pure relative causal essential fluid. Abiding within the energy channels in the manner of the principal deity and retinue, this is

145. *dpung pa bzang po'i rgyud, The Noble Shoulder Tantra.*
146. *rgya mtsho.*

called the basic space mandala of vajradhatu.[147] Just as it says in the basis of the developing stage Mahayoga teachings, this mandala that abides as the basis is developed by depending on the three samadhis,[148] which predominantly reveal the developing stage. The three samadhis are the samadhi of Dharmakaya great emptiness wisdom, which is just as it is; the samadhi of Sambhogakaya, which is always light appearances; and the samadhi of Nirmanakaya, which is the cause of wisdom deities, palaces, and purelands, such as the syllable of the deity and mandala that manifest. Just as it is said in the teachings on the completion stage transmission of Anuyoga, the completion stage with characteristics is predominantly revealed and practiced by depending on the energy channels, vital energies, and essential fluids. The connection between the mind and the brain from a Buddhist point of view must be distinguished from the nihilist idea that the mind is part of the brain. Since both nihilists and Buddhists acknowledge a connection between mind and brain, it may seem as if they have a similar idea about the relationship between mind and brain, but the Buddhist view is entirely different.

Just as within substance, pillars and beams support a building, so the brain and heart support the whole body. Except the wisdom body of Buddhas, any kind of form has a support, including the human body. Nihilists think that the mind is part of the brain and that mental activity arises out of biological functions. Buddhists, however, consider mind as able to be independent of the body and the brain, and the brain, like all phenomena, as originating from mind.

If mind were merely a part of the brain, this would not explain why the mind can travel everywhere in dreams without the physical brain while the brain remains with the body in bed. However, it cannot be said that the mind is completely free from the brain. Although one physical body can be left in the bed and another mental body can be traveling, there is still a habit of the mind going together with the brain of the physical body. Nihilists believe that this habit is all there is, and that the brain manipulates beings by controlling their experience and behavior. In Buddhism, mind is not part of the brain; it is the basis of all.

147. Vajradhatu is forever indestructible stainless space. Dharmadhatu is unobstructed stainless space phenomena. Vajradhatu and dharmadhatu are indivisible, but to discern between them only for practice, vajradhatu is explained as indestructible and dharmadhatu is explained as appearances.
148. chos sku de bzhin nyid kyi ting nge 'dzin; longs sku kun tu snang ba'i ting nge 'dzin; and sprul sku rgyu yi ting nge 'dzin.

New practitioners may consider it very strange that, according to inner Vajrayana theory, wrathful deities are abiding in the palace of the skull, which holds the brain, and are the reflection of peaceful deities abiding in the palace of the heart. According to science, everything functions through the brain, so why can't wrathful manifestations function? It is a much vaster image because it is the manifestation of deities, and deities are immeasurable, limitless phenomena. Even nihilists must acknowledge that mind can create infinite phenomena. Buddhists believe that unobstructed mind can manifest anything, and that includes the belief that wrathful deities manifest from peaceful deities.

Some New School followers have criticized the Nyingma teachings about deities in the heart. They say that since the Nyingmapas teach that there are many deities running from the heart to the brain, it is lucky that this does not make people crazy. These materialistic followers do not understand these teachings in a spiritual way, because they only accept a physical level of reality and cannot imagine or believe in what is beyond their perception. Since mind is unobstructed, any phenomena can appear. There is only one mind, but it is obvious that even if one never goes anywhere, one's mind can go everywhere because it has infinite phenomena. Mind is actually indestructible dharmadhatu and dharmata openness, but its aspect can be anything and anywhere because that is the quality of mind. Therefore, a view that denies deities in the heart and brain is a sign of ignorance and unawareness of the characteristics of mind.

The analogy is given of a house with four windows: from outside the house, it looks as if there are four different lights, one in each window; yet inside the house, there is only one light. This is like the mind, which has one essence but can reflect everywhere. If one does not materialize each phenomenon and reject spiritual appearances, one will not be deluded. If one materializes, one cannot have any wrathful deities in the skull or peaceful deities in the heart, because one prevents oneself from realizing them. By visualizing them, one can see them.

Having eyes so that one can see with circumstances, having ears so that one can hear with circumstances, having a nose so that one can smell with circumstances, having a tongue so that one can taste with circumstances, and having a sense of touch so that one can feel with circumstances, the qualities of these senses appear to ordinary beings to be different. All of these are the manifestations of one mind, so it is unnecessary to think that each sense is different and coming from a part of the mind, and that each of these parts of the mind is traveling through each of these senses. Wisdom mind is oneness, so the senses are not divided for Buddha. Seeing, hearing, smelling, tasting, and touching become divided for ordinary beings because they have to see, hear, smell, taste, and touch separately. Buddha has purified cognitive obscurations, so all the senses are simultaneous.

If one does not accept the manifestation of wisdom mind's reflection, and if one thinks it is strange for deities to travel from the heart to the brain, then instead of trying to deny the appearances of the inner phenomena of practice and the recognition of the naturally pure phenomena of deities, one should consider how one's own senses travel toward outer objects. When one sees, is one's mind going to one's eyes and traveling with them, and when one hears, is one's mind going to one's ears? According to Buddhist teachings, when mind is transformed, it becomes dharmadhatu wisdom, but momentarily, as long as sentient beings have the five senses and a body, they are seeing and perceiving each phenomenon differently with each sense, even though mind is oneness. By analogy, suppose a monkey is in an empty room with five windows. The monkey can move about freely everywhere within the room. But someone looking at the windows from the outside might think that there were many different monkeys appearing now in one window, now in the next, although there is actually only one monkey. Likewise, even though the senses are differentiated for sentient beings, they are actually all coming from the oneness of sole mind. Sole mind is the source of all peaceful and wrathful deities. According to Buddhist teachings, the divided senses that are distracted toward the outer objects of ordinary mind are transformed into undivided wisdom senses that are inseparable from wisdom appearances, so all immeasurable Buddhas abide as the mandalas of the peaceful and wrathful deities.

While one has a body with the five skandhas, it can be considered the support of the mind, but not in the way that nihilists regard the body as the basis of the mind. Nihilists think that when they die, their mind also dies, because they do not believe in the continuity of mind beyond the life of the body. In Buddhism, even when the physical karmic body dies, there will still be a habit body. Although it is unnecessary for anyone to have a brain after death, whether or not the individual has the conception of having a brain will depend on previous habit. One cannot say, however, that there is a brain or there is not a brain once the physical karmic body has been left by the mind. In any case, the mind is not part of the brain at all, and continues after death. Since mind is continuous until the state of enlightenment is attained through practice, any kind of forms can exist according to mind's phenomena. When one is released from the karmic body, those who have believed in all of the peaceful and wrathful deities can open the mandala of the peaceful and wrathful deities so that they fill the sky. It is said that one can attain fully enlightened Buddhahood in the in-between state, especially in the dharmata bardo, when the mandala opens by realizing one's own self-manifestation.

The Buddhist description of peaceful deities abiding in the heart does not mean that they abide in a flesh heart with flesh bodies. The heart actually means wisdom, the essence of all phenomena. Likewise, the description of wrathful deities abiding in the brain in the skull does not refer to the gray matter of the physical brain. One should also not think that the heart is made of flesh but the wisdom deities are different, as though there are two different levels occurring at one time. The point is that the heart and brain are the essence of the physical body, and that the essence is to be transformed into wisdom mandala, which is beyond the fleshly heart and brain.

One should also not think, as some nihilist scientists do, that mind is part of the brain. Mind is everything, not only the brain and heart, and not something that exists only while beings are living in this world. When practitioners pass away, their minds are continuous with wisdom deities. Mind is not abandoned, and does not diminish after the physical brain and heart have been left behind. Mind is continuous with wisdom mandala, for those who believe this and who practice. Also, the mind cannot faint, because it is free from the ordinary brain and heart, so it does not rely only on a substantial brain and heart. Therefore, when practitioners die, mind is transformed into peaceful and wrathful deities, and practitioners have no conception that they have left their heart and brain with their corpse from a habit of materializing them. As a simple analogy, someone is determined to go to an island and reside there without returning to his former place on the mainland. Once he arrives with his necessities at the island and establishes himself there, he does not need to think about going back to his previous place or about a boat, because he has already fulfilled his wish to settle on the island.

Peacefulness and wrathfulness are not completely different in some kind of material way. The essence of both peaceful and wrathful deities is Dharmakaya, which is indestructible, and they are the unobstructed qualities of wisdom mind. When ordinary people become upset with circumstances, they become wrathful, demonstrating a sign of wrathful deity. When people are happy, their energy becomes serene, demonstrating a sign of peaceful deity. Within one being's mind, wrath and peace exist as manifestations of wrathful and peaceful deities. Practitioners are actually developing these wrathful wisdom deities and peaceful wisdom deities.

In developing stage and completion stage practice, during abiding in evenness, there is the complete purification of grasping mind, never wavering from the wisdom of the great nature of stainless emptiness of Dharmakaya. During the state after abiding in evenness, there is the purification of grasping at ordinary, impure objects, so that only purelands, celestial palaces, and male and female deities as the appearance of enlightened bodies and wisdom are seen. Through seeing in that way and practicing, any grasping at the object, which is the space of phenomena, and the subject, which is deity, will be fully purified without exception. At that time, not even a subtle trace of a particle of reality substance can be found. This is formless Dharmakaya. From the self-radiance of formless Dharmakaya manifests extremely pure empty form. This is the supreme form of the Sambhogakaya with the seven aspects of union of the ocean of enlightened bodies and purelands, pervaded by the power of empty form. From the blessings of those enlightened bodies and purelands, the form of the Nirmanakaya manifests. As it says in *Revealing the Names of Manjushri:*[149]

> Formlessness, form, and supreme form.

Thus, as it says, these Three Kayas can be attained by practitioners.

For all of the above, according to the doctrine of the supremely sublime tradition of upadesha, there is the Great Perfection of Atiyoga. For those with keen faculties or even those who are lazy yet have profound faith, although there is not even the subtlest substance to meditate upon, by directly recognizing this uncontrived nature introduced by one's wisdom teacher and with the determination to abide in Dharmakaya, cyclic existence and the phenomena of enlightenment are simultaneously self-liberated in Dharmakaya by the teachings of cutting through all substantial and insubstantial phenomena.[150] Those who are diligent will carry the path of the appearances of the Three Kayas directly, which is the appearance of the luminosity that abides as the basis. Purifying the karmic body into light, to become fully enlightened, is the practice of the teaching of passing simultaneously to the direct clear light manifestation of Buddhas,[151] which is

149. *'phags pa 'jam dpal gyi mtshan yang dag par brjod pa.*
150. khregs chod.
151. thod rgal.

Sambhogakaya and Nirmanakaya. Gradually, through practice, the qualities of the four appearances are perfected, and the four stages of becoming a pure awareness holder become fully apparent.

In *Revealing the Names of Manjushri,* it says:

> The appearance of wisdom is illuminated.
> The light of beings is wisdom light.
> The glorious rosary is so beautiful to behold.

Thus it says. The essence of the continuity of mind of all sentient beings does not exist materially, but its aspects appear unobstructedly. According to the Dharma terms of the Mahayana, this is called Buddha nature. According to the Dharma terms of the Great Perfection, it is called essence, nature, and compassion. This threefold wisdom abiding as the basis has unobstructed qualities and is the origin of all immeasurable peaceful, wrathful, and semi-wrathful aspects of Buddhas, which are practiced with skillful means.

Through the power of practice, when the deities of light form actually start to become apparent, this is the appearance of directly seeing the nature of dharmata. As these manifestations increase, the movement of the vital energy of the five elements is purified as the space of the five wisdoms. The arising of the phenomena of purelands is the appearance of increasing manifestation. From becoming more and more apparent, all appearances encompassing everything are seen as the five Buddha families, the male and female Bodhisattvas, and the inconceivable appearances of all purelands and palaces of mandalas. This is the appearance of attaining the culmination of ultimate awareness. Then, the ordinary impure karmic vital energy of the five elements is exhausted in the space of the five wisdoms. There are no longer any conditioned phenomena of either appearance or non-appearance. Like the cloudless sky in autumn, this is the appearance of the exhaustion of the phenomena of dharmata.

The four pure awareness holders are described as follows. Although not yet free from the trap of the previous residue of the karmic body, from practice the mind has already ripened as the enlightened body of wisdom deity. At the time of death, when the mind is free from the trap of the karmic body, the enlightened body of deity becomes apparent. This is called the fully ripened Vidyadhara. Without leaving the residual karmic body, transforming it into the body of wisdom deity, ultimately to join the state of enlightenment, is called the immortal Vidyadhara. One's own body becomes the wisdom body of whatever deity one is practicing, called the Mahamudra Vidyadhara. Finally, fully perfecting all qualities of purification and realization without exception is attainment of the state called the completely accomplished Vidyadhara.

When seeing the appearances of directly seeing dharmata and increasing manifestation while still within a residual karmic body, it is the state of the fully ripened Vidyadhara. When seeing the appearance of attaining the culmination of ultimate awareness, it is the state of attaining the immortal Vidyadhara. When seeing the appearance of the exhaustion of the phenomena of dharmata, it is the state of the great pervasiveness Vidyadhara. When all of these are perfected, it is said that the completely accomplished Vidyadhara is attained, the supreme state of Buddha.

Although the state of Buddha is one essence, according to the aspect of different qualities, many different names of characteristics are revealed. As Great Omniscient Rongzompa said:

> The supreme state among all states is called the state of being a Vidyadhara. It is also called the state of a vajra holder. It is also called the supreme state of sublime wisdom and skillful means. It is also called the thirteenth stage of Buddha. This is the stage to abide in.

Thus it is said. Although there are distinctions concerning the state of Buddha, it is as said in *The Tantra of the Ornament of the Vajra Essence:*[152]

> Although it is said that there are twelve stages of Buddha, the distinction that the stages are higher or lower was not said. The nature of emptiness and compassion, these two, the five wisdoms, and the five Buddha families are said to be the twelve stages. Furthermore, the three states of Buddha are said to indicate the aspect of the connection with Dharmakaya, wisdom, and compassion. By that blessing, it is said that there are the qualities of enlightened body and wisdom. This is not said in order to define gradual stages of being higher or lower.

152. *rdo rje snying po rgyan gyi rgyud.*

From *The Glorious Lasso of Skillful Means:*[153]

> This transcends the stage of All-Pervasive Light.
>
> Thus it is said. What this means is that in the space of Dharmakaya without characteristics, nonconceptual wisdom and the blessing of compassion are the self-occurring effortless mandala of enlightened body and wisdom. It[154] did not mention stages that gradually ascend. From other upadesha teachings, it is said that the stage of Kuntuzangpo is without distinctions, revealing the greatness of the nature of beginningless purity. This is unlike the lower vehicles of traveling and progressing on a path toward attainment. Thus it is said.
>
> Also, in the sutras revealing the meaning of absolute truth, it is said that there are uncommon characteristics, uncommon complete liberation, the uncommon wisdom of complete liberation, uncommon perfectly pure objects of activity, the uncommon way of entering without contradiction, and so on. Although taught in this way, nevertheless, it can never be said that the stage of Buddha can be systematized into higher and lower divisions. If someone says this, it is against the speech of Buddha and against logic.

Thus said Omniscient Rongzompa.

Great Omniscient Longchen Rabjam said:

> The appearance of wisdom and the nonattachment of great compassion is the twelfth stage, Lotus of Nonattachment.[155] The final attainment of the power of all phenomena is the thirteenth stage, Spontaneously Perfect Vajra Holder, or the Great Gathering of the Wheel of Holy Dharma Sounds Manifesting Sambhogakaya, or the Great Sublime Stage, or the Stage of Vidyadhara, which are all simultaneously contained in the perfection of complete accomplishment. Because the thirteenth stage is Dharmakaya, free from elaboration, it is the Great Sublime stage. From that

153. *dpal thabs kyi zhags pa.*

154. The passage just quoted.

155. The lotus blooms from the mud but is not affected by it, just as Buddhas are always in the realms of sentient beings out of compassion but are not affected by samsara.

state of Dharmakaya, the Sambhogakaya purelands appear, called The Great Gathering of the Wheel of Holy Dharma Sounds. This is also called Vajra Holder, because it is the Buddha of all. It is the essence of all ultimate awareness, called Vidyadhara. These stages are not like steps on a staircase, where one is higher than the other. Even though the essence of Buddha is oneness, the aspects are the Three Kayas. If one discerns the aspects of the qualities, there are more than that, it is said. Because of immeasurable bliss, there is the fourteenth stage, Great Bliss. The fifteenth stage is Samadhi. The sixteenth stage is Unsurpassed Wisdom. There is no need to establish or reject the essence of the meaning. The essence of the meaning is free from existing or not existing, so these stages are explained as only one state. Since Kuntuzangpo has no separation, the Great Perfection is oneness. So therefore, from *The All-Doing Great King:*[156]

> Only oneness is doing everything. It is the state
> of enlightenment.

Thus it is said.

Therefore, even though there are subtle differences in the way in which the two Great Omniscient Ones, Rongzompa and Longchenpa, explain the state of Buddha, because all appearances of qualities of Buddhas' enlightened bodies and wisdom are the inconceivable aspects of appearances, no matter how it is explained, it will always be the supreme resonance of the pristine. Since the essential nature of the state of Kuntuzangpo with no distinctions is inconceivably secret, any attempt to use the reasoning of worldly conventions or the attachment-based logic of intellectuals is a tiring contradiction. Even if one exerts oneself with hardship, it is impossible to find any contradiction in the knowledge of sublime speech about the state of Kuntuzangpo. According to the practitioner's faculties, however, the qualities of the stages of the path can be attained gradually or swiftly. So, according to the experience of individuals and the guidance of their holy teachers, these stages will develop. The meaning cannot be entirely explained here for the many varieties of practitioners.

Thus, relying on the mind, when the meaning of tranquil stillness, true seeing, abiding in evenness, after-evenness, and so on, is understood, when

156. *kun byed rgyal po.*

naturally settling, one finally can attain the wisdom of Buddhas, which does not originate from the mind. As it says in *The Tantra Containing the Actual Meaning of the Great Perfection:*[157]

> By following the elephant's footprints, the elephant is found.
> If one tries to find the king of wisdom, first one has to go
> with ordinary mind.
> Through ordinary mind, if one searches for the meaning,
> Then one definitely finds the self-awareness wisdom king,
> But not grasping at finding this wisdom king is freedom
> from clinging.
> Whatever is free from clinging is not ordinary clinging mind;
> It is self-occurring wisdom body.
> Not originating from ordinary mind, Buddha is found.

Thus it is said.

The reason for this much explanation here on the benefits of samadhi is given in *The Sutra Requested by Jewel Crown:*[158]

> Compared with hearing and contemplating for many eons,
> Meditating for a single day on the meaning of Dharma has
> greater merit.
> The reason is that meditation brings freedom from the path
> of birth and death.

Thus, as said, remember this and sustain mindfulness.

Now, concerning knowledge, the knowable sciences include art, medicine, language, logic and philosophy, and inner awareness, which are the five major fields of study. Within language, there are poetry, semantics, composition, dance and drama, and astrology, which are the five minor fields of study, which when brought together comprise the ten sciences. The study of inner awareness is taught in the Vinaya, the Sutra, and the Abhidharma, which are called the Tripitaka, or the teachings of the three categories. These teachings are trainings on predominantly practicing the meaning of

157. *rdzogs chen nges don 'dus pa'i rgyud.*
158. *gtor rin po ches zhus pa'i mdo.*

morality, predominantly practicing samadhi, and predominantly practicing knowledge.

The meaning of the teachings of the three categories is synthesized in the categories of the secret Mantrayana of the Vidyadharas as follows. The essence of the teachings of the Vinaya and its practice of morality are contained in general and special samaya. The essence of the Sutra and its teachings of samadhi are contained within the developing stage and the completion stage with characteristics, such as practices using channels and airs, or the completion stage without characteristics, such as the practice of tranquil stillness or true seeing. The essence of the Abhidharma and its teachings on prajna are contained within Mahasandhi by perfectly establishing the Mantrayana view of absolute, simultaneously born wisdom, or great uncompounded self-occurring wisdom, dharmata. Therefore, Omniscient Rongzompa explained that practicing all of the knowledge of the Vinaya, Sutra, and Abhidharma is upwardly contained in the Vajrayana, so it is not necessary for the knowledge of the Vajrayana to descend down into the Sutra tradition.

In this way, when the knowledge of the ten fields of study is understood according to the teachings, it is knowing the nature as it is, and knowing countless aspects of Dharma, from all to all.[159] Or it is knowing the truth of conditional relative phenomena and knowing the unconditional absolute truth of dharmata.

The definition of relative truth, or *kun rdzob bden pa*, then, is as follows: *kun* means all phenomena, and *rdzob* means illusion, which is impermanent and deceptive; *bden pa* means each individual's deluded appearances, whether positive or negative, which are perceived as being true, or trueness according to the individual of whatever is perceived as good or bad. This is relative truth.

The definition of absolute truth, or *don dam bden pa*, is as follows. *Don* is the meaning or purpose of those who wish for liberation in unmistaken knowledge. That dharmata is not going to deceive, and therefore it is sublime, or *dam pa*. Truth, or *bden pa*, is unmistaken knowing, or trueness in the essence of dharmata, which therefore is called absolute truth.

Whatever appears as the truth of relative conditional phenomena, if it has the ability to fulfill its own purpose according to time, like the moon in

159. The expression "from all to all" or "from everything to everything" means "including everything."

the sky having the ability to dispel darkness, is called actual relative truth, *yang dag kun rdzob*. Whatever appearances manifest that do not have the ability to fulfill a purpose, such as the moon's reflection on water, are called inverted relative truth, *log pa'i kun rdzob*. As it says in *The Two Truths:*[160]

> Even though the appearances are similar, whether
> a purpose is fulfilled
> Is due to the power to function or not to function:
> Actual relative truth or inverted relative truth,
> These are the distinctions of relative truth.

Thus it is said.

To explain this according to the doctrine of the general Madhyamika, there are four characteristics of the appearances of relative truth. First, there is agreement about the relative appearances of outer and inner existence, from the highest learned scholar to the lowest uneducated simpleton. The next characteristic is the ability to function, such as the solid earth that functions as the support of beings and all other substances. The next characteristic is creation by root causes and contributing circumstances, which means that all compounded phenomena occur from myriad root causes and contributing circumstances, such as the four elements, and so on. The final characteristic is that if one examines whatever functions, it comes from conditions, so it naturally cannot be true.

According to the doctrine of the Great Madhyamika, all theories from worldly theories up to the Yogachara doctrine are inverted relative truth. Why is this? All ordinary individuals of the world think that appearances are real, and then they grasp at them and become attached. All eternalists believe in permanence, and all nihilists believe that there is nothing beyond what is experienced by the five senses. All the Hearers of the Vaibhashika school believe that all phenomena are composed of irreducible particles of substance, and that mind is nondual and partless, as a subtle consciousness. This is their absolute truth and the support of the karma of cause and effect. The Yogachara[161] followers believe that nongrasping mind exists independently, so that is their absolute truth. The Madhyamika followers say that in all of these doctrines, by holding false doctrines as true through being

160. *bden gnyis.*
161. Yogachara is *sems tsam pa,* or the Mind Only school.

attached to them, there is no ability to abandon samsara or attain liberation.

The tradition of the Great Madhyamika of actual relative truth is as said in *The Root of Knowledge:*[162]

> Whatever arises comes from interdependency, is unobstructed, unborn, unceasing, not eternal, not coming, not going, not different, and not oneness.

Thus, it is said that all practitioners who correctly realize the view of the great Madhyamika will experience the appearances of after-evenness meditation as actual relative truth. These appearances are unobstructed like magic; unborn like a dream; unceasing like the moon in water; not eternal, like an echo; not coming, like an optical illusion; not going, like a mirage; not separate from form, like a reflection; and not the same as form or not oneness, like an emanation. Like these eight magical examples, appearances are without true existence, but they appear to everyone. Seeing all appearances as magical, and therefore abandoning attachment to existence as true, there is the ability to fulfill the meaning of liberation. Realizing that appearances naturally resemble magic comes about through the root and contributing circumstances of receiving teachings from one's own root Lama, by one who has the special sign of the handprint of having previously created merit and wisdom. Deceptive appearances do not exist in absolute truth, because if all phenomena are recognized as empty of existence, non-existence, being true, and being false, then false theories do not even exist. Thus, the four characteristics of actual relative truth are explained.

To explain this according to Vajrayana: Thinking that the ordinary universe and its contents are real and being attached to them constitute inverted relative truth. Seeing the container of all outer appearances as purelands and palaces, and the inner essence of all sentient beings as male and female wisdom deities, which are only naturally pure, is actual relative truth.

In conclusion, the two truths are seen in three ways. Perceiving appearances as individually self-existent through attachment is the stage of ordinary beings, so it is inverted relative truth. Recognizing that appearances are deluded while still having attachment is the stage of the general sublime, so it is actual relative truth. When there is neither the conception of appearance nor non-appearance, so therefore there is no attachment to

162. *rtsa ba shes rab.*

conception or nonattachment to conception, this is the state of Buddha, which is absolute truth. It is said:

> The impure, the impure pure,
> And the extremely pure
> Are the stages of sentient beings, Bodhisattvas,
> And Buddhas.[163]

Thus it is said.

Furthermore, regarding absolute truth, there is the absolute truth of having cut all doubt with the three states of knowledge, which are the states of hearing many Dharma teachings, contemplation, and meditation. There is also the absolute truth of the practitioner's experience and the absolute truth of the ordinary individual's general inference. The absolute truth of all sublime beings is seeing the nature of the characteristics of absolute truth directly. There is also the absolute truth of enumeration and the absolute truth without enumeration of philosophers, including many different distinctions explained in various teachings. The quintessence of them all is synthesized in *The Five Stages*[164] by the Glorious Protector Nagarjuna:

> Both relative truth and absolute truth
> Must be discerned.
> When they become indivisible,
> Then it is called union.
> This is the nature of nondual wisdom,
> Which, without abiding, has transcended suffering.

Also, Shantideva said:

> When tangible and intangible conceptions
> Are not appearing in the mind,
> At that time, there are no other forms.
> Aimlessness is great peace.

163. Sentient beings have impure phenomena. Bodhisattvas have both impure and pure phenomena. They have the previous karmic residue of impure phenomena, but they do not believe in its reality because they are practicing, so they are excelling to the state of Buddhas. The extremely pure state is Buddhahood.
164. *rim lnga.*

Also, it says in *Gone to Lanka:*

> That which is unborn is only a single truth,
> But children keep repeating that there are four truths.
> If the essence of enlightenment is attained, not even
> a single truth exists,
> So how can there then be four?

Thus it is said. Also, Lord Atisha said:

> Sublime wisdom is always without grasping at existence as true.

Thus, as said, whoever knows and whatever is known with no attachment and no obstruction is the essence of prajnaparamita. This essence of knowledge is knowing the meaning of emptiness just as it is and achieving the depth of confidence. In other texts, it is said:

> If emptiness is seen in the wrong way
> By those with less knowledge, they will fail to achieve confidence.

As it is said, separating appearances and emptiness, like separating hairs, and disparaging appearances of skillful means by only focusing on the nature of emptiness with attachment, are deviations toward the nihilist view. This is said in order not to deny phenomena through having a wrong point of view about emptiness. Misinterpreting emptiness as nothingness will cause doubt about the system of the basis of the inseparability of the two truths, the path of the inseparability of the two accumulations of merit and wisdom, and the result of the inseparability of the Two Kayas, causing this system to be misinterpreted. For that purpose, it is said:

> The perfection of knowledge is free from speech, thought,
> or expression.
> Unborn, unceasing, like the essential nature of sky,
> Only the wisdom of discerning self-awareness sustains this.
> Homage to the mother of all the Victors of the three times.

Thus, as said, from emptiness, the view of the essential nature is free from limitations. Like the nature of sky, this will never fall into the limitation of appearances. From the view of appearances, wisdom's discerning self-awareness is self-sustaining, so it will never fall into the limitation of emptiness. The wisdom of the great equality of nonduality has no object, no place, and not even the subtlest trace of a particle of substance. Great stainless emptiness is the origin of all pure appearances. This is the wisdom vajra that dispels all fear. From the speech of Great Omniscient Rongzom Chökyi Zangpo:

> Since all fear is dispelled from the nature of emptiness, whoever grasps at material substance will be unprotected and not liberated. How is this to be understood? Hearers are self-liberated by realizing the selflessness of the self, but they are not totally liberated, because they have not realized the selflessness of phenomena. Solitary Realizers are liberated by realizing the selflessness of the self and part of the selflessness of the phenomena of objects, but they are not totally liberated, because they still hold to the existence of grasping mind. Yogachara practitioners are liberated by realizing that there is no dualistic mind, but they are not totally liberated, because they still think there is an independent wisdom without duality. Madhyamika practitioners are liberated by realizing that there is nothing that is absolute, but they are not totally liberated, because they hold the view of seeing relative truth.
>
> Well, then, suppose it is said, "If there is a view that not even the slightest material substance exists, then the activity of skillful means would cease and separate from compassion, so that wisdom and compassion would not be united and liberation could not occur." The reply to this is as follows. Compassion arises with the aim of sentient beings, but it is not necessary to think of establishing the view that sentient beings are material. Without establishing the existence of sentient beings, benefiting sentient beings with all their appearances of happiness and suffering is just magical. This is pure, untiring great compassion without attachment. So, it is unnecessary to view the activity of skillful means as material. Therefore, since the nature of emptiness dispels all forms of fear, do not be afraid in shunyata.

Thus it is said.

Nihilists do not believe in anything, including a self, that exists beyond the experience of the momentary five senses and five skandhas. They do not accept the continuity of mind or try to attain enlightenment, but they cannot make dualistic mind cease, whether they are dead or alive. Mind is continuous, even though its manifestations are sometimes negative and sometimes positive, since the basis of mind exists intangibly. Therefore, nihilists cause samsara. Eternalists believe in everlasting gods who are creators. From a Buddhist point of view, this means that eternalists believe in a permanent self, since eternalist gods have a self because they create objects. According to Buddhism, if beings keep a self, they cannot become enlightened. Therefore, even though eternalists are unlike nihilists who do not accept the continuity of mind or try to attain enlightenment, the eternalist belief in a permanent, continuous self, like the nihilist lack of belief, also causes samsara.

As long as beings have a self, the self is a subject, and subjects have objects. If Hinayana followers realize that there is no individual self, they will not cause passions, since the individual self is the origin of the passions. Hinayana followers thus acknowledge individual selflessness, but they leave objective phenomena as they are. The Solitary Realizers believe there is no self, just as the Hearers do, but their special additional attribute is that they think phenomena have no independent self, even though they believe that grasping mind is there. The higher vehicles refer to this attribute as "one and a half selflessnesses." Rongzompa explains this in the passage quoted above. According to the Mahayana and Vajrayana, one cannot be totally liberated without entering the Mahayana and Vajrayana. Because Hearers leave objective phenomena, there is a potential to come back, and because Solitary Realizers leave grasping mind, there is a potential to come back. Actually, their ideas of liberation are much better than nihilism or eternalism, and by attaining their kind of liberation according to their intention, they can be in peace for many eons, as long as their previous cognitive obscurations do not arise. When their previous residual habit of a limited view eventually reemerges, however, causing their obstacles to delay fully enlightened Buddhahood, then they must enter the path of Mahayana or Vajrayana. Without entering them, there is no way to be totally liberated.

The benefits of developing bodhichitta are as Shantideva said:

> Since instantly, when bodhichitta vows are taken, one becomes the object of worship of worldly gods and human beings imprisoned in samsara, one is called the heir of all Sugatas.

Thus, as said, in this way, ordinary beings transform into objects of worship. As said in *The Sutra of the Adornment of Stalks:*

> Sons of the lineage,
> Whoever develops the supreme mind of bodhichitta,
> All effort of that person's body, speech, and mind that
> is made from intention
> Will always become one taste of virtue.

Thus, just as it is said, from everything to everything, there will always be immeasurable benefit.

The Accumulation of Merit through Mandala Offerings

The Meaning of Mandala and Buddhist Cosmology

The third uncommon inner preliminary practice is the mandala offering, and here one must accept traditional Buddhist cosmology as represented in the mandala, or assembly of deities. For those who are learned in Buddhist theory and have no doubt about the speech of Buddha, it is unnecessary to explain the difference between general ideas about cosmology and the Buddhist cosmological system of viewing all existence. However, for new practitioners who have faith, are learning how to practice, and are searching for an understanding of Buddhist theory, it is necessary to clearly analyze this difference in order to clean contradiction and misconception. Dharma practice means engaging and developing one's own phenomena through pure view, so practitioners must have a correct view from the beginning in order to believe in how one can open and develop wisdom mind to attain fully enlightened Buddhahood.

Whoever is Buddhist must believe in Buddhist cosmology. According to the metaphysical category of Abhidharma from the Sutra tradition, there are teachings about Mount Meru and the four continents, and according to the inner Mantrayana tradition, there are teachings about purelands, such as the Kalachakra, which describes the outer Kalachakra universe, the inner Kalachakra vajra body, and other Kalachakra mandala systems. These teachings are totally different from ordinary contemporary ideas about the continents of the material world and explanations of the material universe.

The Buddhist cosmological system of the sutras and the mandala tradition of Mantrayana are not accepted by those who only believe in a small part of material existence and choose material explanations of phenomena over a spiritual view. Followers of Buddhism are not supposed to be affected by this. Those who believe in spiritual doctrines have to uphold them according to each of their theories, without adjusting to a view of disbelief in spirituality.

Nihilists do not believe in what is beyond the perception of their senses, so the spiritual phenomena of Buddhist cosmology, including Mount Meru, are unbelievable to them. Of course, nihilists accept the existence of the world in which we are living, called Dzambuling[165] in Buddhist cosmology, but they do not accept the existence of other worlds and universes described in Buddhist scriptures because they cannot perceive them. Even if they openly doubt Buddhist cosmology, however, it is doubtlessly true because it comes from the teachings of the Buddha, and there is no greater omniscience than that of the Buddha, who manifested whatever teachings would benefit beings according to their capacity for understanding.

From a Buddhist point of view, worlds that exist beyond the perception of beings with obscured karmic senses cannot be denied. Other beings with clearer senses can perceive them, since their perception depends on individual phenomena. Until the spiritual appearances revealed by the Buddha become perceptible, one has to believe in them with faith, and then what is imperceptible can become perceptible. There is no negation in believing the speech of the Buddha, because the Buddha's speech is flawless. If one believes only in what modern nihilists can see, one cannot believe that there is anything beyond ordinary existence. With this view, there cannot be any religion with a spiritual foundation. If one only wants to believe what ordinary nihilists believe, one cannot be spiritual, because being spiritual means believing in what is sacred and beyond the ordinary.

A rejection of Buddhist cosmology occurs when spiritual phenomena are denied rather than proven by faith and the experience of practice. Faith is not stagnant but arises when a spiritual connection is made and increases through practice. Without the effort to make a spiritual connection, faith does not develop, so spiritual phenomena are not accepted and perceptible reality is seen as the ultimate truth.

It is especially strange if Buddhists deny the existence of the mandala of

165. dzam bu gling; Skt. Jambudvipa.

the universe described in Buddhist cosmology, because for many hundreds of years, Buddhists have been visualizing and offering immeasurable mandalas of universes to the Three Jewels, including their sublime teachers, saying:

> OM. The golden foundation of the earth, strewn with flowers,
> Adorned by Mount Meru, the four continents, the sun and the moon:
> By dedicating and offering these toward Buddhas' purelands,
> May all beings attain pureland.

Even if some Buddhists do not see Mount Meru from their habit of reality, they still offer these mandalas with many auspicious substances and visualizations of infinite positive phenomena. How can they offer mandalas without believing in what they are offering? To reject the existence of Mount Meru is to cancel these offerings and the entire tradition of making mandala offerings. Since mandala offerings are taught in the Buddha's own speech, which is always extremely positive and infallible, there is no reason to try to disprove them from a nihilist point of view.

Defined simply, nihilism is disbelief in anything beyond what is perceived by ordinary, shortsighted senses, and spirituality is belief in what is beyond these senses, which is the basis that sustains all religions. If Buddhists only follow what is said in nonreligious science, there is no basis of spirituality, because one cannot be truly spiritual if one only believes in what is materially evident. If one were to believe only in material reality, there would be no immaterial object of faith as a basis for belief, and therefore no spiritual path to follow or result of enlightenment to attain. Especially, Buddhists must believe that Buddha is omniscient in order to attain the all-knowing state of Buddhahood.

Ordinary beings have cognitive obscurations, so they cannot see spiritual phenomena. Buddhas have purified cognitive obscurations, so they can see anything, and because they see what is true and what brings permanent happiness, they have revealed sublime phenomena to ordinary beings in order for them to become sublime. If there is no belief in spiritual appearances, then one cannot create positive phenomena, because no matter what religion is followed, positive phenomena originally come from believing in spirituality. At least being a believer is better than being a nonbeliever. Being a nonbeliever is like being an animal; even though a nonbeliever coincidentally appears in a human body, it is not actually completely human because of the mind's limitation of disbelief. All the messages of the Koran, the Vedas, the Bible, and the Buddhist scriptures, as well as all celestial appearances of heavens, gods, and purelands, cannot be canceled just because they are not perceived with obscured senses. Even if ordinary beings cannot perceive what is taught by sublime beings, they still need to revere these teachings, never dismissing what they cannot see. If they dismiss what is imperceptible to them, it can cause darkness, because they are dismissing the light that shows them where to go.

All religions recognize that there is something beyond ordinary reality that cannot be seen by everyone, and followers are taught to pray and receive blessings through believing in what they may not yet be able to see. Even if spiritual phenomena are temporarily imperceptible to them, they will still create positive energy through faith and belief, increasing their spiritual connection. Even though inexperienced religious people do not see spiritual phenomena with their physical senses, they believe that they exist and can definitely be seen. In Islam, there are angels and entire cities of jinn that only the prophets can perceive. In Judaism, different Kabbalah texts describe up to five different realms of angels. Hindus believe that divine beings live in realms not seen by those who do not believe in them, but that the faithful can communicate with them through worship. Christians believe in heaven, God, and the Holy Spirit, all of which are imperceptible to the senses of nonbelievers. Buddhists believe that cyclic existence occurs from dualistic habit but can be transformed into immeasurable purelands of Buddhas by believing in them with faith, through prayer and meditation.

It is important to understand the characteristics of phenomena and not only to be drawn to substantialization. Obviously, beings have different phenomena, and beings are countless, so countless different beings have countless different phenomena. Some beings can perceive phenomena that other beings cannot perceive. Even within one day, some beings perceive the same phenomena together, but other beings situated in a different location cannot perceive those phenomena at the same time. Likewise, even though there are different religions in this world, and even though each religion talks about a basis of oneness, they still preach various beliefs, such as the Christian belief in Jesus and the Islamic belief in Muhammad, due to different perceptions of phenomena.

According to relative truth, if Buddhists reject the existence of Mount Meru, they must also say that all the objects of faith of eternalist religions not seen by nihilists or proven by science do not exist. By the logic of this view, the spiritual beliefs of all religious traditions are invalidated because it is thought that no one sees what is believed, and no one is supposed to believe in anything that is not immediately visible. This kind of logic does not take into account that the phenomena of beings are different because of their different habits, and therefore spiritual phenomena are not always invisible. Those who have spiritual phenomena see positive spiritual appearances, believe in them, and write texts about them. Then their followers believe their teachings, and through their faith and pure phenomena, these followers can also see spiritual appearances.

The existence of spiritual appearances cannot be verified from a nihilist view of accepting only what can be materially seen with ordinary perception. Whatever seems to exist or not exist is the phenomena of beings, including all negative and positive appearances of the universe. It is sad when supposedly spiritual Buddhists become too excited about modern scientific ideas and begin to think that spiritual phenomena do not exist because they cannot be explained by scientific theories or detected by scientific instruments. Nihilists are born to be nihilists, but those who are spiritual should not agree with them by believing one-sidedly in nihilist ideas.

Mind is not only in negation or just senselessly empty, but has unobstructed qualities. Why not use these unobstructed qualities in a positive way until attaining fully enlightened Buddhahood? In Buddhism, models of Buddhist cosmology represented by mandalas are used for everything, including offerings, paintings, and practice, and only create positive phenomena. One has to think that mandalas exist, including pure and impure material mandalas according to Nirmanakaya, and pure nonmaterial stainless phenomena according to Sambhogakaya. Both pure material and immaterial mandalas are indivisible from the forever stainless, inconceivable mandala of Dharmakaya. Why not believe this? Since one has mind, and mind has phenomena, why not use these phenomena to expand pure, flawless ecstasy mandala?

Buddhism distinguishes between compounded phenomena and the uncompounded. Compounded phenomena arise from root and contributing circumstances gathered within substance, whereas the uncompounded is not gathered within substance and therefore does not appear as ordinary, material phenomena. Nihilists only believe in the compounded phenomena of circumstances they can perceive, and think that the uncompounded that is not gathered within substance is non-existent. There is no expectation to see or believe in anything beyond what is compounded. In Buddhism, even though the uncompounded is not seen by those with obscured senses, any phenomena can potentially arise whenever root and contributing circumstances meet, which can appear in the mind and also to the senses. Phenomena cannot be limited by imposing the idea that something cannot exist. Belief in what is beyond obvious substantial existence is spiritual, and causes spiritual phenomena to become apparent.

Believing strongly in commonly accepted nihilist explanations of phenomena and attempting to use the discoveries of modern science to disprove spiritual explanations of ancient Buddhist cosmology demonstrate attraction to material thinking and ignorance about the nature of phenomena. Nonspiritual science considers each phenomenon to be seriously real, which is why scientists always disagree with one another and are continually proving and disproving theories that invariably change. Countless new conditioned phenomena can be discovered because phenomena are endless, but whatever is found exists within the root and contributing circumstances of temporary compounded substantial phenomena. Although scientists may think they have found what is ultimate, it will not last, because it only exists within the circumstance of conception. The Buddhist view of phenomena does not generate disagreement between beings over what is temporarily wrong and right. Buddhists do not have to torment themselves over hallucinatory ideas as though they were something that belonged to them, because they recognize that whatever conceptions are created, there is nothing that can belong to anyone.

With this point of view, if one has faith and follows sublime beings, one will not create contradiction through attachment to the reality of phenomena while living in this world, and therefore one will not cause disagreement or suffering. There will only be freedom for everyone. After one passes away, one will not leave any imprint of negativity for others to follow, like a condor who flies with skillful wings in the sky, soaring freely, perfectly, and silently without noise or disturbance, leaving no tracks.

Because mind is continuous, the phenomena of existence are continuous and do not permanently cease. Even death and birth are only names. Death is actually not death, as nihilists believe, but only habit. Mind recedes and appears, but it does not end.

In the Three Sections on Mind, Expanse, and Precious Teachings,[166] which came from Vajrasattva through Garab Dorje and were described by

166. sems sde; klong sde; and man ngag gi sde.

many Old Tradition saints, including Kunkhyen Longchenpa, it is explained that mind is the all-doing king, since everything is made by mind. All phenomena come from one's own mind, so mind is the basis of all negative and positive karma until enlightenment is attained. Whatever karma is created by mind within the compounded, conditioned phenomena of cyclic existence must diminish and disappear. Whenever these phenomena disappear, nihilists assume there is nothing and call it death because they do not believe that mind continues beyond the life of the physical body. Actually, death is only the mind receding. Since mind is continuous, it has to appear again somewhere if wisdom body is not attained. Buddhists believe that death is not nothingness, but that mind is still there, continuing even though conditional phenomena temporarily separate. When beings no longer appear in this realm, they will still reappear elsewhere according to their habit. Until all the phenomena of dualistic habit are completely purified in stainless nonduality, everything moves between dormancy and appearance as the phenomena of mind change. For ordinary beings, how long phenomena are dormant when they recede and how long phenomena endure when they appear depend on the conditions of karma.

Therefore, Buddhists believe that invisible phenomena can appear, even though they are not emerging at the moment. If what does not exist could not come into existence, the word *appearance* would not be in use. Again, as it is said in *The King of Samadhi Sutra:*

> Before, many eons ago, the world occurred,
> And again, after occurring, it dissolved, and there was no world.
> As it was, it will be, coming and going.

Since the subjective mind exists, any objective phenomena can exist, both tangibly and intangibly. Mind is intangible and cannot be destroyed, so infinite phenomena continuously appear and recede to the ordinary senses of beings; yet there is nothing within compounded substance that has any essence. What seems to exist or not exist is only the reflection of particular appearances of one's own habit within time. If this is recognized, everything in reality becomes flexible, and one will not torture oneself by becoming caught within any limitation. When the nature of phenomena is understood, the existence of intangible spiritual phenomena cannot be denied. The result of the Buddhist belief that existence is created by mind is always positive, because by acknowledging that phenomena continuously recede and appear and recede and appear from the mind, Buddhists can use the mind to create the positive phenomena of spiritual appearances.

Many beings with excessively materialistic minds believe strongly in the existence of whatever appears before them and doubt the possibility of the existence of phenomena that are not immediately apparent to them, but they do not pretend to be Buddhist or to represent Buddhism. Their individual opinions about what they believe truly exists arise from their lack of a vast understanding about the basis of phenomena. Therefore, whatever is apparent is considered to be true, and whatever recedes is considered to be finished or non-existent. Then these beings disagree or agree about these phenomena, which continuously come and go, since the characteristic of phenomena is to continuously change within time and place. This does not mean that only one set of phenomena continuously exists and other phenomena do not exist. Likewise, if phenomena dissolve, it does not mean they will not reappear in a different time and place, even though beings with deluded minds think they have vanished forever. Although whatever arises will recede, beings with deluded minds think that whatever arises will always be as it is and that whatever is dormant will never exist.

If one cannot pierce through the limits of substantialization to a truly expansive view, one stabs oneself into the ground like a dagger that becomes stuck in one position, immobilized in a tight hole. One is then unable to move anywhere else or see anything beyond one's position, so one's view is obstructed. When one's ideas are vast, one will never become stuck anywhere, because one will not be limited by a constricted view.

One who holds modern nihilist ideas of only believing in the perceptible physical world cannot understand Buddhist cosmology, which is not limited to the physical world. Although all models of the universe are the phenomena of sentient beings, when scientific ideas about the universe become predominant because of the habit of reality, so that people think that science holds the ultimate answers and spirituality is no longer useful, spiritual ideas recede. At that time, those who believe in a modern scientific perspective may think that spiritual ideas have been permanently invalidated and are therefore finished, but according to the Buddhist view, at another time, when scientific ideas recede, spirituality will naturally return and flourish.

As theories of the origin, evolution, and future of the universe are introduced according to time and circumstance, people seriously believe in them, without recognizing that these ideas are related to the circumstances of particular times and places or considering other times and places that are not simultaneously apparent. This is also true of spiritual beliefs. When spiritual phenomena arise, nonspiritual phenomena recede.

Even when spiritual phenomena arise, if they are not the phenomena of full enlightenment, they are inconsistent and may sink into dormancy through lack of practice. Likewise, various ways of understanding cosmology may arise according to time and place but can later sink into dormancy, like certain kinds of plants that appear at a particular time due to the circumstances of climate and season. The appearance of these plants does not mean that other plants have permanently ceased to exist; it is only that they are dormant. When circumstances change, plants that have already appeared can recede, and other kinds of plants can appear in their place.

Since phenomena are always coming and going, all ideas about the universe are temporary appearances, so any idea can exist. Western science cannot say that Eastern mystics are wrong, since it is only conception. Instead of debating about differing explanations of the universe or phenomena, it is better to let others think what they wish. There is no need to be concerned if some people think the world is round and moving, and others think the world is flat and still, since it is all delusion. It is not necessary to explain each detail of phenomena, just to understand that all phenomena, including all material judgments, can be recognized as manifestation, so there is no reality to each single explanation and no need to endlessly analyze conceptions.

People in Asia have traditionally had faith in Buddhism, but because of Western influence, they now listen to modern ideas and imitate Western culture, not recognizing how deep and valuable Asian traditions are. Also, many Westerners who are learning about Buddhism pay more attention to Western views because they are used to them and attracted to what they know. Although it is not indispensable to use modern examples of Western thinking, if one only speaks nicely according to Dharma tradition, people consider it unfamiliar and invalidate it; if modern examples are used, they can make a connection.

Scientific explanations of phenomena are always related to relative truth, whereas spiritual explanations are connected with absolute truth. For example, science explains the manifestation of material energy within interdependent phenomena, such as light defined as a wave of an oscillating electromagnetic field in which the oscillation of charged particles that create light is produced from the interaction of positively and negatively charged particles, so that positively charged nuclei confine negatively charged electrons and keep them from wandering off into space. From a scientific point of view, just as light is caused by and depends on this interaction, all substance needs the interaction of negative and positive charges in balance. From a spiritual point of view, Buddhism explains that all relative phenomena come from interdependence, but that is only true of relative phenomena, according to the path of enlightenment and the phenomena of practitioners. The phenomena of enlightenment are not relative or dependent on any interaction. Buddha does not rely on any dualistic phenomena, but is just one immeasurable natural light of enlightenment.

Buddhist spiritual teachings can never be replaced by scientific ideas, because nonreligious, scientific ideas generally deal only with substance, whether within form or within conception, and substance decreases and becomes exhausted. Buddhist teachings lead through substance to substanceless enlightenment.

One should never reject the speech of the Buddhas. When modern people misunderstand Buddhist explanations of existence and dismiss them as insignificant or incorrect, it is because they miss their inner meanings and spiritual significance. These teachings are never only about substance but always reveal spiritual phenomena and the natural qualities of insubstantial mind. Buddhist explanations cannot be compared to nonreligious, scientific explanations, because Buddhism encompasses levels not addressed by science.

A scientific understanding of cosmology that is modern today will not be considered valid forever. After a few generations, there will be another, more modern version. Also, nihilist scientists are always disagreeing and disputing each other's theories, just as, in response to Einstein's statement "God does not play dice with the universe," the theoretical physicist Stephen Hawking said, "God does play dice." Material ideas change and cannot be kept forever, and the people who believe in them are also impermanent. Those who think scientific explanations of the universe supersede Buddhist spiritual explanations do not realize the impermanence of scientific theories, although whatever exists in this world, including even their own bodies, can show them that everything is changing.

Ideas about the universe that come from knowledge of new information do not change the basic problem of believing in a material rather than a spiritual point of view, so one is still caught within change rather than understanding the nature of change. Buddhists see all samsaric existence as changing, including the theories and discoveries of science, and rely on a spiritual view to go beyond change. According to the Buddhist point of view, whatever phenomena arise and whatever phenomena one chooses to accept, inconceivable space is always present within both general and individual phenomena, whether or not it is recognized. If phenomena are impure, space is alaya. If phenomena are pure, space is Dharmakaya. Without basic space, phenomena cannot arise, yet materialistic people ignore space and grab phenomena, creating new phenomena within interdependent relative links without recognizing their source. Even though nonspiritual, materially oriented scientists do not acknowledge anything resembling spiritual space, they still use space as the source of new phenomena arising whenever they form new ideas, while former phenomena recede. This does not mean phenomena that recede are completely finished or phenomena that arise are permanent, but just means phenomena are changing.

When one uses a calculator, one starts with the temporary appearance of a zero as a beginning point from which all other numbers can appear. After finishing one's calculations, one cancels whatever numbers have appeared in order to return to the zero, from which the next calculation can appear. While numbers are being used and the zero is not apparent, one cannot say there is no zero, because its potential to appear still exists whenever the calculator is used, and it is related to the appearance of numbers. Even though this small zero can disappear and become dormant when the calculator is not being used, it is still connected with the immeasurable, unappearing zero of space, which is always openness.

According to the samsaric phenomena of dualistic mind, whatever appears continually comes from and recedes into alaya, unless these appearances are transformed through practice into wisdom manifestation. Then, samsaric phenomena do not exist. For those who do not believe in immaterial, intangible mind, whatever phenomena exist are seen as real. Without changing alaya into Dharmakaya, alaya becomes the basis of all samsaric phenomena. Until beings have purified dualistic phenomena by attaining fully enlightened Buddhahood, all interdependent phenomena are continuously changing, and any phenomena can disappear and appear.

Each time a new circumstance appears, it may be thought that previous circumstances are completely finished, but this is not true. No matter how many times one goes toward a different direction, ultimately one lands somewhere again. Even though one thinks one has landed at the top of the world, there must still be a bottom of the world. It is unnecessary to take this difference between the top and bottom seriously. It can just be understood that everything is relative and that someday the top can become the bottom and the bottom can become the top, just as the highest mountains were once the ocean floor. Nothing within ordinary phenomena becomes permanently absent, but just recedes.

By knowing that all phenomena are coming, going, and abiding in the basis of space, one can recognize that all changing phenomena cause suffering. Buddhists try to abide in the pure basis of space through faith and meditation, so that all circling phenomena are transformed into manifestation. In this case, manifestation is not the deluded phenomena of ordinary dualistic mind, so whatever appears is not the cause of suffering but only the illumination of wisdom. By practicing in this way, the disagreement and agreement that come from dualistic clinging to each phenomenon is reduced, and nondualistic pure immeasurable space expands to destinationless space with awareness mind.

Omniscient Longchenpa said:

> In a brief way, the immeasurable phenomena of existence
> and non-existing phenomena beyond existence
> Never moved even an iota from stainless wisdom space.

If nihilists hear that nothing in existence or non-existence ever moved away from stainless space from the beginning up to now, they can misinterpret it to reinstill nihilism. They can think that if nothing ever moved from the basis of space, there is nothing for them to obtain and nothing to lose, so they will not practice, trapped between what recedes and what appears. The meaning of the words of Kunkhyen Longchenpa is to abide in the stainless, inconceivable state of wisdom. Then there is no cause of temporarily receding and appearing phenomena.

It is weird that nonreligious people do not believe Buddhist teachings and think they are just imaginary, but can be interested in metaphysics. Buddhist metaphysical theories are sublime and excel beyond ordinary metaphysical theories believed by many people, but what excels and is not ordinary is not believed and what is ordinary is accepted. It is extremely valuable to believe in Buddhist visualization, but people do not believe in it; yet they visualize rivers, mountains, and beautiful scenery to relax.

Most nonreligious people believe that this world exists only in the form of a planet within a solar system, do not believe in other levels of existence that are imperceptible, and easily accept the ideas of science. Nonspiritual science is generally based on the physical, while Buddhism is based on what is beyond the physical. Science can be contained within Buddhist theory, but Buddhism cannot fit within scientific explanations, because Buddhism explains both physical and metaphysical phenomena. By only acknowledging a physical universe, one cannot know anything about metaphysical truth; yet nihilists attempt to evaluate spirituality with a material point of view. Nihilist scientists need to understand mind before they can understand theories based on mind rather than substance. All theories of physical phenomena are conceptions created by mind, but nihilists generally depend on substance as though it had a separate existence apart from mind, whereas Buddhist metaphysical theories do not consider substance as existing apart from mind. From a Buddhist point of view, physical explanations of phenomena are extremely limited because they ignore intangible mind as the source of all physical existence.

Even if one holds a nihilist view of believing only in phenomena that are materially evident to the perception of the five limited senses, one undeniably uses metaphysical phenomena anyway by creating the phenomena of mind. Although the mental forms created for whatever one thinks or does can be considered mentally substantial since they exist within conception, they can also be called metaphysical since they do not exist in gross form. Those who accept metaphysical phenomena differ from those who do not, in the way they recognize and use their own phenomena. The difference is that the former can use phenomena positively to transform them into spiritual appearances. In this way, those who believe with faith in metaphysical appearances create a positive connection between the object of metaphysical phenomena and the subject of the believer, so that their spiritual qualities can increase. If metaphysical phenomena are denied, one cannot even plan how to survive in this life, because all future plans for physical phenomena first have to be imagined before they can become real, and any imagined plan begins as metaphysical phenomena. It is not until a plan becomes actualized within material substance that it can be called physical.

Moreover, physical phenomena can undeniably become metaphysical. For example, suppose an earthquake destroyed an entire city and everyone in it so that nothing was left. If one person who had been born and grew up in that city still remained alive and strongly reminisced about it through habit, although the previous physical existence of the city would be gone, its metaphysical existence could still be imagined. Even though nihilists deny that a metaphysical phenomenon exists, the only reason the phenomenon does not appear to exist for them is their temporary lack of belief in its existence and consequent inability to perceive it. Whenever they believe in the existence of the metaphysical, they can make their beliefs function within material existence so that they become physically evident.

Many modern people are interested in metaphysical ideas about what is beyond material reality. Of course, it is much better to believe in metaphysics than only to believe in a fragmented material reality, but there is no comparison to believing in Buddhism, including Buddhist teachings about Buddha nature, inherent wisdom deity, and the continuity of mind. These beliefs are the basis for attaining the state of enlightenment, so they are not only for temporary worldly comfort using one's imagination and thought, but benefit throughout one's lives up to full enlightenment. When full enlightenment is attained, one does not need metaphysics, because dualistic reality's believer is cleansed in the state of wisdom phenomena.

The actual cause of fully enlightened Buddhahood is beyond metaphysics. Until that state happens, one develops positive phenomena on the path, from the phenomena of worldly deities up to fully enlightened inconceivable wisdom deities. If one is not actually connected to Buddhist ideas such as Buddha nature and wisdom deities, whatever metaphysics are followed cannot last long or lift one to more and more positive states, because of the lack of a correct point of view. Without an expansive, continuous idea of wisdom deities, from the lack of a point of view of how to develop that which is immeasurable, phenomena will naturally become limited and will have to cease in a certain way because they will be fragmented and only temporary imagination.

It is strange that people can talk about worldly metaphysical ideas and others will believe what they say even though it is only imaginary and does not bring wisdom phenomena, yet what the Buddha has shown is not believed even though it is true. For example, many people accept the existence of archetypes; yet there is no result from believing in archetypes, because there is no belief in the continuity of Buddha nature until full enlightenment is reached, no point of view, no wisdom deity, no path of enlightenment, and no guidance about how to practice up to enlightenment. Why do they not believe in Buddha nature? Belief in Buddha nature and wisdom is most meaningful, because there is nothing in it that causes a limitation of qualities, for this life or up to enlightenment. The problem is that even though beings, including human beings, have Buddha nature, they do not believe in allowing it to blossom. Instead, many people have the conception that it is imaginary, while accepting as real anything that can be used in a temporary, ordinary way.

Nonbelievers do not accept Mount Meru as taught in the Abhidharma, but for whoever believes in it, it will become present. Belief in any positive appearance makes that appearance come back again in the believer's phenomena. The explanations in the Abhidharma are not apparent, but they can be apparent.

From the Buddhist point of view, one can only discriminate between the physical and metaphysical attributes of all existence according to time, place, and the different phenomena that rely on conditions perceived by different beings. Neither physical nor metaphysical phenomena exist permanently. They are only like two different kinds of magic being shown by a magician, one after another. While one is being shown, the other is dormant, but it is coming. According to material time and circumstance, the magic of existence continually comes and goes as the different phenomena that appear to beings. Reality is itself metaphysical because it does not remain continuously within physical phenomena but changes and disappears. When metaphysical power is solidified into form, it becomes physical, and when physical power dissipates into formlessness, it becomes metaphysical.

Buddhism teaches that all samsaric phenomena originate from alaya, the basis of all phenomena, until all phenomena are liberated in Dharmakaya. One who recognizes that all samsaric phenomena are impermanent will neither consider nonspiritual scientific ideas to be ultimately true nor reject spiritual ideas as false. If people try to modernize spiritual traditions by replacing spiritual teachings with scientific explanations of the universe as the most accurate descriptions of phenomena, they will have to give up their practice, since practice is based not on perpetuating the habit of materialization but on illuminating spiritual energy. If people give up their practice, they will suffer, because it is through practice that the natural unconditioned state beyond suffering can be enlivened. If some people wish to choose the basis of suffering over the benefit of practicing to attain enlightenment, that is their choice, but there is no reason for actual Buddhists to listen to them or believe what they say.

Buddhists are sometimes accused of being superstitious by those who do not recognize their own negative superstition. Superstition is belief in what is thought not to exist. Since the entire world acknowledges the Buddha and that Buddhism exists, if they call this superstitious, isn't that in itself superstition? Even those who criticize Buddhist views depend on Buddhism as a basis for all of their contrary ideas. This is the meaning of interdependent relative truth. There are no phenomena that do not rely on interdependence unless confidence is attained in wisdom mind. Until then, everything is interdependent.

When scientific explanations of phenomena predominate, and spirituality becomes dormant, nonspiritual scientists who do not accept spiritual ideas have no method to create lasting beneficial phenomena, even though it seems that they are developing material within the momentary phenomena of this short life. If beings have good karma, spirituality can reappear, and when positive spiritual phenomena arise strongly, scientific ideas recede. For example, if there were a third world war, scientifically developed weapons could destroy the world as we know it. When those who experienced this war or existed in its aftermath examined what was left of the world, they could recognize that the circumstance that caused this destruction was the product of science. From their reaction to this tragedy, they could understand that excessive substantialization leads to its own destruction, so substantial power and energy could become dormant for a while. As intangible mind reemerged again, fresh spiritual ideas could arise, and people with incisive minds or those who were guided by the manifestations of sublime beings could step toward spiritual explanations, creating peace and developing spiritual energy. So, substantial phenomena could become dormant and spiritual phenomena could flourish again for a while, although its duration would not be certain. Why would it be uncertain? Because of the limitation of the habit of karma of different beings. During that time, beings could think that science had been invalidated. Since human minds would not have been exhausted, however, science would not have been eliminated; it would only have receded. When the sadness of former tragedies had faded and material ideas arose once more, science could reappear again. With the understanding of this continual movement between the material and the immaterial, hopefully science will not be used to try to invalidate spirituality, but all samsaric beings will be liberated through the compassionate weapon of wisdom.

Those who believe only in material reality within general phenomena and are attached to material explanations have to praise material qualities, since they only conceive of the material world. That is why they are attached to a worldly system of thinking and worldly phenomena, so they cannot be blamed for that. At a spiritual level, however, and especially from the Buddhist point of view, one must never fall into material or immaterial extremes. Enlightened mind pervades the material and immaterial yet is free from remaining within the material or immaterial. If one wishes to attain that state, one should never say that immaterial spiritual explanations are nullified by material scientific explanations.

According to Buddhism, Buddha Shakyamuni is omniscient. There is nothing that is not known to Buddha, including science, because Buddha has purified cognitive obscurations. Buddha predominantly taught from the lower yanas to Mahayana up to Vajrayana to liberate beings from suffering to attain fully enlightened Buddhahood, which is forever abiding in evenness, happiness, and peacefulness. The reason Buddha did not predominantly teach science is that beings are already attached to materialism and reality, so they can become distracted by material ideas. Instead of only increasing materialism, Buddha taught how to believe in karma, how to develop good karma, and how to purify karma to go beyond karma on the path of enlightenment. Buddha taught beings to have faith in sublime beings because ordinary beings do not know the right direction; they can only know through faith in sublime beings who can show them the correct path. This kind of teaching is so much more powerful than ordinary materialism because it shows how not to create negative karma and how to create positive energy until attaining enlightenment. Spiritual ideas cannot be compared to the material ideas of science, and Buddhist spiritual ideas cannot be changed to accommodate scientific ideas. In Buddhism, the sciences that are taught are never totally material, because they are connected with spirituality, since they are understood to be reflections of the mind and do not deal solely with material existence.

Since modern science generally deals with material existence, people often mistakenly think that it is important for them to know more about it. By miscalculating that a material rather than a spiritual orientation will help them sustain themselves and prosper within their immediate lives, they become more concerned with materialism than with spirituality. This is the antithesis of a spiritual point of view. Since the mind does not end, it is the mind's development of spiritual qualities that is important, and these qualities endure from one life to the next throughout the succession of one's lives.

Material is material, and can change from anything to anything. From the material development of science and technology, nuclear power became the most expensive, advanced, and powerful form of defense, but when chemical weapons were considered, which were easily made by anyone, inexpensive, and easy to use, the most powerful became powerless. To adjust to nihilism by thinking that science is more advanced than spirituality is totally wrong, not only because the ideas of science change, but because these ideas have no basis of happiness, morality, belief in karma, faith, or compassion. Accepting Buddhist teachings about the nature of phenomena never causes suffering.

What is wrong with believing in Buddhas and deities, even if one cannot see them due to obscurations, and trying to visualize or even imagine them according to teachings or sadhanas? It is much more meaningful than anything else. Because mind is continuous, even though it seems as if what is imagined is created by mind and is compounded, instant, and disappearable, it is not like that. Since the nature of mind is uncompounded and continuous, whatever positive image is created by mind will be apparent someday, so it is beneficial and self-correcting. It is very strange to believe in changing television channels, where there is no continuity of pleasure because there is no worth in anything that appears; yet people still believe in whatever extremely temporary compounded circumstances and neurotic conceptions come from television. Until interdependent relative truth is exhausted through practice, it is necessary to rely on positive interdependent phenomena. For those who believe in practice, interdependent relative circumstances can be transformed through meditation into oneness, like the sun. Then, reliance on the duality of all that is perceived as negative and positive will be reduced, just as black clouds and white clouds only temporarily obscure the sun. When dualistic habit, which only exists within interdependent relative truth, is cleansed by meditation, interdependent relative phenomena are reduced, just as the fresh wind of practice cleanses all clouds of conception until mind is purified. Then there is only the sole, stainless, shining sun of enlightenment. This sun is not a new sun; it is the same sun as it has always been from the beginning. This is the Old Tradition's precious teaching.

Ordinary reality is only real and true according to beings' beliefs, and does not exist independently as real and true. Everything material is relative. Since relative truth is only true according to deluded mind, everything that is relative will have to change. To think that what cannot be perceived is not true and that modern science is true because it is based on the perceptible and conceivable is to ignore the truth that the nature of phenomena is to arise and recede. For example, an island that has previously existed can disappear into the ocean, and an island can appear where land did not exist before. Likewise, planets or stars that existed before can disappear, and new planets or stars can be discovered. Even the reality of the physical world shows that the nature of relative truth is always to change due to the truth of impermanence.

It is the culmination of science to understand that all substance comes from and exists within temporary relative circumstances, which turns the mind toward its natural spiritual qualities. Buddhists who are familiar with contemporary scientific explanations of the universe believe in Buddhist cosmology with the awareness that these explanations are not just materialistic but are maps of the basis of mind, drawn by mind. Without mind, nothing can exist.

Trying to prove that scientific, material explanations of cosmology are true and spiritual teachings are false is unwise from a spiritual point of view, because material explanations rely on material circumstances that are very, very temporary and eventually must fall apart. When one trusts only material phenomena that cannot always exist, immaterial spiritual power becomes dormant. As Buddha Shakyamuni taught according to the general yanas, there are the four conclusions:

> Whatever is collected is always impermanent because it will disperse.
> Whatever is collected by ordinary mind will always cause suffering.
> Whatever phenomena arise, their essence is empty and selfless.
> Whenever realizing and abiding in selflessness, this is peace.

This is not like the nihilist understanding of phenomena, which one minute can be seen and the next minute cannot be seen, so that one thinks there is nothing. It is selflessness. Of course, non-Buddhists can contemplate selflessness or emptiness, but those who are spiritual should not materialize selflessness and emptiness as nihilists do, simply thinking about these as ideas and later attempting to devalue or invalidate them. Phenomena do not exist forever as substance only but are empty. There is no continuity to any kind of substance. Only intangible mind is continuous. By believing in Buddha and letting one's own Buddha nature blossom by practicing with belief, faith, and devotion, one can open the unending continuity of wisdom.

Buddha is always abiding in the uncompounded flawless wisdom of Dharmakaya, inseparable from the uncompounded immeasurable purelands of Sambhogakaya, emanating effortlessly and unobstructedly as uncompounded Nirmanakaya manifestations to guide and awaken beings with compounded phenomena from delusion. One might ask, "If Buddhas have no impure phenomena and are only pure, how can their stainless wisdom eyes see the impure phenomena of existence?" The answer is that this impurity is not Buddha's own phenomena, because Buddha has no phenomena of suffering or happiness. Buddha is always abiding in stainless sole awareness.

Buddha guides sentient beings and shows them that all the impure and pure phenomena that appear are the reflection of one's own mind, awakening them from the delusion of ignorance. It is told that there are people who are sound asleep in a palace of jewels. Some are disturbed by the impure phenomena of turbulent nightmares, while others are enjoying pleasant dreams of happiness. There is also someone who is not sleeping but is awakening these people by telling them, "All the suffering and happiness you experience in your dreams have no true essence and will change, one after another, because they have no holdable, keepable reality. Anything that is not material reality cannot cause suffering and is naturally pure. You are just temporarily intoxicated by sleep, unaware that the suffering and happiness of nightmares and dreams do not exist. It is just your dreams, because you are here with me in the same immeasurable palace of jewels."

The universal existence of mandalas has been observed and accepted by many scholars who have studied them as spontaneously appearing phenomena of the mind as well as profound representations of the mind and existence.[167] They are dismissed, however, by others, who consider their own scientific explanations of phenomena to be truer maps of existence. Nonetheless, mandalas continue to arise in beings' minds. Materialist thinking reduces the limitless meaning of the metaphysical phenomena of mandalas to a mere form of geography that is imperceptible to the ordinary senses; mandalas are thereby separated from mind rather than recognized as the mind's creation. The mandala of existence is a vast mirror of the mind; all phenomena are the mind's reflections. Whether one offers Mount Meru and the continents according to the Sutra tradition, enlivens the mandala of the wisdom channels, airs, and sole essence of the inner Mantrayana tradition, or recognizes the mandala of the secret Vajrayana tradition, every aspect is positive.

167. See, e.g., C. G. Jung, *The Archetypes and the Collective Unconscious* (Princeton: Princeton University Press, 1990), pp. 357–359.

The basis mandala is all immeasurable natural phenomena. Also, the meaning of mandala can be explained as the infinite circle of all-encompassing totality. Mandala is immeasurable, inconceivable limitlessness. This does not mean only the round shape of a circle, since the shape can be anything according to beings' phenomena. The quality of the mandala is that it is unending, and its unbounded edgelessness is symbolized by the endlessness of circling, which is the quality of perfection. As an example, in the mandalas of deities, the principal wisdom deity is in the center, encircled by the manifestation of countless retinues, with immeasurable purelands and palaces. If this is analyzed according to actual relative truth, all outer phenomena, including the elements, are pureland, and all inner beings are naturally wisdom deities. These unending wisdom phenomena are equally pure. According to absolute truth, there are no ordinary beings' phenomena of ordinary impure material existence, so there is no contradiction between scientific and Buddhist traditions of phenomena of the universe. There is no contradiction, because phenomena are the unending circling of wisdom.

When practitioners realize the basis mandala, in order for it to fully blossom and expand in an immeasurable way, there is the path mandala. This has many methods with different sadhanas of deities according to different individuals' faculties, including the painting and visualization of mandalas. According to inner Mantrayana tradition, one does not think of one's karmic body but develops the aspect of the wisdom body of inherent deity. This is the mandala of wisdom body. By reciting mantra according to one's sadhana, without thinking about karmic speech or air, all sounds are carried into wisdom mantra. This is the mandala of wisdom speech. As the five wisdoms of the original sole wisdom of Dharmakaya and its manifestations are realized, the effortless countless aspects of discerning wisdom unobstructedly emanate and benefit all beings. This is the mandala of wisdom mind.

Through practicing with faith and belief, whenever the aspect of the principal deity appears, the essence of the quality of wisdom is not differentiated from the retinue of the deity. It is not that the quality of the principal deity is higher or that the quality of the retinue is lower; they are the equally even illumination of nondualistic wisdom mandala. Wisdom mind is indivisible, evenly abiding in oneness forever, but at the same time, the quality of unobstructed wisdom manifestation is everywhere, as everything, at any time, unendingly and inconceivably, with flawless wisdom body, wisdom speech, and wisdom mind. That is the actual meaning of mandala.

Accumulation of Merit through Mandala Offerings

Third, the mandala offerings. The root verses read: **My bodies, wealth, and glories of all my lives I offer to the Three Jewels in order to complete the two accumulations** of merit and wisdom. As it says, to offer the mandala, there is the mandala of offering[168] and the mandala of accomplishment.[169] The purpose of the mandala of accomplishment is that it establishes the Three Jewels as the unsurpassed field through which merit is accumulated. In this case, the field is the object to which accumulations are made. Just as when one grows crops, one needs a field of land, so if one accumulates virtue, one needs the field of the Three Jewels.

Since the purelands of all Buddhas are inconceivable and as pervasive as the immeasurable space of phenomena, there is no partiality of a particular direction. If all purelands are synthesized, all enlightened bodies and purelands are perfectly contained within the immeasurable five Buddha families, who are represented by the five gatherings made of rice or torma arranged as the mandala of accomplishment. This is symbolic of the object of visualization, in order for practitioners to concentrate on them and to have pure phenomena.

In the tradition of one wish-fulfilling jewel as the entire field of refuge, the sublime purelands of the five Buddha families, beyond the objects of mind, are understood to be perfectly complete throughout the three times as the inexhaustible ornaments of the fivefold mandala of Guru Rinpoche's enlightened body, speech, mind, qualities, and activities. This is because Guru Rinpoche's enlightened body is Vairochana of the Buddha family, and any aspect of any kind of appearance manifesting. His enlightened speech is Amitabha of the Lotus family. His enlightened mind is Akshobhya or Vajrasattva of the Vajra family. His enlightened qualities are Ratnasambhava of the Jewel family. His enlightened activities are Amoghasiddhi of the Karma family. All qualities of the arrangement of the Sambhogakaya's enlightened bodies and purelands are perfectly contained. From all of this, the magical manifestation of wisdom is the Great Orgyen Guru Rinpoche. Therefore, five gatherings and one gathering are both acceptable without contradiction, because oneness is the origin of all and manifests all immeasurable Buddha phenomena. Even though the mandalas of deities manifest unobstructedly as many different aspects, there is no lesser or higher quality of wisdom manifestation. Inconceivable varieties of different qualities still

168. mchod pa'i man dal.
169. sgrub pa'i man dal.

come from oneness. Do not think that the single one has a lesser quality because it is single, or that more is vaster and therefore has a greater quality. There is neither less nor more. For the mandala of accomplishment, it is also acceptable to use an image of Guru Rinpoche, whether it is a statue or a thangka, as the support, in place of the gatherings.

Then, in preparing the mandala of offering, the best-quality base of support to use for the placement of the gatherings is one made of gold, silver, or other precious substances. A medium-quality base of support is one made of bronze or a similar substance. The lowest-quality base of support is one made of a substance that is not bumpy or rough but smooth, like a stone or a piece of flat wood. As long as it is not broken or flawed, it is said to be acceptable. One should make sure that the base of support is clean.

Next, the best offering substances to use to make the gatherings include gold, silver, turquoise, coral, pearls, diamonds, rubies, sapphires, or other precious gems. Medium-quality substances include the two kinds of myrobalan called *a ru* and *ba ru,* the medicinal fruit called *skyu ru,* and other medicinal herbs. If one cannot find these precious substances or medium-quality substances because of one's capacity, then one can use any kinds of grains or beans, such as wheat, peas, or rice. If, due to poverty, it is still too difficult to acquire any of these substances, then as long as there is faith, there is no need to become discouraged. It is as said:

> Since I have no merit and have great poverty,
> With no other wealth besides this to offer,
> Accept this for me, you who have the power to
> accumulate immeasurably,
> Protector with the wisdom to benefit others.

Thus, remembering the meaning of these words, carefully cleanse pebbles, sand, or whatever substance is available. If one visualizes that this represents the inconceivable wealth and glory of the phenomena of existence and enlightenment, and offers this, by the power of the Three Jewels, the sublime field of refuge, the purpose will be completely fulfilled.

In any case, whether one is able to acquire the best, middling, or inferior substances, the offering represents **my bodies, wealth, and glories of all my lives** that **I offer to the Three Jewels in order to complete the two accumulations** of merit and wisdom.

Thus, from beginningless time until now, in all the countless rebirths that have been taken, by focusing on the result of temporary bliss, one has acquired positive virtue with the power to produce the state of rebirth as a god or human being. This is *zag bcas kyi dge ba,* virtue with flaws, which means that this virtue is connected with intention, passions, and the material. *Zag med kyi dge ba* is virtue with wisdom, so it is called flawless virtue.

During all past lifetimes, it is entirely possible that rebirth was taken enjoying the full glory of the vast arrangement of the outer container of the universe and inner essence of beings. In this lifetime, it is a sign that previous accumulations were not lacking, since a precious human rebirth with eighteen eases and obtainments has been acquired. Once having acquired this, until the state of complete omniscience is reached, one will always remain under the protection of the Three Jewels, who are the unsurpassed limitless field through which the two accumulations are perfected. The limitless field is the limitless Buddhafields[170] of the Three Jewels. The limitless offerings are the substances of limitless virtue. The limitless intention is not the wish for material rewards but the intention that all sentient beings, including oneself, shall attain enlightenment. By awakening the phenomena of the Mahayana and developing the supreme enlightened mind, the excellent appearances of gods and humans will endure until the supreme appearances of the state of fully enlightened Buddhahood manifest. Then, in future rebirths, there will be the sovereignty of higher rebirth taken in any of the four continents, subcontinents, the realms of the gods, and so on. There will also be the power to take rebirth as a Hearer, Solitary Realizer, Bodhisattva, Vidyadhara, Dakini, and so on, with the pure appearance of the universe and contents. Have no doubt that the power to take extraordinary rebirth will occur from the virtue of these limitless offerings.

By considering **my bodies, wealth, and glories of all my lives,** not just offering limited material or to fulfill small matters for oneself but **in order** for all sentient beings as all-pervasive as sky to cleanse the two obscurations and **complete the two accumulations**, these are **offered** to the Lama, the **Three Jewels.** This is the limitless intention for all beings, including oneself, to attain enlightenment.

The two obscurations are understood as follows:

> Whenever there is any conception such of greed and so on,
> This is called the obscuration of the passions.[171]

170. Purelands of Buddhas.
171. nyon mongs sgrib pa.

> Whenever there is the conception of the three circles,[172]
> This is called cognitive obscuration.[173]

Thus, as it is said, depending on positive and negative objects, the karma of attachment and aversion is accumulated, which is the attachment of the obscurations of the passions. Grasping any phenomena of existence and enlightenment as substantial, grasping them as insubstantial, grasping at both, grasping at neither, grasping at the whole, and so on, are all the habit of the duality of subject and object.

Nothing exists within the phenomena of sentient beings that is not included within the three circles. One example is in relation to offerings, in which there are the three circles of the offerer, the offering, and the one to whom the offering is made. Through meditation, one purifies these three circles by abiding in evenness, so there is no more cause of the three circles.

By constructing the thick wall of the conception of the three circles, the unimpeded characteristics of all that is knowable, including existence, enlightenment, and the path, are not understood. This is called obstructed cognitive obscurations. Therefore, when an ordinary individual cleanses the attachment of the obscurations of the passions by realizing the selflessness of the self and purifies the obstructed cognitive obscurations by realizing that phenomena do not exist as reality, this purifies the two obscurations. Accumulating vast amounts of merit to attain Rupakaya, and accumulating merit sealed without the aim of the three circles, which is wisdom, in order to perfect wisdom merit to attain Dharmakaya, offerings are made.

At the time of arranging the gatherings for the offering mandala, hold the mandala plate in the left hand. Think that one is cleansing all the particles of dust from the basis of the earth, and with the right inner forearm, clean the base of the mandala three times while reciting the long one-hundred syllable mantra or the short six-syllable mantra of Vajrasattva. To prevent dust from arising from the basis of the earth, or to symbolize the great powerful golden foundation of the earth, anoint the base with the essence of saffron water, and place one large gathering in the center of the mandala to represent the king of all mountains, Mount Meru. To represent the four continents, place gatherings in each of the four directions. Then, in the east

172. 'khor gsum.
173. shes bya'i sgrib.

and west, place gatherings to symbolize the sun and moon. These seven gatherings are presented as the offering.

The reason the mandala practice comes after refuge and bodhichitta in this preliminary practice is that when taking refuge and developing bodhichitta, Guru Rinpoche as the embodiment of all Buddhas is the object of refuge and the witness to one's promise never to abandon the aspiration to accomplish the purpose of sentient beings. At the time of the mandala offering, Guru Rinpoche continues to be the field through which merit is accumulated. With remembrance of the meaning during each of these occasions, one hundred thousand accumulations are made. If this is not possible, then at least once each day, the verses of refuge, bodhichitta, and mandala should be repeated three times each. At the time of dissolution, from the enlightened body of Guru Rinpoche, boundless light rays emanate and dissolve into oneself and all sentient beings, purifying and cleansing the two obscurations and perfecting the two accumulations. The one who is making the offering and all sentient beings then dissolve into the offering mandala. The offering mandala dissolves into light, which then dissolves into Guru Rinpoche. Abide in the equanimity of the uncontrived nature of the conceptionless three circles.

In this way, the benefit of making actual and visualized offerings to all the Victorious Ones sows the seed of the positive habit of inexhaustible merit in the continuity of mind. This ensures that in all lifetimes there will be rebirth in the god and human realms with expansive full glory. Ultimately, this will become the actual state of the Sambhogakaya Buddha. As it says in *The Secret Essence:*[174]

> The wish-granting tree, wish-fulfilling jewel, and all elements
> Do not have actual, independent substance.
> One's own mind's merit is sown in one's own mind.
> The wondrous, magical manifestation of the marvel of Dharma
> Is not coming from somewhere else.
> The union of skillful means and wisdom
> In oneness occurs like that.

Thus it is said that the benefits of mandala offerings are beyond the limitations of objects.

174. *gsang snying.*

Purification of Obscurations: The Vajrasattva Meditation and Recitation

Fourth is the Vajrasattva meditation and recitation. **Above the crown of my head is Vajrasattva, who is inseparable from the Lama. From Vajrasattva's body flows a continuous stream of nectar, and all obscurations are purified.**

Thus, previously, during refuge, bodhichitta, and mandala, depending on Guru Rinpoche, who contains all Buddhas, the effort was made for accumulation and purification. Here, one may wonder why, once again, one depends on the meditation and recitation of Vajrasattva to purify nonvirtue, as if something were not included in the earlier practices. As mentioned before, the essence of all Buddhas is indivisible oneness, while the aspects of the qualities manifest in every way. This is not a contradiction or a repetition; it demonstrates the immeasurable and varied qualities of Buddhas. The inconceivable, absolute qualities of all Buddhas are contained in one's own Lama, who embodies the Three Jewels. The power of the signs, meanings, and gestures of the Guru are unobstructedly manifesting in every aspect. This is not like ordinary individuals who substantialize themselves as separate and, by the strength of their view that self is better than others and in order to compete and show their abilities, engage in different actions. It is the emanation of wisdom.

According to the ordinary perceptions of the objects to tame, all Buddhas before their enlightenment developed bodhichitta, and there are accounts of how each one, having taken rebirth as a Bodhisattva, made their own individual prayers of aspiration. According to these accounts, the way in which the great Vajrasattva, who is the same as Guru Rinpoche, manifested as Vajrasattva's body was through the dedication of his prayers.

> May I remain above the heads of all extremely negative sentient beings, to cleanse all of their suffering without a single exception.

By the power of this prayer, even those with seriously sinful karma that is extremely difficult to cleanse can be purified instantly by the obvious revelation of the power of truth.

For example, previously, when Arya Tara first developed bodhichitta, she prayed:

> Since there are more males who have taken rebirth to accomplish the benefit of sentient beings and fewer females, may I only take rebirth in the form of a female in order to fulfill the purpose of beings.

Avalokiteshvara vowed:

> Until cyclic existence is emptied of sentient beings,
> I will not become enlightened.

Manjushri prayed:

> May I dispel the darkness of ignorance in the minds of all sentient beings through the light of wisdom.

Vajrapani prayed:

> May I subdue all the obstructing forces that prevent all sentient beings from achieving the state of Buddha.

Also, it says in *The Accomplishment of the Supreme Buddha Called the Treasure of Blessings:*[175]

> By your great compassion for those in the turbulent realms of degeneration,
> Holding them with the power of five hundred great prayers,
> You are praised by the Buddhas as a white lotus. Just hearing your name is never to return to samsara.
> I prostrate to the Guide of Great Compassion.

Thus, just as the meaning of this is clarified in the supportive teachings written by Mipham Rinpoche called *White Lotus,*[176] our Buddha came as the great guide to lead sentient beings in these degenerate times when other Buddhas could not subdue us. Also, the incomparable Buddha, Thubpai

175. *thub mchog byin rlabs gter mdzod.*
176. *padma dkarpo.*

Wangpo,[177] Fulfiller of All Meaning,[178] made his prayers of aspiration. Similarly, in the past, Buddha predicted that the Greatest Khenpo (Shantarakshita), the King (Trisong Detsen), and the Supreme Vajra Master (Padmasambhava) would spread the teachings of Buddha from the north to the north.

To fulfill this prophecy, long ago in the country of Nepal, the daughter of the chicken keeper Sallei, whose name was Supreme Bliss,[179] began building the Boudhanath Stupa.[180] Although the stupa was still incomplete at the time of her death, her four sons continued its construction. Upon completion of the stupa, the four brothers offered prayers of dedication together. Exactly in accordance with their prayers, three of the sons' rebirths united them in Samye Monastery as the Khenpo, the King, and the Vajra Master. Like the rising sun, their reunion enriched and expanded the teachings of Buddha. Just as all of the Victorious Ones and their Heirs of the three times have developed the supreme enlightened mind in order to lead all beings to perfect liberation, the truth of the strength and power of prayer was shown in order for future disciples to follow this example. Thus, this has been a brief explanation of the general meaning.

Now, the actual practice is that in one's ordinary karmic body, above the crown of one's head is a white thousand-petaled lotus, upon which is a stainless full moon. Upon that is Vajrasattva, who is indivisible with one's extremely kind root Lama. The body of Vajrasattva has the glory of beauty, youth, and complete perfection, pure like a stainless moon. The blessing of his radiant splendor is incomparable, and his unwavering immaculate wisdom is ablaze like the sun. His right hand holds a five-pointed vajra to his heart, and his left hand holds a bell supported in front of his hip. He is embracing his consort, Nyema Karmo. His legs rest in the vajra cross-legged posture. His deep blue hair is tied in a knot at his crown, beautified with a precious jewel. He wears an upper garment of white silk, a lower skirtlike garment with patterned designs, variously colored silk scarves, a blue silk patterned scarf, and sleeves as for dancing. These are the five silk garments. The precious jeweled crown, earrings, short throat necklace, middle neck-

177. thub pa'i dbang po.

178. don kun grub pa.

179. Sallei is gsal le in Tibetan transliteration, and her daughter's name, Supreme Bliss, is bde mchog (Skt. Shamvara).

180. bya rung kha shor, which means permission to act blurted from the mouth. This refers to the permission given to Sallei to build the Boudhanath Stupa.

lace that reaches to the breasts, bracelets, anklets, belt, and long necklace that reaches just below the navel are the eight jeweled ornaments of adornment.

On his lap is Nyema Karmo, a youthful sixteen years of age. A wheel on her crown symbolizing the wisdom of dharmadhatu, earrings on the ears symbolizing discerning wisdom, a necklace symbolizing the wisdom of equanimity, a belt symbolizing all-accomplishing wisdom, and bracelets symbolizing mirrorlike wisdom are the five mudras that adorn her. In her right hand she holds a curved vajra blade, and in her left she holds a skull. She embraces her consort with her arm around his neck. Her two legs are in the lotus mudra of embrace as they abide in union. Both male and female consorts are delicate, flexible, intertwined, graceful, youthful, light, shining, glorious, and radiant, as the nine signs of wisdom body of the peaceful wisdom deities who abide in the nondual essence of bliss and emptiness. In Vajrasattva's heart is a full moon disk with a five-pointed crystal vajra standing upright upon it. In the center of the vajra is a radiantly luminous white syllable HUNG, standing upright surrounded by the syllables of the hundred-syllable mantra beginning in front of the HUNG.

> OM is the supreme mantra, most excellent beginning praise.
> VAJRA SATTVA SAMAYA, the tantric vow of Vajrasattva.
> MANU PALAYA VAJRA SATTVA, I beseech you, Vajrasattva,
> to grant me your protection.
> TENOPA TIK'THRA DRIDHO MEBHAWA, abide firmly in me.
> SU TO KHAYO MEBHAWA, make me totally satisfied.
> SU PO KHAYO MEBHAWA, increase perfectly within me.
> ANU RAKTO MEBHAWA, be compassionate toward me.
> SARWA SIDDHI ME PRA YATTSA, by your blessing, bestow
> all attainments upon me.
> SARWA KARMA SU TSA ME, may I also attain the power
> of all activities.
> TSITTAM SHRI YAM KURU, make my mind virtuous. HUNG is the
> essence of wisdom heart.
> HA HA HA HA, the four boundless wishes of bodhichitta,
> the four joys, the four empowerments, and the Four Kayas;
> Ho is the exclamation of joy.
> BHAGAWAN SARWA TA T'HAGATA, Victorious One who embodies
> all the Tathagatas.
> VAJRA MA ME MUNTSA, Vajrasattva, may you never abandon me.

VAJRI BHAWA, I pray, please make me a vajra holder.
MAHA SAMAYA SATTVA, Great Samaya Deity.
AH is to unite indivisibly.

Visualize that with the self-sounding of the mantra, the syllables circle to the right. This is the power of the support. Then, with great faith in Guru Vajrasattva from the depth of one's heart, the ten nonvirtues, the five heinous crimes, the five crimes that are close to heinous crimes, transgressions of Vinaya vows, bodhichitta training, secret mantra samaya, and so on—everything that falls in the negative direction of nonvirtue from beginningless past lifetimes until the present should be confessed with intense remorse from the heart. Taking the vow that from this time onward one will never again repeat these negative deeds, even if one's life is at stake, is the power of regret.

Then, from the rosary of syllables in the heart of Guru Vajrasattva's **body flows a continuous stream of crystal moonbeam nectar** down through the union of male and female consorts. The nectar continues to flow and swirl around down the lotus stem that is about four finger-widths in length connecting into one's crown chakra. Entering one's crown, the nectar fills one's entire body. All illness, demonic force, negativity, and **all obscurations** pour out from the cleansing path of excrement and path of urine, and every single pore. Flowing down nine levels below the earth, these enter into the mouths of the males and females to whom karmic debts are owed by oneself and all sentient beings. By receiving these transformed into inexhaustible desirable qualities, all of them are fully satisfied so that all karmic debts without exception are completely cleansed and **purified**. One's body and mind become pure like stainless crystal. Visualizing being filled with flawless great bliss, and so on, is the power of the antidote.

In this way, through reliance on the power of the support, the power of remorse, and the power of the antidote, by this offering of confession, Guru Vajrasattva is greatly pleased, saying, "My son, lineage holder of Buddhas, all of your negativity, obscurations, shortcomings, and faults are completely purified without any residue." Thus giving approval, Guru Vajrasattva and consort dissolve into the essence of great bliss, which dissolves into light, and dissolves into oneself. One becomes indivisible as one taste with the appearance of the body and wisdom of Vajrasattva. The white seed syllable HUNG in one's heart as Vajrasattva is surrounded by OM VAJRA SATTVA HUNG. By reciting these essence of essence syllables, they circle and radiate inconceivable light rays. All appearances of the outer universe become the pureland of Manifest Joy.[181] The inner essence, all sentient beings without exception, become the assembly of Vajrasattva deities. From each one, the natural sound of the mantra melodiously resonates.

Finally, the outer universe and inner essence of beings, including all enlightened bodies and purelands, dissolve into one. One dissolves into the seed syllable HUNG in one's heart. The HUNG also gradually vanishes upward into the nada.

The nada is the final sign of becoming subtler and subtler before disappearing in stainless Dharmakaya. Any kind of phenomena come from the subtlest energy of phenomena and are supposed to be connected to the subtlest of all, which is no more substance. In order to be liberated and not trapped from the material habit of cause and effect, there are meditation and visualization. However much one visualizes, there are phenomena, and visualization always goes with phenomena. That means not remaining in only nothingness. But in order not to be trapped in phenomena, there is wisdom, and there is dissolution up to the nada in order not to remain in substance and cause more compounded substance, which is the meaning of nada: dissolving in stainless sky, never permanently remaining in material, never permanently remaining in nothingness, in indivisible clarity and emptiness, to finally disappear in Dharmakaya's state. The nada is not necessary to visualize; it is a demonstration or sign to abide in stainless, sole tig-le,[182] immeasurable Dharmakaya. The ultimate phenomenon is the nada. It is not necessary to make something into nada phenomena; it is not gross, but can disappear. The view of Buddhism is never remaining in the two extremes of eternalist substantialization with conception or in nihilist nothingness only. This view is not made up; the nature is like that.

Then, abiding within the equanimity of the state of the nonconceptual clear light of great emptiness is the power of never returning or the power of restoring pure wisdom energy.

It is said:

> Self-awareness is from the beginning unchanging as the
> manifestation of Dharmakaya.
> In the freshness of this present awareness,

181. mngon par dga' ba'i zhing khams.
182. thig le.

The uncontrived practitioner who abides naturally
Will find his own mind to be Vajrasattva.

Thus, one only needs to maintain awareness of these words that are spoken directly from the Lord Father, Great Treasure Revealer, King of Dharma.

After arising from the wisdom of equanimity, then it is as said:

Born in the Vajra family,
Revealing the secret teachings of Vajrasattva,
Having compassion toward sentient beings and faith in my Guru,
May I be born and born in this way until attaining the state
of Vajrasattva.
Holding the vajra and bell in my hands,
Reading profound upadesha,
Evenly eating the nectar of the wisdom vajra queen,
May I be born and born in this way until attaining the state
of Vajrasattva.
Whatever merit I have accumulated through this practice
Is dedicated to all limitless sentient beings.
May all attain the supreme state beyond suffering,
The glorious enlightened body of Vajrasattva.

Thus, dedicate and pray by reciting these words blessed as vajra speech.

According to absolute truth, especially in the inner Vajrayana, eating the wisdom nectar of the vajra queen means abiding in the secret place of the vajra queen,[183] which is inconceivable stainless space where all immeasurable Buddhas abide always. This is also the meaning of the speech of Kunkhyen Longchenpa, "Eating the samadhi meal."

According to the path of practice, in the inner Vajrayana, one is always supposed to practice to develop great emptiness wisdom bliss with the developing stage and completion stage in order to attain the phenomena of fully enlightened Detong Dorje Sempa,[184] filling the universe, which is the state of the immeasurable five Buddha families in union. One first practices with the consort of one's own mind,[185] with male and female energies that

183. rdo rje btsun mo'i bha ga.
184. bde stong rdo rje sems dpa', indivisible emptiness wisdom bliss Vajrasattva.
185. yid rig.

exist inherently, including the visualization of channels and chakras according to instructions of upadesha, in order not to be attached substantially to actual male and female consorts with karmic bodies. One visualizes the female wisdom vajra queen or male wisdom vajra king. Then, when the consort of one's own mind develops and one attains confidence in this practice, if one wishes to develop further by practicing with a physical consort, one must ask one's own root Lama Vajra Master whether it is necessary. This will depend on whether one is attached substantially to physical bliss or detached from the power of exaltation and therefore from the creation of karma due to causing samsaric pleasure. If one has gained full confidence in the consort of one's own mind, it may not be necessary to have a physical consort. According to what is appropriate for one's practice, one's consorts can have extremely positive spiritual energy with wisdom mind, or at least doubtless faith in the Vajrayana tradition. If one has no capacity oneself to develop one's own mind's consort, one can find a consort with wisdom mind in order to develop one's practice.

It is necessary to receive these teachings in detail by voice transmission from teachers who have full confidence, and then practice, not just forcing this by oneself through reading books and guessing what to do, because if any obstacles occur, a material book cannot purify disturbed vital energy according to the time at which it is necessary to do so, and it cannot develop wisdom energy. If one does not have the capacity to practice the path of skillful means,[186] the best way is meditation with faith and belief.

Since Vajrasattva and Kuntuzangpo are one, it is as Great Omniscient Rongzompa said:

> To synthesize, since the nature of all form is the essence
> of sky,
> Likewise, the nature of all phenomena is enlightened
> as the nature of Buddha Vajrasattva.

Thus, that is the meaning.

> By the sound of the always sublime enlightened mind,
> It is shown that all phenomena are naturally enlightened.

186. thabs lam.

Thus it is said.

> Then, the meaning of the sound of "always," *kun*, is that there is no distortion, and that all phenomena are perfectly complete. The meaning of no distortion, *ma 'dres pa*, is that the aspects of phenomena appear differently. The meaning of perfectly complete, *yongs su rdzogs pa*, is natural nonduality. From everything to everything, there is never any negativity to discard, so it is Kuntuzangpo, Always Noble. This is the sole essence of all phenomena. For example, the sky is naturally abiding in all form, open and without restriction. All inconceivable phenomena are unsurpassed and not left somewhere independently: all of them are contained in the nature of Kuntuzangpo. Therefore, this is called dharmadhatu. In brief, all phenomena are enlightened mind. The nature of Vajrasattva is enlightened mind, or enlightened in the nature of Kuntuzangpo. From everything to everything is always great and vast. Therefore, the meaning of Vajrasattva and Kuntuzangpo is the same; their greatness and vastness is the same. Thus:
>
> > Kuntuzangpo is the nature of Vajrasattva.
>
> As it is said:
>
> > So open, so great, great Dharma.

Thus it is said by Omniscient Rongzompa.

The Tibetan words *sherab* (*shes rab;* Skt. *prajna*) and *yeshe* (*ye shes;* Skt. *jnana*) appear again and again in this commentary because they are connected with enlightenment. It is important to explain these words because of the tendency to materialize and separate them, which is incompatible with the meaning of Dharma, which is to make everything noncontradictory. For sentient beings, body and mind are different, but for Buddhas, body is pureland, pureland is body, speech is body, body is speech, wisdom mind is wisdom Buddha, and wisdom Buddha is wisdom mind.

Sherab or *prajna* can be translated as "incisiveness," while *yeshe* or *jnana* can be translated as "wisdom." Sometimes, however, the Sanskrit word *prajna* is translated as "wisdom," and the word *wisdom* can be used for sublime intelligence. Some people think of jnana as always higher than prajna, and believe that jnana is an aspect of Buddha, while prajna is below Buddhahood. It is definitely not correct to say that prajna is something other than jnana, or that jnana is always the purest. The only way to know the meaning of these words is from the context of the level of attainment to which they are applied.

There are many different levels of sherab or prajna, and many different levels of yeshe or jnana. For example, even ordinary people have worldly knowledge and worldly wisdom, but when ordinary beings are compared with the Hearers, the prajna and jnana of the Hearers are higher. When the prajna and jnana of the Hearers are compared with those of the Solitary Realizers, the prajna and jnana of the Solitary Realizers are higher. When the prajna and jnana of the Solitary Realizers are compared with those of the Yogachara, the prajna and jnana of the Yogachara are vaster. The prajna and jnana of the Yogachara is surpassed by those of the Madhyamika. The prajna and jnana of the Madhyamika are surpassed by the Vajrayana. When the state of complete enlightenment is attained, there is no more thought of either prajna or jnana.

Prajna or sherab can be understood as the lower levels of the prajna of human beings, and also as the higher levels of prajna from the first up to the tenth bhumi. Therefore, *prajna* can be used in various contexts to mean worldly intelligence; the realization of practitioners; the realization of Bodhisattvas, which transcends ordinary intelligence; and one of the aspects of Buddha. When prajna is used for Buddha, who has surpassed all, it is the ultimate prajna called prajnaparamita, which is beyond prajna.

Likewise, the word *jnana* or *yeshe* can be understood in many different ways. The word for wisdom is used by followers of other religions, including Muslims and Hindus, although the meaning is different. In Buddhism, even though the same word, *wisdom*, is used, it has many different meanings according to the context. *Jnana* can refer to worldly wisdom; to the impure pure wisdom of practitioners; to the wisdom of Bodhisattvas from the first to the tenth bhumi, according to the different stages of realization of the state after evenness; and to the nondual wisdom of Buddhas. It cannot be fixed with conceptualization as having only one particular meaning. In the great speech of Buddha and its shastras, worldly wisdom is referred to as *dag pa' jig rten gyi ye shes,* but this wisdom is not the same as *ma dag pa dag pa'i ye shes,* which is the wisdom of the path of enlightenment and is used for practitioners and for Bodhisattvas from the first to the tenth bhumi. Also, the wisdom of practitioners and Bodhisattvas is not the same as Buddha's wisdom, which is fully enlightened.

In its pure form, the word *wisdom* is used for the five wisdoms. It should not be conceptualized, however, that Buddha has wisdom and that practitioners do not. Practitioners have these five wisdoms inherently, and these wisdoms are blossoming through practice but have not yet fully expanded.

For example, there are many different levels of bodies, including both bad and good karmic bodies. Also, there is the body of manifestation. Likewise, there are many different levels of mind, including many different levels of ordinary mind with dualistic habit, since beings vary in intelligence and faculties. Some people have intelligence that is more worldly, some have intelligence that is more spiritual, while others have sublime intelligence. The state of Buddha means that all worldly levels of prajna have been surpassed, and that is why it is called prajnaparamita. Wisdom is also like that, since there are many different levels of wisdom. Even among ordinary beings, some with good hearts are more kind and compassionate than others, which is related to wisdom, although it is not sublime wisdom as in the first to tenth stages of the realization of nondualistic wisdom mind. Even when this wisdom has been realized, from the first up to the tenth stage, the realization of wisdom has to develop more and more. This is because previous karmic residual habit still persists; however, wisdom is transforming into higher and higher stages, even though the same word, *wisdom,* is used for all of these stages.

When fully enlightened Buddhahood is attained, it becomes the stainless sky of *ye shes chen po,* or Greatest Wisdom, because there is nothing more to be developed. So, even the one word *jnana* encompasses many levels of meaning, due to the different purposes for which it is used, including whether it refers to karmic phenomena, practice, or realization.

According to the Mahayana, each sentient being has Buddha nature, and even Buddha nature has jnana. If there were no jnana in the minds of practitioners, what would there be to develop? Whenever one is developing spiritually, there are many different levels of development according to the different faculties of beings, and that is why there are different levels and descriptions of prajna and jnana. This means that jnana exists inherently, and also prajna exists inherently. As explained, jnana does not mean only fully enlightened Buddhahood, because each being has prajna and jnana inherently. Even though these two words are explained differently, the essence is Buddha nature. That is why it is not necessary to conceptualize them as separate or as only belonging to a particular state. As prajna and jnana develop, their qualities become increasingly vast and profound as nondual wisdom mind opens. They cannot be intellectualized. They are different aspects of the qualities of mind, but their essence is oneness, which is sole dharmata.

When wisdom is fully enlightened, it is extremely perfect, so it does not matter what it is called, whether prajna and sherab or jnana and yeshe. If one conceptualizes the meaning of prajna or jnana, then one cannot be in dhatu. The Sanskrit *dhatu* is *ying* in Tibetan, or *space* in English, and is always, no matter what different phenomena appear. Since dhatu is always, prajna is always, because dhatu opens prajna; so prajna cannot be materialized as distinct from wisdom. That is why they are called noncontradictory.

According to the aspect of discerning wisdom, one can call this by many different names, such as dharmadhatu or vajradhatu. *Dharmadhatu* means that all dharmas are contained within space. Since all qualities are contained in dharmadhatu, it becomes indestructible vajradhatu, which is not separate from dharmadhatu or dharmata. There are also ratnadhatu, padmadhatu, karmadhatu, and Buddhadhatu. Whatever is said about these qualities, which are aspects of appearance that are discerned as qualities of Buddhas, all of these dhatus are always based in oneness, according to Mahayana and especially Vajrayana tradition, so by keeping this doctrine, one is not going to cause the materialization of each aspect as separate from each other aspect. The repeating dhatu is a sign that they cannot be divided. If one divides each of these dhatus and tries to make five different dhatus, then there is no sole oneness and no basic, inconceivable vastness. If there is no sole oneness, then from where do manifestations come and to where do they go? There would be no answer. Even though one calls these dhatus by different names, they must be only oneness.

If prajna and jnana are divided, they cannot be integrated. One can only say that according to sublime beings, jnana is nondual. Prajna is discernment, but without jnana, there is no prajna. If there is jnana, prajna is always there. Also, sherab is not something of less quality. It is called a quality of enlightenment in many texts. It is said that the Dharmakaya Buddha has dharmata eyes; the Sambhogakaya Buddha has wisdom eyes; and the Nirmanakaya Buddha has prajna eyes. The essence of the Three Kayas is oneness, and these are only descriptions of different aspects of these eyes. It does not mean that they are totally independent and separate in a material way. Also, there are five eyes of wisdom.

Receiving the Blessings of Guru Yoga

Fifth, the essence of all paths, Lama'i Naljor,[187] or Guru Yoga, is as follows. The essence of Kuntuzangpo's inconceivable object of sublime appearances of skillful means as dharmata is the actual empty nature of great prajna, Kuntuzangmo. Unchanging throughout the three times, this limitless sphere of space, which is the source of the manifesting and gathering of all Buddhas, is not from the path of learning and practice. This is the enlightened Lama who has attained the nondual union of Vajradhara, which only means the result of Buddha, the Three Kayas. Therefore, the term *yoga* is not appropriate in this context. It is for those practitioners who have the joy of devotion and diligence to try to achieve the state of the enlightened Lama. Whatever Dharma is practiced, the subject who is the practitioner is practicing in order to increase and enhance the union of skillful means, or phenomena, and prajna, or emptiness, which is for the benefit of the practitioner. That is why this is called Yoga.

In a brief way, all yogas are contained in the two yanas: the causal yana, or Mahayana tradition, and the result yana, or Vajrayana tradition. The result yana of Vajrayana is as said in *The Lamp of the Three Ways:*[188]

> Even one meaning is understood, it excels beyond ignorance;
> It has many methods; it has no hardship;
> And it belongs to those with keen faculties. So therefore,
> Vajrayana surpasses all other vehicles.

Thus, as it says, Vajrayana surpasses the causal vehicle with characteristics in these four ways.

In particular, as our incomparable Lord Buddha Shakyamuni said:

> Do not rely on an ordinary individual; rely on Dharma.
> Do not rely on the words; rely on their meaning.
> Do not rely on relative truth; rely on absolute truth.
> Do not rely on consciousness; rely on wisdom.

Thus, this teaching from the glorious voice of Buddha on the four ways of

187. bla ma'i rnal 'byor.
188. *tshul gsum sgron me.*

relying completely reveals the meaning of everything, which is the way of taking wisdom as the path and the pinnacle and king of all vehicles.

It is as said in *The Precious Treasure of the Supreme Vehicle:*[189]

> In the aim of the common, conceptual vehicle, even though mind is the basis, path, and result, all of these do not arrive at the meaning. In this vehicle of Vajrayana, wisdom is the basis, path, and result of Buddha, so by establishing wisdom, liberation from samsara is swift. In other vehicles, although there is hope to attain enlightenment, the basis is the root of samsara, which is ordinary mind. Not only does that path take a long time, but the result is extremely difficult to accomplish because the way of establishing the basis is mistaken.

As it says in *The Mirror of the Mind of Kuntuzangpo:*[190]

> To desire to attain Buddhahood through the mind is to
> misunderstand me.

Thus, this way of misunderstanding is both logically and philosophically incorrect. If there is this expectation to achieve the basis, the path, and the state of the result of Buddhahood with the mind, since the basis of this construction is dualistic mind, it follows that the entire basis, path, and result will be dualistic. If one believes this, then Buddhahood will not be accomplished. Even if it were possible, it would have to be mistaken, because there could still be no liberation from duality. Furthermore, just as one has collected various karma and habits, then, if one believes that there will be a basis, path, and result, there will be the fault of delusion. Suppose someone were to say, "If there is no mind, there cannot be Buddhahood, since all Bodhisattvas who were enlightened depended on mind. You accept that, don't you?" The answer is that Buddha does not depend on whether or not there is a mind, but only depends on whether or not there is the wisdom of Dharmakaya. That is how it is. Also, Ngari Panchen Padma Wang-gi Gyalpo[191] said:

189. *theg mchog rin po che'i mdzod.*
190. *kun tu bzang po thugs kyi me long.*
191. mnga' ris pan chen pad ma dbang gi rgyal po.

The Great Perfection is the form of all wisdom.
The perfectly pure embodiment of the great Vajradhara
Is the ultimate result, the oneness of Buddha.

Thus, since the pith of all practice is complete within the meaning of the Great Perfection, if one is able to engage in practice that is connected with Lama'i Naljor, then all that is to be abandoned and realized on the stages and paths will be perfectly complete. Je Gotsangpa[192] said:

Even though there are many developing stage visualizations,
None is higher than visualizing the Lama.
Even though there are many completion stage meditations,
None is more reliable or all-encompassing than meditating
on the Lama.

Thus it is said.

In *The Tantra of All-Containing Jewels,*[193] it says:

No matter who practices for one hundred thousand eons
By meditating on one hundred thousand deities,
Just remembering the Lama is supreme.
The merit of this is limitless.
More than practicing and reciting a million mantras,
Praying once to the Lama is supreme.

Thus it is said.

Saraha said:

For those who hold the Lama's speech in their heart,
It will be like seeing a precious treasure in the palm of their hand.

Thus, there are many such teachings. In *The Commentary on the Advice of the Holy Father and Son*[194] by Jigme Gyalwa'i Nyugu and his disciples, it says:

192. rje rgod tshangs pa.
193. *kun 'dus rin po che'i rgyud.*
194. *yab sras kyi zhal rgyun khrid yig.*

In particular, the natural Great Perfection is the vehicle of the vajra heart essence. According to the lower vehicles, the profound meaning of the absolute is established through analysis and theoretical reasoning, and so on; that is not said in the Great Perfection. According to the lower tantric schools, by relying on common siddhi, ultimately supreme siddhi will be attained; that is not said in the Great Perfection. According to other high tantric schools, by relying on the third empowerment of the example of wisdom, one attempts to be introduced to absolute wisdom; that is not said in the Great Perfection. This lineage, like a golden chain that has never been tarnished, can only be received from a supreme and highly realized Lama who is recognized to be the actual Buddha. Then, by praying with irreversible intense devotion and combining one's mind inseparably with the Lama's wisdom, through the strength of the bestowal of blessings, realization will blossom within one's own mind.

It is as said:

The simultaneously born wisdom of absolute truth
Only comes from the handprint of the accumulation of merit, the purification of obscurations, and the blessings of a highly realized Lama.
Other than that, if someone thinks there is another method, it is foolish.

Thus it is said.
From Kunkhyen Longchenpa's *Magical Resting:*[195]

The developing and completion stages, and so on, are not able to liberate by the essence of their path; they depend on conduct and advantageous circumstances. Lama'i Naljor is only the essence of the path itself, so the realization of the unconditioned nature is born in the mind, and one becomes liberated. Therefore, Lama'i Naljor is more profound than all other paths.

195. *sgyu ma ngal gso.*

Thus it is said.

In this way, all sublime scholars and saints of the past are in agreement on the ways in which Lama'i Naljor is the most profound of all practices. Their wisdom minds and voices are one in praise of Lama'i Naljor. These are the reasons one should never think that the preliminary practices need to be done in order to be able to begin an actual practice. Without anticipating another actual practice in the future, holding the actual practice of Lama'i Naljor as the life of the main practice, if one is able to practice like the unceasing flow of a river, it is like one hundred rivers flowing under a single bridge. By arriving at this essential point, one's practice will be greatly enhanced.

All Dharma to be practiced is the speech of Buddha and the limitless enlightened commentaries based only on Buddha's speech. We ordinary individuals lack methods because of ignorance, so the correct way of practicing is not understood. If one creates complexity with many conceptions like a net, just forget about enhancing one's practice; one is completely overwhelmed by discouragement, tiredness, hope, fear, irritability, and procrastination. Due to this, the time for liberation never arrives. This is because of materializing Dharma as being tangible, intangible, with characteristics, without characteristics, and so on. Always distinguishing between good and bad, like separating hairs from each other, one deviates from the path. It is as Orgyen Rinpoche said to King Trisong Detsen:

> Great King, the view of this, my secret mantra, is foremost. Do not lose conduct to the direction of the view. Not believing in virtue, sin, or anything, one will be lost to the direction of darkness and demonic views. Likewise, do not lose the view to the direction of conduct. If this happens, one will then be caught by the materialization and characterization of Dharma, and the time of liberation will not come.

Thus, we can understand through this speech.

All of the profound and expansive nine yanas can be contained in the preliminary practices, and specifically in Lama'i Naljor, like an ocean of Dharma including everything. Through one-pointed devotion, if one knows how to practice by synthesizing the essence of all practices, then, even if one dies right now, it will never be possible to fall from the towering cliffs of a wrong place. The Glorious Lord Nagarjuna[196] said:

196. dpal mgon klu sgrub.

If someone were to fall from the peak of the king of all mountains,
Although this may seem impossible for the mind to comprehend,
it could still occur.
If, through the Lama's kindness, a beneficial teaching is received,
Even if liberation is not desired, it could still occur.

Thus it is said. Like that quotation and so many others throughout the sutras and tantras, it is solely the Lama who is praised as the quintessence of the Three Jewels. Therefore, by practicing the path of receiving the Lama's blessings, the result of the state of Buddha is actually accomplished. It is impossible to find a better, more meaningful result.

Whatever the case, it should be known that from Buddha Kuntuzangpo and consort and the manifestation of Kuntuzangpo, the five Buddha families and consorts, to Vajrasattva is the Wisdom Mind Lineage of the Victorious Ones. From Garab Dorje, Jampal Shenyen, Shri Singha, Vimalamitra, and the Great Master Padma Jungne is the Gesture Lineage of the Vidyadharas. Without relying on an elaborate way of teaching, all teachings are fully realized just from gestures. From King Trisong Detsen, the subject Berotsana, and the companion Kharchen Za Yeshe Tsogyal, who are the King, Subject, and Companion, from these three to the first and following incarnations of Düdjom Lingpa to the root Lama is the Lineage of Personally Hearing Teachings Given by Voice. The order of these lineages is clearly and extensively described in the commentary from the New Treasures of Düdjom Rinpoche called *Heart Essence of the Dakini.*[197] If this meaning is synthesized, the root Lama of great kindness is the embodiment of all Lamas of the lineages of Wisdom Mind, Gesture, and Personally Heard Teachings Given by Voice. All of the root Lamas in the three lineages that are contained within the root Lama of great kindness appear to beings to be subdued with the appropriate appearances according to the time, in various manifestations without interruption like an unbroken bridge that has continued to the present time, with only wondrous, incomparable histories of Buddhas ripening the minds of fortunate beings to be subdued.

It is unthinkable even to consider that these teachers could have differences like the distinctions made between the pure essence and impure aspects of food. One should never think that at the time of the Wisdom Mind Lineage of the Victorious Ones and the Gesture Lineage of the Vid-

197. *mkha' 'gro'i snying thig.*

yadharas that appearances are at the level of sublime beings, and that at the time of the Lineage of Personally Hearing Teachings Given by Voice, appearances are those of ordinary human beings. For those who are Vidyadharas practicing the categories of Vajrayana, it does not matter how the lineage is transmitted. Whether transmitted from one wisdom mind to another wisdom mind, from one who is showing a gesture to another who is receiving the gesture, or from one who is giving a teaching by voice to another who is hearing the teaching, the way these three lineages are transmitted according to time and place is through Lamas who continuously appear. Though their names appear differently, ultimately the wisdom minds of the lineage holders are absolutely inseparable. Therefore, it is said that it is never, ever acceptable to view good and bad distinctions between lineages and lineage holders, and especially never to view one's own root Lama, who is the holder of the blessings of the three lineages, as an ordinary person. Buddha said:

> Whoever shows disrespect
> To the future Vajradhara
> Insults me,
> So I will completely abandon them all.

Thus Buddha said. Also, the quotation continues:

> Since I am within the body of the Lama,
> I will accept the worship of practitioners.
> By pleasing me in this way,
> They will purify the karmic obscurations of their minds.

Thus it is said.

From *The Commentary on "The New Treasure Preliminary Practices"*:[198]

> If there is no devotion for the Lama, even if one completes the requirements of sadhana practice according to the six tantric teachings[199] of meditation deities, supreme spiritual attainment will never be obtained. Even many of the common spiritual

198. *gter gsar sngon 'gro'i khrid yig.*
199. The six tantric teachings are Kriya, Upa, Yoga, Maha, Anu, and Ati.

> attainments such as long life, prosperity, magnetizing, and so on, will not be accomplished. If by chance there is some minor accomplishment, it requires great hardship and the path will not be profound. If unerring devotion develops in the mind, obstacles on the path will be cleared, advancement will be made, and all common and supreme spiritual attainments will be accomplished without relying on anything else. These are the reasons this practice is called the profound path of Lama'i Naljor.

Thus it is said.

Having faith in the Lama, however, is very difficult. Among the six realms of beings, birth in the human realm is very rare compared with birth in other realms. As a simple, obvious example, everybody knows there are many more beings in the ocean than beings in the human realm. Among human beings, there are many more savages who from ignorance know nothing about spirituality and do not believe in it, because of the lack of prayers in many previous lives, than there are spiritual people. Even if there is an idea of spirituality, it is often occupied by a wrong message. If there is belief, only human realms are accepted as objects of consideration. In some religions, according to their god's message, only the adherents of the same religion are objects of consideration, while those who follow other religions are sacrificed or harmed with the thought that it is virtuous.

So having faith in Buddhism is as rare as a daytime star, due to the lack of good karma of human beings. Especially, due to believing in the importance of self-determination and self-reliance, many people become unnecessarily paranoid about having faith in a Lama at a spiritual level and indiscriminately see Lamas with distrust as potentially interfering with their personal autonomy. There used to be spiritual countries in Asia holding Buddhist lineage, but through attachment to this short life, many Easterners are interested in science and technological advances, and even Eastern scholars are catching the contagion of nihilism. Instead of quoting Buddha's speech, they quote Western scientists and imitate Westerners, which is most moronic, letting the vast culture and teachings of Asia decay for the sake of self-interest and momentary material gain. This is just mentioned in the hope that in this kaliyuga, some white crows who have faith in Buddha and Dharma will follow and rely on many sublime beings' teachings, including the speech of the omniscient Buddha.

In addition to the three lineages explained earlier, there are three special lineages of Guru Rinpoche's treasures,[200] known as Wisdom Prophecies, Empowered by Prayer, and Sealed Treasures from Guru Rinpoche Entrusted to Dakinis to be Given to Treasure Revealers. If these three treasure lineages are added to the three lineages of Wisdom Mind, Gestures of Vidyadharas, and Personally Hearing Teachings Given by Voice, then there are six lineages, which are all contained within one's own root Lama.

This has been a brief explanation of the general meaning to be understood. In the actual practice of Lama'i Naljor, one visualizes oneself as Dorje Naljorma[201] and the Lama as Guru Rinpoche in space in front of oneself. First, as it is said in the tantras, the meaning of Dorje Naljorma is:

> Vajra is the nature of emptiness.

Thus it is said. Also, it says in the *Prajnaparamita:*

> The perfection of knowledge is free from speech, thought, or expression,
> Unborn, unceasing, like the essential nature of sky.
> Only the wisdom of discerning self-awareness sustains this.
> Homage to the mother of all the Victorious Ones of the three times.

Thus, just as said in many of the profound categories of Sutra and Tantra, the Dharmakaya wisdom Dakini is the absolute vajra space of emptiness, the mother of the expanse of all Buddhas of the three times. Natural unobstructed clarity is the spontaneous presence of the qualities of Sambhogakaya as the completely enlightened body of the five families of Vajra Varahi. Pervading throughout immeasurable purelands, sustaining in sky, they are the five consorts of the space of Akanishtha. From this state, manifesting in holy places and sacred lands according to the appearances of the objects to be subdued, there are Dakinis born from the lineage of Vajrayana teachings, Dakinis born from holy places, Dakinis born with inherent wisdom Dakini qualities blossoming, and others. They are the inconceivable emanations radiating from the Nirmanakaya Vajrayogini with serene, desirable, and wrathful aspects, accomplishing the purpose of sentient beings.

Like that, the embodiment of all of these immeasurable Dakinis of the Three Kayas is praised by the Triumphant Omniscient Lord, Mipham

200. gter ma, terma.
201. rdo rje rnal 'byor ma; Skt. Vajrayogini.

Rinpoche, in his prayer to the Dakini Queen Yeshe Tsogyal called *The Longing Melody of Faith:*[202]

E MA HO! Wondrous!
Vajrayogini, mother of all Victors,
Yangchenma, keeper of an ocean of melodies,
Jetsunma, compassionate liberator of beings,
Dakini of great kindness in Tibet,
Consort who pleases the enlightened mind of the
  Lotus-Born Vidyadhara,
Sole mother and only refuge of the people of Tibet,
Source of the profound secret Vajrayana teachings,
Conqueress of supreme knowledge, compassion, and power,
Vidyadhara accomplished in the supreme attainment
  of immortality,
Yogini who has perfected all the stages and paths,
Mother of skillful means, compassionately manifesting
  whatever form is necessary to subdue beings,
Goddess whose benefit for others is equal to the sky,
Ruler with naturally limitless, all-pervasive enlightened activity,
Jetsunma, if called upon, your compassion is swift.
If one is accomplishing you, you are a Dakini of most
  profound blessings,
Greatly kind one, whose compassion is like the love
  of a mother watching over her children;
My sole protectress, who contains all objects of refuge,
Yeshe Tsogyal, to you I pray.
Queen of Dakinis, to you I pray.
The manifestation of power, to you I pray.
Radiant One of blue light, to you I pray.
Sole consort of the Lotus Guru, to you I pray.
Sole mother lineage holder, to you I pray.
Holder of profound treasures, to you I pray.
The one whose blessings enter quickly, to you I pray.
Glorious one who fulfills all wishes, to you I pray.
The one who accomplishes the hopes of beings, to you I pray.

202. *dad pa'i gdung dbyangs.*

Wish-fulfilling jewel, to you I pray.
Deceitless compassionate one, to you I pray.
Constant protector, to you I pray.
Dispeller of suffering, to you I pray.
Supreme guide of beings, to you I pray.
You are my Lama, you are my Yidam,
You are my Dakini, you are my Dharmapala.
Jetsunma, for an unfortunate being like me, you are
my sole source of refuge.
I pray to you with devotion from my heart.

Thus, Mipham Rinpoche wrote. Also, the fifteenth Karmapa[203] prayed:

Mother of all Victorious Ones, Kuntuzangmo of the dharmadhatu,
Guardian of all Tibetans, sole mother of great kindness,
Bestowing supreme spiritual attainment, Dakini Queen of great bliss,
To the feet of Yeshe Tsogyal I pray.

Thus, as said, this explains the intangible Kuntuzangmo who appears within form as Yeshe Tsogyal, whose glorious auspicious signs and noble marks are in full bloom.

Therefore, it is said that if the auspicious connection is made within the body, realization will dawn in the mind. Just as sublime scholars and saints who came before have said, in order for blessings to enter the mind quickly, one should not see one's ordinary body as a karmic body. If one knows that one's essence is the Queen of the Dakinis of the Three Kayas, Yeshe Tsogyal, appearing in the aspect of Vajrayogini, then, unstained by obscuration, one becomes a supreme vessel for empowerment, using the sublime way of realizing the meaning of taking the result as the path. Thus clearly visualize.

All of one's appearances, wherever they are, become the Akanishtha pureland of Lotus Light and the perfect arrangement of the fully ornamented palace. Visualize that in the middle of this are a lotus as a sign of nonattachment and a sun as a sign that the darkness of ignorance has been dispelled. Upon a seat of a corpse, which is a sign that the conception of self has been purified, appears Jetsun Queen Abiding in Sky,[204] transparently

203. rgyal dbang mkha' khyab rdo rje; Gyalwang Khakhyab Dorje.
204. Vajrayogini.

red in color. Her face is serene and slightly wrathful from the enlightened aspect of desire, and her manner is extremely attracting. From her opening lips, a garland of stainless teeth with four budding fangs are shown, beaming like moonlight. Her two eyes are a sign of the two form Kayas, and the single eye in the center of her forehead is a sign of Dharmakaya. All three eyes are eagerly gazing into space where the Lama is seated. With the single-pointed joy of seeing the Lama, her only focus is the Lama's heart, in the manner of intense longing.

Her body blossoms with the youthfulness of a sixteen-year-old maiden. Her breasts are full, and her secret lotus is flowering. The sign that the net of passions has been cut from the root is the curved copper blade she raises up in her right hand, next to her right ear. In her left hand she holds a skull filled with wisdom nectar beside her waist in the manner of offering, which is a sign of unobstructedly bestowing supreme and common attainments. She stands in the dancing posture with her right leg balanced evenly while the left leg is drawn slightly up. Half of her hair is tied on top of her head and adorned with a brilliant wish-fulfilling jewel. The other half is flowing freely down her back. Her jeweled crown is beautifully decorated with a garland of amaranthine flowers. At the beginning of the spiral of her upwardly gathered hair is a wheel, and her two ears are ornamented with golden wheel earrings with tiny dangling bells. Her golden arm bracelets and leg anklets have delicate ringing bells. Her belt is made of the five mudras of bone, and her long middle necklace is beautified with lapis lazuli, rubies, diamonds, pearls, and various precious jewels. To the right and left of her crown are silk scarves with loosely flowing, graceful layers that flutter. Her beauty is so captivating that just looking at her cannot bring satisfaction. Her exquisite enlightened body appears within an expanse of the swirling, vibrant radiance of the five wisdom light rays. Like phenomena appearing in the mind, without a single particle of substance, as a rainbow appears in space, clearly meditate in this way.

It is as said in *Revealing the Names of Manjushri:*[205]

> The glorious Buddha born from a lotus
> Is an omniscient treasure holder of wisdom.
> King of various magical manifestations,
> Great Buddha, lineage holder of Vajrayana.

205. *'jam dpal gyi mtshan yang dag par brjod pa.*

Thus, as predicted, this is the Lotus-Born Padmasambhava, who is the refuge and protector of beings in the degenerate times. As Khandro Yeshe Tsogyal said:

> In general, for future sentient beings of Tibet,
> The Lama of their karmic connection will be the Lotus-Born.
> Everyone should diligently practice their Lama,
> Each visualizing their Lama in the form of Guru Rinpoche,
> Because extraordinary blessings and compassion will be received,
> So one should practice either the concise or extensive heart accomplishments of the Lama according to the sadhana.
> I swear to you that Buddhahood will be accomplished in one lifetime.

Thus she spoke. Also, in *The Vajra Speech of Guru Rinpoche,*[206] it says:

> Whoever is a fortunate being with faith
> Should pray to me with yearning devotion.
> By the interdependent connection of root and contributing circumstances and sublime aspiration,
> My compassion will be swifter than other Buddhas.

Thus, it is also said in *Confidential Speech:*[207]

> If you accomplish me, you accomplish all Buddhas.
> If you see me, you see all Buddhas.
> I am the epitome of all Sugatas.

Thus, just as the truth of this vajra speech is his own speech, it is only necessary to practice the accomplishment of Guru Rinpoche.

The way of practicing the gathering of the refuge field is as follows. Above the crown of the root Lama Orgyen Chenpo,[208] Guru Padmasambhava, clearly visualize the Gurus of the lineage extending upward all the way to Kuntuzangpo. At the time of Vajrasattva practice, Vajrasattva is the only Lama visualized above the crown of one's head, as the embodiment of all

206. *rdo rje'i gsung.*
207. *gsang thems.*
208. o rgyan chen po.

lineage Lamas synthesized in a single wish-fulfilling jewel. At the time of Lama'i Naljor practice, it is taught to clearly visualize all lineage Lamas and the entire assembly of the deities of the Three Roots and the Dharma Protectors surrounding the enlightened embodiment of Orgyen Dorje Chang (Vajra Holder of Orgyen), like a gathering of a town. Since there are these differences in the manner in which to visualize, it is best to visualize in accordance with the teachings given for the practice being done. If one is unable to visualize, as mentioned earlier, one can synthesize all the lineage Lamas into the single body of the great Orgyen Rinpoche. This is called the tradition of synthesizing all objects of refuge into a single wish-fulfilling jewel. This way of practicing will never cause contradiction, and not only that, it is the most excellent. As the Mahaguru said:

> Previously as Amitabha, the Buddha of Boundless Light,
> In Mount Tala as the Lord Avalokiteshvara,
> I am the Lotus-Born of Dhanakosha,
> Manifesting the appearance of the Three Kayas,
> Which are actually inseparable and not different from each other,
> Abiding in the space of phenomena as Kuntuzangpo, and
> In the pureland of Rich Adornment[209] as Great Vajradhara,
> In Bodhgaya as Buddha Shakyamuni,
> Who are all inseparable as me, Padma,
> And spontaneously present within me.
> Therefore, you must always pray to me.

Thus, only pray from the heart with trust and devotion.

As explained before, clearly visualize that **oneself is transformed into Dorje Naljorma, and in the sky in front of oneself,** the form that contains all Buddhas of the three times, one's own **root Lama of great kindness appears in the form of Padmasambhava.** Clearly visualize the aspect of Orgyen Rinpoche. It is said in the commentary to *Heart Essence of the Dakini:*

> In the space directly above one's head, within a tentlike shimmering expanse of five-colored rainbow light rays of the self-illumination of the five wisdoms, is a broad and high precious

209. stug po bkod pa, the pureland in the center of Akanishtha.

jeweled throne. The throne is lifted up by eight majestic lions and draped with exquisite brocade silks of the gods. Upon the throne rest the layers of a variegated lotus with one hundred thousand petals, a sun, and a moon. Upon this is the essence of all Buddhas as the root Lama of great kindness, appearing in the form of Guru Padma Thötreng Tsal.[210] His complexion is most desirably radiant white with red. He is an extremely youthful eight years of age, radiant with the splendor and presence of the auspicious signs and noble marks. His joyful face is smiling with a slightly wrathful expression, and his round eyes are lovingly gazing upon one. His right hand holds a five-pointed golden vajra in the conquering mudra above his heart, and his left hand is in the mudra of evenness, holding a kapala[211] filled with wisdom nectar. Within this rests the excellent vase of immortality ornamented with a sprig from a wish-granting tree. His consort Mandarava appears as the three-pointed khatvanga hidden under his left arm. The shaft of the khatvanga is waterwood,[212] on top of which are two vajras crossed at the navel, and on top of them is a vase, three kinds of skulls, nine iron rings suspended from the base of the three points, and floating silk scarves, adorned with a damaru[213] and bells. He is clothed in the layers of an inner white-colored secret vajra garment, with a long-sleeved deep blue Vajrayana garment above that, with a red Dharma robe with spiraling gold patterns above that, and with a brocade cloak of the red color of power above that. He is crowned with the magnificent lotus petal hat that grants liberation upon seeing it, and abides with two legs in the manner of the kingly gesture. From his exceedingly radiant body, immeasurable stainless light rays emanate. His body is shining with the undistorted splendor[214] of majestic presence and the glory of the auspicious signs and noble marks. His voice is stainless resonance[215] resounding with the sixty branches of

210. gu ru pad ma thod phreng rtsal, Lotus Guru Skull Rosary Manifestation.
211. Skull cup.
212. chu shing, a kind of dark hardwood from a large tree that grows in India.
213. Skull drum used for invocation in the tradition of inner Vajrayana. When played, the damaru awakens beings from ignorance toward awareness by the sound of Dharma, to the phenomena of wisdom Dakas and Dakinis.
214. lhang nge.
215. lhan ne.

> melodious enlightened speech. His enlightened mind is unwavering immaculate wisdom[216] with profoundly secret nondual wisdom, compassion, and power. His unique enlightened presence naturally encompasses all the Buddhalands of the ten directions without exception. Within every single pore of his body, all purelands are perfectly complete. Think of his countenance as like a magical manifestation, containing the essence of the Three Jewels, Three Roots, and all objects of refuge, actually present before one.

Thus, as said, one should visualize. Through this visualization, ordinary appearances naturally cease. As clarified above, it is said that the qualities of his enlightened body are undistorted splendor. The qualities of his enlightened speech are stainless resonance. The qualities of his enlightened mind are unwavering immaculate wisdom. Elsewhere, in *The Mantrayana Sutra of the Ten Divine Prophecies Contained in Three Points,*[217] it says that undistorted splendor means appearance that has no substance. The qualities of his enlightened body, although apparent, have no material existence, like the flawless moon's reflection on water. Stainless resonance means to be unobscured, since the qualities of his enlightened voice are exceptionally clear. Unwavering immaculate wisdom means without elation or dullness, since the qualities of his enlightened mind resemble the light of a precious wish-fulfilling jewel. The comparisons made in these teachings are not contradictory, because they explain the essence just as it is. Since the qualities of the Buddhas' three secrets are in accord with the aspirations of the objects to be subdued, they appear in every aspect.

Then, from one's heart, light rays of fervent devotion radiate inconceivably, reaching the heart of the Mahaguru who contains all Buddha families, who resides in the Southwest Palace of Lotus Light. Immediately, Guru Rinpoche's omniscient wisdom mind knows the time has arrived to bless the mind of that fortunate being. Visualize that the Mahaguru together with his great assembly of a billion Vidyadharas, Dakas, and Dakinis, like clouds gathering in space, instantaneously arrive before one. Visualize the samayasattva abiding indivisibly with the wisdom energy of the jnanasattva.[218]

216. lham me.

217. *lha'i lung bcu ru bstan pa'i don mdo gsum du 'dus pa.*

218. Samayasattva (Tib. dam tshig sems dpa') is the tantric vow of the inherent mind of bodhichitta, and jnanasattva (Tib. ye shes sems dpa') is fully enlightened wisdom mind. These terms are connected with rituals. First, one visualizes whatever deity is practiced as the

HUNG. In the center of the Southwest Continent on the
peak of the glorious Copper-Colored Mountain,
In the palace of Great Bliss Lotus Light,
The Nirmanakaya Lord Lama Orgyen,
Together with your great assembly of Vidyadharas, Dakas,
and Dakinis,
May you please come to bless the holders of your lineage.
OM AH HUNG VAJRA GURU PADMA SIDDHI PHA LA HUNG AH.

Thus, as said in *The Extensive New Treasure Preliminary Practices,* the verses are recited while doing the visualization together with the invocation.

Or, visualize that oneself is Dorje Naljorma and Guru Rinpoche is in the sky in front of one with the signs, meanings, and gestures explained earlier. If one believes with firm faith and certainty from the heart in the same instant of remembering, the jnanasattva and samayasattva are inseparable. Therefore, it is not necessary to rely on elaborate invocations of the jnanasattva from purelands, and so on. There is no doubt that blessings will be received. In the sutras, it says:

For those who think of the Victorious Ones,
They will be present before them.
Bestowing constant blessings,
They will fully liberate them from all faults.

Thus it is said. Orgyen Rinpoche said:

Before each one who has faith, I will be there.

And again:

For those who wish, I will be with them.

Thus he said. Whether one does the extensive or simple visualizations, adapting to one's capacity, there will be no contradiction, and this will greatly benefit and develop one's practice.

---

samayasattva, and then, to that deity, fully enlightened Buddhas, or jnanasattva, are invoked from purelands to become indivisible with the samayasattva.

In these concise preliminary practices, each word of the seven-branch offering prayer is not explicitly mentioned as it is in extensive versions of the preliminary practices, but the meaning is contained in the four verses recited here. **The complete embodiment of all Buddhas of the three times, supreme root Lama, I pray to you. In this life, the next lives, and between lives, hold me with your compassion. May your blessings flow unceasingly throughout the three times.**

Thus, first, the antidote that purifies pride is prostrations. The characteristic of pride is holding self as supreme and looking down on others. In particular, it is prideful to show disrespect to the constant source of refuge, the Three Jewels and the Lamas who show the path to liberation, to one's parents of great kindness, and to those whose qualities surpass one's own. By disparaging and harming those whose qualities are less than one's own through negative conduct of body, speech, and mind, the result occurs of being disliked by others in this lifetime. In future lifetimes, rebirth will be taken as a suffering, vicious, hostile beast. The method to destroy these tendencies is obviously to show respect humbly from one's heart for the Three Jewels and the Lamas of great kindness. It is also important to have great respect for one's parents of great kindness and those who are older, noble, and knowledgeable, and not only that, but to support other sentient beings through genuine loving-kindness. It is as Bodhisattva Shantideva said:

> Even just looking toward sentient beings with one's eyes,
> One should think, "For them, I will become a Buddha.
> Therefore, I must look at them with an honest mind and loving manner."

Thus it is said.

The actual offering of prostrations is as follows. The hands are joined together in the lotus-bud mudra. While bringing the hands to touch the forehead, the obscurations of the body are purified. While bringing the hands to touch the throat, the obscurations of speech are purified. While bringing the hands to touch the heart, the obscurations of mind are purified. Thinking in this way, having touched one's three places, and then touching the five places of the forehead, the palms of both hands, and the knees to the ground is a prostration of the five main branches of the body. This is taught according to the teachings in the tradition of the common vehicles. Stretching the body out to make a full prostration as mentioned in *The Tantra of Stainless Confession*[219] and others is taught according to the tradition of the uncommon Vajrayana. Of these two traditions, the sublime Lamas who have come in the past have said that if one performs full prostrations in the Vajrayana tradition, because they take more effort and hardship, there is that much more power for purifying obscurations. The benefits of prostration are as said in *The Distinctions of Transmissions:*[220]

> A beautiful complexion, inspiring speech,
> A retinue that is disciplined by one's splendor, adored
> by gods and humans,
> Accompanied by holy companions, a grand, majestic presence,
> The higher realms of gods and humans, prosperity,
> and the attainment of liberation.

Thus, it is as said.

Second, the antidote that purifies greed is offering. Offering varieties of aspects of perfection, including inconceivable offerings of actual material substance and offerings that are manifested from the mind, in the same way that Kuntuzangpo offered to fully enlightened Buddhas and male and female Bodhisattvas, brings the benefit of the results of enjoying the happiness of gods and humans, and becoming an object of all beings' offering and honor, which continues until the state of Buddhahood is attained.

Third, the antidote that purifies hatred is confession. No matter how great the negativity of self and all other beings may be, confess by applying the essential method of the four powers with great remorse, and all negativity will be purified. The benefit of confession is never being reborn in the lower realms. By taking rebirth in the higher realms of gods and humans, all the qualities of liberation will be obtained.

Fourth, the antidote that purifies jealousy is rejoicing. Instead of being jealous about the prosperity and happiness of other beings, one should always rejoice. The benefits of rejoicing are expressed in *The Great Bliss Prayer to Be Reborn in the Pureland of Amitabha:*[221]

> When hearing about the virtue others are making,
> By abandoning the jealous mind of nonvirtue

219. *dri med bshags rgyud.*
220. *lung rnam 'byed.*
221. *chags med bde smon.*

> And sincerely rejoicing from the heart,
> It is said that one will receive the same merit.

And so it is.

Fifth, the antidote that purifies ignorance is requesting the wheel of Dharma to be turned. Wherever all Buddhas, Bodhisattvas, and sublime beings are, pray to them to turn the wheel of Dharma according to the minds of beings by offering precious jewels or whatever one can offer, including offerings manifested by the mind. The benefit of doing this is to purify the obscuration of abandoning the Dharma and to always increase the appearances of profound, immaculate knowing and wisdom in all future lifetimes. By sustaining the precious Dharma, the state of perfect omniscience will be attained.

Sixth, the antidote for wrong view is praying to request the enlightened ones not to abandon sentient beings. In this realm and others, when all Buddhas, Bodhisattvas, and sublime beings, including our own holy teachers, have completed manifesting their activity for the benefit of beings, they then focus on abiding in their fully enlightened Buddhafields. As a simple example, the sun and its rays are unceasing, but according to time and place, the rays manifest and draw back continuously, always indivisible from the sun. Again, as time and place align, the sun's rays manifest, dispelling beings' darkness and blossoming lotuses. Likewise, just as the sun's rays never cease, actual compassion never ceases, so wherever sentient beings' good fortune arises, enlightened manifestations emanate for the blossoming of Buddha nature. As said in the *Guhyagarbha Tantra:*

> Great compassion is always related to beings.
> Therefore, beneficial activities manifest in time and
> place, again and again.

Prayers must thus be made requesting enlightened beings to remain until cyclic existence is empty in order to fulfill the purpose of all sentient beings. The benefit of this prayer is the total purification of short life, untimely death, and all types of nonvirtue such as killing and harming others. One will be able to achieve immeasurable long life.

Seventh, the antidote for doubt is the dedication of merit. Whatever virtue has been accomplished, rather than having the motivation that it be for this life's gain and reputation or for happiness in future lives, it is necessary to dedicate it to the enlightenment of self and all other sentient beings. It is as Acharya Ashvaghosha said:

> The root of all virtue that is accomplished, whatever it is,
> Must not be with the hope for fame, reputation, and the
>   result of the happiness of gods and humans.
> Be free of the mind that cherishes samsara
> And make the dedication only to go beyond the world.

Thus it is said.

Whether virtue that is accumulated is tiny or great, if it is not dedicated to the state of enlightenment, then according to the teachings in the sutras, there are four root causes that exhaust the root of virtue. These four are: not dedicating virtue to the state of enlightenment; dedicating in order to subdue enemies, protect loved ones, and achieve gain in this life; dedicating with a reverse point of view; and regretting virtuous deeds. The importance of dedicating all virtue to attain the state of enlightenment, whether it is tiny or great, is as Buddha said in *The Sutra Requested by Ocean of Knowledge:*[222]

> It is like this. If a drop of spittle is thrown on the sand, it will quickly dry. If that same drop of spittle is thrown in the great ocean, then it will never dry. Ocean of Knowledge, even though the result will ripen, the root of whatever virtue has been made will not be long-lasting if one has regret, hesitation, weakness, and incorrect dedication. If virtue is dedicated to enlightenment, it will never be exhausted, but will continue to increase forever.

Thus it is said.

In the same way, since the aspects of virtue vary according to time and circumstance, whether the virtue accumulated is great or small, if all virtue is made with the supreme dedication to the state of enlightenment, it will be as said in *The Sky Treasure Sutra:*[223]

> Just as many rivers that come from different directions
> Eventually converge as one taste in the great ocean,

222. *blo gros rgya mtshos zhus pa'i mdo.*
223. *nam mkha' mdzod kyi mdo.*

Whatever virtues come from different directions
Become one taste by dedicating them all to enlightenment.

Thus it is said.

The difference between a dedication prayer and aspiration prayer is that a dedication prayer is preceded by the root cause of virtue. When this is combined with recitations and aspirations, it becomes a dedication. An aspiration prayer does not need to be preceded by the root cause of virtue, but is wishing from the heart. This explanation comes from the Omniscient Longchenpa.

Then, the root verses are, **The complete embodiment of all Buddhas of the three times, supreme root Lama, I pray to you. In this life, the next lives, and between lives, hold me with your compassion. May your blessings flow unceasingly throughout the three times.** Thus, to explain these specific words here about **the Buddhas of the three times**: The Buddhas of the past include the Buddha Marmedzad, Khorwa Jig, Serthub, Odsung,[224] and so on. The Buddhas of the present include our guide, the incomparable Buddha Shakyamuni, and all other Buddhas who come in this time. The Buddhas of the future include Maitreya Buddha and all Buddhas up to Mopa Tayei.[225] Especially, in the Great Perfection, there are the twelve Buddhas of the Great Perfection, all Lamas of the lineages of wisdom mind, gesture, and personally heard teachings given by voice, the five tertön kings, the one hundred great tertöns, the one thousand tertöns, the three aspects of the supreme Nirmanakaya, and others. **The complete embodiment of** all Buddhas of the three times who have come in the past, come in the present, and will come in the future are contained without exception in the one form of the wisdom body of one's own root Lama.

The meaning of root Lama is, from *The Self-Occurring Tantra:*[226]

The categories of the Lama include the general Lama,
the guide, the samaya Lama,
The Lama who shows upadesha, and the Lama
who bestows empowerment.

224. mar me mdzad (Skt. Dipamkara); 'khor ba 'jig (Skt. Krakuchanda); gser thub (Skt. Kankamuni); 'od srung (Skt. Kashyapa).
225. mos pa mtha' yas.
226. *rgyud rang shar.*

Thus, according to this, the general Lama is revered and respected by all regardless of their sect as their Lama, who is their spiritual guide. The guiding Lama has the capacity to guide and lead beings from the result of the state of the happiness of gods and humans, all the way to the path to liberation. The Lama of the samaya of empowerment, through empowerment in either the outer or inner tantras, teaches how to sustain the samaya of wisdom deities. The Lama who reveals upadesha grants entrance into the mandala of the tantra of unsurpassed Vajrayana, gives empowerment, explains the tantras, and gives special upadesha teachings that introduce uncontrived pure awareness. Because this Lama places the disciple in the state of Buddhahood very swiftly, more than any other Lama, this Lama's kindness is the most supreme, like one's own heart. Thus, this teacher is called the **root Lama.** Since it is impossible for there to be another Lama more exalted than this, this is the highest, **supreme** Lama. Prostrating **to** the Lama with great devotion from one's body, **praying** with great devotion from one's speech, and sustaining single-pointed faith with great devotion from one's mind, the words are said: **In this life, the next lives, and between lives, hold me with your compassion.**

Here, there is reference to this life, future lives, and between lives. In general, *bardo* means between. Until fully enlightened Buddhahood is attained, since beings always exist within time and place, wherever they exist, they are always in between because they have not gone beyond reality phenomena. Therefore, they have bardo phenomena. The appearances of this life are called the natural bardo. The dream bardo and meditation bardo are both contained within the natural bardo, so that all together are counted as one.

From the time when one is caught by the contributing circumstance of death until the inner breath is completely gone is called the bardo of death. After breathing ceases, there is no covering like the brightness of the sun, darkness, clouds, or the three obscuring influences such as fluid received from the father, fluid received from the mother, or vital airs. Everything appears like unobscured sky in autumn, free from these three circumstances. It is said that this is the arising of the appearance of original purity, like stainless space. This is uncontrived awareness, unaffected by fabrication. If one can recognize this immutable state and abide there, one will be liberated in Dharmakaya.

If one cannot stay in that state, then the natural manifestation of the nature of phenomena will become the self-manifesting appearances of the gathering of peaceful and wrathful deities. The arising of these various appearances is the bardo of dharmata. If one can recognize that these are all self-manifesting appearances, with the confidence to sustain the recognition of the immutable state, one is liberated in the clear light of Sambhogakaya.

By not recognizing self-phenomena, thinking that the gathering of peaceful and wrathful deities is coming from somewhere else with personal minds, there is delusion. When this starts, it is called the bardo of existence. A being in this state no longer has a gross karmic body the same as in the previous life, and this bardo is characterized by not having a gross karmic body, but a mental body of habit. Since there is no gross karmic body, there is no ability to use gross substances such as food and drink, but a being in this state can still use smells, so those in this state are called surrounding smell-eaters. In rituals done for people after death, substances called sur[227] are burned and given to the dead as smoke. For people who were vegetarian, karsur[228] are burned, such as herbs, rice, and whatever foods do not contain meat, and for people who liked meat, marsur[229] are burned, which are foods with meat. The dead can smell these foods. The habit of mind to acquire a body is very strong, which is called expecting to join with a body. From the previous strong habit of feeling, it seems as though a being has all the senses, which is called having unobstructed senses. The experience of the combination of these four characteristics,[230] which are the four skandhas excluding the skandha of form, is the appearance of the bardo of existence. If one's practice is not complete in this situation, then by praying to the root Lama and wisdom deities with single-pointed devotion, through the power of profound prayers of aspiration, one can be relieved by exhaling a great breath to be liberated in purelands or to again obtain a precious human birth. All of whatever is left of one's previous practice can then be accomplished, and one can reach the state of fully enlightened Buddhahood.

Thus, the natural bardo, the bardo of death, the bardo of dharmata, and the bardo of existence have to be recognized in time, whenever they occur. One prays for liberation: "Hold me with your compassion."

It says in *The Prayer to Kuntuzangpo:*[231]

227. gsur.
228. dkar gsur.
229. dmar gsur.
230. Not having a gross karmic body, rags pa'i gzugs khams med pa; surrounding smell-eaters, dri za nye ba 'khor; expecting to join with a body, nyer len gyi mtshams sbyor; and having unobstructed senses, dbang po kun tshang thogs med ldan.
231. *kun bzang smon lam.*

The basis of all is uncompounded.
The self-occurring, all-pervasive expanse is inexpressible.
There is no name of either samsara or enlightenment.
To see this nature is Buddha.

Thus, it is as said. If we can abide like Buddhas, without wavering from that state of the wisdom mind of Dharmakaya, since there is no way for delusion to occur, there is not even the name of bardo. "There is no name of either samsara or enlightenment" is not like the nihilist way of believing, which denies that samsara and enlightenment exist, and says that nothing occurs except for the independently existing appearances of the six gatherings of consciousness of this present life arising. Dharmakaya, which is completely beyond the relative views of nihilism and eternalism, is as the Glorious Lord Nagarjuna said:

Material and immaterial are both compounded.
Enlightenment is uncompounded.

Thus he said.

What is the meaning of "compounded"? "Compounded" refers to all phenomena that occur from root and contributing circumstances. All these phenomena are impermanent and destructible. For example, if there is an undamaged seed, with the contributing circumstances of water, fertilizer, heat, moisture, and so on, a sprout will grow and bear fruit. This occurs due to the connection between root and contributing circumstances. Therefore, this means that when compounded phenomena join with the negative contributing circumstance of the worldly conception of grasping at a self and what belongs to a self, this becomes the root cause. By relying on the view of a self, there is delusion about the contributing circumstance of being attracted to positive objects and repelled by negative objects, and karma based on attachment and aversion is accumulated; so, all phenomena become the overwhelming appearances of the causes and results of suffering. If compounded phenomena are joined with positive root and contributing circumstances, then the root circumstance of one's own Buddha nature is awakened by the positive contributing circumstance of meeting a sublime Lama. Then, by diligently accumulating merit and purifying obscurations, all the qualities of enlightenment will increase. It is said:

> Material is born from interdependent circumstances.

This is said because all material is compounded due to relying on root and contributing circumstances. One may think, "If all compounded phenomena are born from relying on root and contributing circumstances, how are immaterial compounded phenomena born?" It is as said:

> The immaterial becomes compounded by being named.

For example, it is impossible for a rabbit to have horns, so there is no conception of a rabbit having horns, but there is a conception that a rabbit does not have horns. This is a sign of the way the mind grasps at non-existence, which is an unreliable mental event based on delusion. As long as there is any designation or conception of anything being immaterial, it is said to be compounded phenomena. In the *Bodhicharyavatara*,[232] it says:

> For example, a barren woman dreams her son is dead.
> When she awakens, she thinks that she has no son.
> That conception of not having a son comes from the
> conception of having a son.
> So, both of these conceptions are obstacles and also delusion.

Thus it is said.

As in the previous quotation, "Enlightenment is uncompounded," thus, the meaning of the absolute truth of dharmata can only be beyond thought or expression.

An individual who goes between the states of abiding in evenness and after-evenness without joining them while on the path of learning will depend on the compounded phenomena of root and contributing circumstances until reaching the path of no more learning, where abiding in evenness and after-evenness are indivisible. This includes all of the various kinds of practices that accumulate merit and purify obscurations. Unlike the perceptions of nonpractitioners, however, this will only be positive root and contributing circumstances that join with flawless virtue.

Then, the verse, **May your blessings flow unceasingly throughout the three times**. Thus, concerning time, as mentioned earlier, conceptualizing

232. *spyod 'jug.*

a non-existent self causes dualistic mind. This produces passions, creating samsara. Whether the appearances of existence are good or bad, and for however long they appear, their appearance depends on the changes of time. If all the different names for determining time, such as seconds, hours, days, months, years, eons, and so on, are brought together, they are synthesized as the times of the past, present, and future. Therefore, the **three times** originate from the deluded appearances of the passions and karma, so that no matter where one wanders in existence during the three times, one must pray to be held **unceasingly** with compassion in order to avoid wandering in samsara. Timeless time is the supreme enemy of time. Until the state of Buddhahood is attained, pray that one's body may receive the blessings of enlightened body, one's speech may receive the blessings of enlightened speech, and one's mind may receive the blessings of enlightened wisdom mind. Thus, pray with the single white power of devotion.

The fourth time, which is the timelessness of the nature of equanimity, is the extremely pure, dustless space of appearance, which is completely free from the elaboration of samsara, enlightenment, hope, fear, happiness, and suffering. As the state of supreme bliss, it is as said in Mipham Rinpoche's *Praise to Manjushri:*[233]

> The most peaceful in peace,
> Supreme, flawless Manjushri,
> Sky-pervading body of great compassion,
> Sustaining in youthfulness, I prostrate to you.
> The most wrathful in wrath,
> Lord of death, annihilating all death phenomena,
> Devouring samsara and enlightenment in the mouth
> of stainless space,
> Great enemy of time, I prostrate to you.

Thus, it is said. Next, receiving the four empowerments. Generally, Guru Yoga practice is the swift path to directly receiving the blessings of all Buddhas, who are contained in the body of the Guru. Since this is the tradition for accomplishing the path of Vajrayana, it is necessary to rely on empowerment. It is said:

233. *'jam dpal la bstod pa.*

Without relying on empowerment in Vajrayana,
There is no accomplishment.
It is like the example of an oarsman without oars.

Thus, it is as said. Therefore, according to the common tradition of Mahayana, the root cause of the seed of Buddha nature ripens from the positive contributing circumstances of the effort of purification and accumulation, so that eventually, over a long time, the result of the state of Buddha is attained. Therefore, in Mahayana, the seed goes before and the result comes after. According to Vajrayana, it is not like that. From the beginning, there is no difference between seed and result. It is like the example of the sun, which from the beginning is the nature of clear light but only temporarily can be obscured by clouds. When the wind blows the clouds away, the sun shines, but this is not a new sun. The sun is from the beginning the sun, and it is its original nature fully manifesting. Likewise, by the power of relying on empowerment, precious teachings, and the visualization and completion stages together, temporary obscurations are purified and the qualities of the Three Kayas, which are from the beginning one's own mind, swiftly open. The Three Kayas are not coming from a new cause. From the beginning, the cause and result are inseparable and completely manifest through skillful means. In the tradition of Vajrayana, the result is perfected from the beginning in the basis of mind.

When empowerment is received directly from the Lama, this is called the empowerment of the basis. Receiving self-empowerment[234] and receiving empowerment during Lama'i Naljor practice is the empowerment of the path. Finally, when the meaning of empowerment manifests as wisdom awareness and the basis and result are inseparable as the perfectly attained state of the Three Kayas, this is the empowerment of the result. Although there are separate explanations throughout the classes of tantra on the differences between empowerments of the basis, path, and result, the essence is the single white power of devotion, so one receives the empowerment of the great light rays from the Lama's three secret places. To receive this empowerment is the most sublime of all empowerments. Since this is the sacred empowerment through which absolute wisdom most swiftly becomes apparent, there is nothing more profound.

Therefore, the four empowerments are received in the following way.

234. bdag 'jug.

From the white OM in the Lama's forehead, extremely clear and bright white light rays emerge. Dissolving into the center of one's forehead, the enlightened body vase empowerment is received. The obscurations of the channels of one's karmic body are cleansed, and one's body is blessed with enlightened vajra body. The fortune to attain the state of the Nirmanakaya is preserved in the mind.

From the red AH in the Lama's throat, extremely clear and bright red light rays emerge. Dissolving into one's throat, the secret empowerment of enlightened speech is received. The obscurations of speech and vital airs are cleansed, and one's speech is blessed with enlightened vajra speech. The fortune to attain the state of the Sambhogakaya is preserved in the mind.

From the deep blue HUNG in the Lama's heart, extremely clear and bright deep blue light rays emerge. Dissolving into one's heart, the obscurations of mind's tig-le are cleansed. In this case, *tig-le* refers to the seed of mind that causes samsaric phenomena, which is the origin of phenomena that have not yet been purified. When tig-le is purified, it is sole stainless Dharmakaya. The prajna wisdom empowerment is received, and one's mind is blessed with enlightened vajra mind. The fortune to attain the state of Dharmakaya is preserved in the mind.

The Lama's mind as the essence of conceptionless wisdom manifests as an extremely clear and bright sphere of five colors that dissolves into one's own heart. Then the two obscurations, including all habits, are completely cleansed and purified. The precious word empowerment is attained, and one is blessed to be inseparable with the victorious qualities and activities of all Buddhas. The Three Kayas are discerned in different aspects of qualities, but their essence is indivisible. The fortune to realize the Svabhavikakaya is preserved in the mind.

The explanation of the meaning of the Guru's essential twelve-syllable mantra is explained according to the extensive commentary on *The New Treasure Preliminary Practices* called *The Lamp Illuminating the Path to Liberation*[235] as follows.

OM, AH, and HUNG are the expression of the three vajras of enlightened body, speech, and mind that begin the mantra.

BENZAR is vajra. *Vajra* means never affected by the elaboration of dualistic conceptions. Abiding as the essence of all-pervasive empty awareness, vajra is Dharmakaya.

GURU means the Sambhogakaya Lama. The nature of this Sambhoga-

235. *thar lam snang sgron.*

kaya deity has the seven branches of union, carrying the inexhaustible opulence of the qualities of enlightened body and vast oceans of purelands arranged like gatherings of clouds. This is Sambhogakaya.

PADMA is the radiant awareness of discerning wisdom, the vajra speech of great bliss. Arising in the form of the supreme Lotus family of miraculous birth, this is Nirmanakaya.

By remembering the greatness of the qualities of this Great Lama Orgyen Dorje Chang, who is the inseparable Three Kayas, pray from the state of the uncontrived nature of one's mind, free from elaboration. By the power of prayer, both common and supreme SIDDHI without exception are requested with HUNG, and received within one's mind right at that moment. Thus, remembering the meaning, recite the mantra.

In this mantra, OM AH HUNG BENZAR GURU PEMA SIDDHI HUNG, the HUNG has a small circle that means it has the sound of the Tibetan MA or English M, which would be said as HUM, but it is actually pronounced with the sound of the Tibetan NGA, as HUNG. Likewise, the Sanskrit word VAJRA is BENZAR. Also, PADMA became PEMA, and RATNA became RENA, pronounced differently due to the difference in the languages spoken. Many sublime scholars have said that if one can translate the meaning and pronounce the words perfectly, of course it is best, but if one has faith and belief and understands the meaning, even though one cannot pronounce the words exactly because of differences in one's own language, there is no mistake and blessings will be evenly received. All the mantras in Buddhism have been blessed by sublime beings, so there is nothing missing.

Many teachers in both East and West think that generally Buddha taught in Sanskrit, and that Sanskrit is the original and essential language of Buddhism. Buddha's unobstructed tongue was not limited only to Sanskrit, however; according to history, Buddha also taught in other languages. If Eastern scholars and especially Western scholars sometimes think that Sanskrit is the only authentic language for Buddha's teachings, it actually implies that they think Buddha is not omniscient. Buddha said that he could teach in the languages of the gods, gandharvas, nagas, yakshas, rakshas, and human beings, so it is incompatible with Buddha's speech to try to confine it to one language.

It is also not always necessary to think that Dharma came only from India and does not exist other than that. Of course, wherever there is a language used for Dharma, it is necessary to study it, but it does not mean everyone must rely on only one language. Other languages also can function for the benefit of others, so to restrict Dharma to one language would be causing a limitation. In India, Buddha's speech was burned by Surya Siddhi, and there were many attempts to destroy Buddhist teachings in India many years ago. So, although Buddhism originated in India, it is not necessary to think that it will always be as it was. According to beings' phenomena, Buddhism can flourish in other places when the time ripens. Historically, many sutras and Mahayana texts have existed in the Chinese language. Even just in this world, there are many places other than India where Buddhism thrived, including in Oddiyana, where many tantric teachings originated, as well as in other Dakini lands, which were brought by sublime beings to this world. So, if the meaning, point of view, contemplation, and explanation of the result are there, whatever language is used, that is the speech of Buddha and also the speech of shastra. It is not wise to hold only one language as authentic by substantializing it. This can cause cognitive obscurations, because whatever is material, including words, always falls apart and vanishes. So, by materializing in that way, one cannot synthesize the meaning of Buddhist teachings into practice.

Also, whatever is written in Sanskrit is not always connected with Dharma. For example, on news broadcasts on the radio in the Himalayas, one can often hear about government ministers who have Sanskrit names, such as Ratnasambha and Padmasambha. These ministers may not belong to the five Buddha families, even though they have this potential, but are involved with government and politics. So Sanskrit is not used only in one way, but in many. The various names and words that are used in religions are also used in other ways, depending on the context. For example, Mary is the name of the mother of Jesus, but there are many other people named Mary in the West, and not all of them are the mother of Jesus. Also, there are many Latinos who are named Jesus, but they are not the crucified Jesus. Likewise, Hindus have many names such as Krishna, but they are not referring to Lord Krishna, and among Muslims there are many people named Muhammad who are not their Prophet.

The Omniscient Dharmabhadra said that regardless of the language that is used, whatever one learns or studies has to be put into meditation. If one does not put what is learned into meditation, one cannot decide how to attain enlightenment. By only studying and not synthesizing what is learned into meditation, all knowledge causes cognitive obscurations. For example, on a long staircase, the highest step makes shade on the step beneath it, not allowing light to shine on it, with each successive step shading the one below it. If one is very attached to education, and also to the experiences of practice, however much one clings, that much one causes cognitive obscurations. In order not to have shade, one needs to let the light come into the expanse of oneness, not seeding but purifying cognitive obscurations through allowing the transparent quality of unobstructed awareness.

In general, people always praise whatever they know because of their attachment to it. Attachment causes samsara. Attachment is not only for males by females or for females by males, but can be for anything. Even meditation can cause attachment, and if it does, it can also cause cognitive obscurations.

Sangye Gyatso, the Fifth Dalai Lama's minister, was an expert astrologer and wrote extensive explanations on astrology. Finally, he regretted that he had spent his life writing. He said that if he had made the same effort to meditate, he could have attained enlightenment, but that the demon Garab Wangchuk had given him a steel pen, so he had been lured to write.

Kyabje Düdjom Rinpoche said:

> Knowing all, but not knowing one.
> Knowing one, and liberating all.

He meant that one must know one essence for knowing all.

In *Jewel Treasure of the Dharmadhatu,*[236] it says:

> Whatever happens, let it happen.
> Whatever is appearing, let it appear.
> Whatever arises, let it arise.
> Whatever is, let it be as it is.
> Whatever is not, let it not be.

The meaning of the supreme attainment as the Four Kayas and five wisdoms, the descriptions of the syllables of the essential mantra as the Three Kayas, the seven branches of union of the Sambhogakaya, and so on, have already been explained during the descriptions identifying the objects of refuge, so they must be understood.

The common spiritual attainments, including the eight accomplishments, the twelve great actions, and so on, can be synthesized according to the meaning as follows. To purify all obstacles of illness, being haunted and

236. *chos dbyings mdzod.*

possessed by demons, and everything that is undesirable and unsuitable, is the activity of pacifying. To increase and extend life, merit, and all wisdom and qualities on the stages and paths is the activity of increasing. To subdue one's own appearances and conquer the appearances of others through splendor is the activity of power. To annihilate and guide beings who harm the teachings of Buddhism and cruel beings who harm other beings, through great compassion, like that of Captain of Great Compassion for Black Man with a Short Spear, is the activity of wrathfulness.

When, as mentioned, the manifestation of the spontaneous presence of the appearance of the basis is not recognized, this becomes the origin of the descent into the interdependence of samsara. The empty essence of one's mind is Dharmakaya; the natural radiance is Sambhogakaya; and the all-pervasive quality of compassion is Nirmanakaya. By not recognizing one's Three Kaya nature that abides as the basis, this nature becomes dormant. By becoming ignorant of the manifestations of the Three Kayas, the root of all passions, the three poisons arise. As these three increase, the skandhas, elements, sense sources, and so on, and all phenomena of the outer universe and inner essence of beings of cyclic existence appear.

By the power of practicing on the path, all these appearances transform into the qualities of the path of the Three Kayas. The sign of this is the arising of the experiences of bliss, clarity, and nonconceptuality. These three experiences indicate the reversal of cyclic existence and the ascent to the Three Kayas.

The sign that the vase empowerment of enlightened body struck one's body is that attachment to the place of one's country, one's own body, belongings, loved ones, and all reality passions is cleansed, and the reality passion of desire is purified. The sign of this is that the mind that grasps at the internal body's earth element of flesh and water element of blood as substances or as characterized by reality is purified. From that power, fixation to the external reality of the objects of grasping of the outer elements of earth and water is being purified. Gradually, when all outer and inner elements of earth and water become purer and purer, lighter and lighter, it is a sign of becoming close to approaching indivisible purity. When the power of grasping at the gross elements of the body, which causes pain and illness, becomes less and less, the sign that one is close to having the profound, immaculate knowing of prajna eyes is that one can see forms that are a long distance away as though they are close. The experience of bliss within the body increases. Then one meditates on this appearance of the empty bliss of Nirmanakaya on the path without attachment. The result is as said by Indrabodhi:

> Great exaltation is not mortal.
> Great exaltation is always immortal.

Also, from *Gyutrul Thalwa:*[237]

> The nature of great bliss
> Is not substantial and not insubstantial.
> It cannot even be imagined to be in the center.
> It is said to be the mudra of great bliss.

Thus it is said. The naturally immaterial enlightened body of the appearance of great bliss, in which all flaws are completely exhausted, which is the result of the state of Nirmanakaya, will occur.

The sign that the secret empowerment of the enlightened speech of the Lama has struck one's speech is that the obscurations of vital energy of speech caused from pleasure, fame, gain, desire, and gossip are cleansed, and the reality passion of anger is purified. The sign of this is that the inner fixating mind that holds to the fire element and inner heat, and the air element and inner breath, as reality is purified. By that power, the external fixation to the reality of the objects of grasping of the outer elements of fire and air is purified. Gradually, when all outer and inner elements of fire and air become purer and purer, lighter and lighter, it is a sign of becoming close to approaching indivisible purity. Then, external fire and air and internal heat, breath, and so on that develop from root and contributing circumstances, producing the potential for ordinary sound, decrease. Without searching for the words of the sound of Dharma, the unborn sound of emptiness occurs and naturally resonates. The sign that indicates the power of the natural sound of dharmata is the ability to clearly hear sounds from a long distance away as though they are close. The sign of attaining wisdom eyes is to clearly see all appearances as only pure. The experience of the clarity of speech increases. That is the appearance of the path as the empty radiance of Sambhogakaya. In that state, having experience without attachment, it is as said:

237. *sgyu 'phrul thal ba.*

You are the one who benefits the world with one word,
But the sound can be heard according to each being's wishes.
Each being thinks, "Buddha taught this to me."

Thus as taught, one word is the inconceivable secret speech of the great sole inconceivability that is free from all elaboration. The meaning of "the sound can be heard according to each being's wishes" is that Buddha's speech resounds in all aspects.

Likewise, in *The Arrangement of the Triple Gems,* it says:

From the attainment of fully enlightened Buddhahood
Until taking parinirvana's state,
I never revealed any teaching,
But from the nature of Buddha,
Whatever beings are wishing,
That many Dharma sounds appear.
This is the naturally secret, inconceivable speech of Buddha.

Thus, the essence of Buddha's speech is inexpressible because it is beyond sounds, names, and words. From inconceivable space, the supreme speech of the various sounds and words of Dharma occur. The nature of all of these is beyond thought. From *The Secret Essence:*

E MA HO! Wondrous awe of Dharma!
The speech of all perfectly enlightened Buddhas
Is beyond all sounds, names, and words,
As endless variations of sounds that clearly occur.
The branches of this mandala of sole enlightened speech
Are incalculably all-pervasive.
Resounding as individual sounds, names, and words,
All of this is the supreme mudra of enlightened speech.

Thus, also, from *Praising the Enlightened Speech of Secret Mantra:*[238]

In the great Akanishtha, beyond ordinary thought,
The basis where dualistic appearances vanish in space,

238. *gsung gsang sngags kyi tshul la bsngags pa.*

The expanse of equanimity, self-appearing and naturally
free from direction,
Is the mandala of enlightened speech, spontaneously present.

Thus, as said, by receiving the power of sole enlightened speech pervading with oceanlike branches of melodious sound, the result of the state of Sambhogakaya will be fully attained.

Through the power of the prajna wisdom empowerment, the sign that the Lama's enlightened mind has struck one's mind is that attachment to worldly conceptions such as the subjugation of enemies, the protection of family and friends, all general and specific attachments to samsara, enlightenment, happiness, suffering, accepting, rejecting, hope, and fear are cleansed, the obscurations of mind's tig-le are cleansed, and the reality passion of ignorance is purified. The sign of this is that as the inner grasping mind is purified, holding to the outer object of the appearance of sky becomes purified. When the outer empty sky and inner awareness sky cannot be divided, this is approaching the expanse of the totally all-encompassing sole inconceivability. When this occurs, dualistic mind or the consciousness that fixates upon subject and object is purified and there is no longer any external or internal obscuration. Attaining the unimpeded wisdom eyes of dharmata, the sign is that the experience of nonconceptuality increases. This is the appearance of the path as the wisdom of nonconceptuality of Dharmakaya. In that state of experience without attachment, then finally it is as said in the sutras:

Peaceful Intelligence,
In the inconceivable secret enlightened mind of Buddhas,
Free from the mind that holds to objects, the mind of
conceptual discrimination, and consciousness,
Samadhi is not lost forever.
This is the inconceivable secret enlightened mind of Buddhas.

Thus, as it is said, the state of the result of Dharmakaya will be fully attained.

Finally, when it is time to conclude the session of practice, the verses read: **The blessings and empowerment of wisdom body, wisdom speech, and wisdom mind are completely and perfectly obtained. One is receiving the attainment of wisdom body, wisdom speech, and wisdom mind from the Vajra Master, Guru Rinpoche.**

Thus reciting, think that one receives from the principal form of all Buddhas, the root Lama, Great Orgyen, the indestructible vajra blessings of enlightened body, the unobstructed vajra blessings of enlightened speech, and the undeluded vajra blessings of enlightened mind. If synthesized, consider that one receives all of the blessings and empowerments of the five inexhaustible mandalas of enlightened body, speech, mind, qualities, and activities. Finally, the Lama's enlightened wisdom body of great rapture transforms upward from the throne and downward from the top of the crown to the heart, transforming into a sphere[239] of five-colored light of white, yellow, red, green, and blue that dissolves into oneself. Think that one becomes indivisible as one taste and recite the root verses:

Lama ö shu rang thim yerme ngang
rig tong dön gyi la-me rang shal ta.[240]

The Lama dissolves into light and is absorbed into oneself.
Abide in indivisible awareness and emptiness, which is
the face of the absolute Lama.

Thus reciting, abide in the equanimity of the inexpressible state of the self-awareness of indivisible clarity and emptiness.

At this time, the meaning of indivisibility is like pouring water into water so that there cannot be any way to know a difference. It is necessary to understand that this means freedom from the conception of fixating on oneself and the Lama as separate. The word *ngang* means nature, which can be used in an ordinary way for personal qualities, such as the nature of someone with a short-tempered disposition or a tolerant disposition. This is the way it is used according to samsaric phenomena, which is the nature of impure phenomena that cannot possibly be permanent and will always depend on the movement of phenomena that are born, cease, and abide. In this case, the meaning of nature is beyond the three states of being born, ceasing, and abiding. This is the unconditioned state of the unending nature, which is completely free from change throughout the three times. This continuity of the empty, pure self-nature of dharmata needs to be sustained.

239. The sphere of light is the size of one's own upper thumb, from the first joint to the tip.
240. bla ma 'od zhu rang thim dbyer med ngang / rig stong don gyi bla ma'i rang zhal blta. In this case, *blta*, or see, means to abide in that inconceivable state, and the face of the absolute Lama means indivisible emptiness and awareness.

Abide in indivisible awareness and emptiness, which is the face of the absolute Lama. Thus, awareness means clarity. Furthermore, to analyze the difference between mind and awareness: this is not the mind; this is awareness. The characteristic of mind is that first there is the mind that holds to objects, and next there is the mind that discriminates by rejecting or accepting objects, which together are the mind that accumulates passions and karma based on attachment and aversion, throwing one into samsara. Awareness mind is not this grasping dualistic mind that is the root of samsara. Awareness mind means the nondual sole wisdom of indivisible clarity and emptiness. As Garab Dorje, the crown ornament of the Vidyadharas, said:

From the pure space of original purity,
Wisdom mind instantly manifests.
Like a jewel discovered in the depths of the ocean,
Dharmakaya is uncreated and uncontrived by anyone.

Thus, as said, from the beginning, the stain of grasping mind is purified. The meaning of space is completely vast, just as the element of stainless space is beyond ordinary mind. Since all faults are exhausted and all qualities are perfected, the suffering of samsara is cleansed. The complete culmination of all qualities of Buddha is enlightened mind.

Also, this explanation is not like the teachings on relative bodhichitta found in the causal vehicle of the paramitas. There, it is said that by considering sentient beings as the object, bodhichitta occurs in the mind of the subject. As Shantideva said:

The essence of emptiness itself is compassion, for some who are accomplishing enlightenment.

Thus, as said, since the subject is originally unborn, it is impossible to find any individually existing objects of sentient beings. This is the absolute truth of the nature of phenomena, the nondual wisdom mind of Buddhas, the great mind of enlightenment. Here, it is unnecessary to become fearful by thinking that if there is no subjective enlightened mind, then the continuity of compassion directed toward the object of sentient beings will cease. It is as said in *Entering the Way of the Great Vehicle:*[241]

241. *theg pa chen po'i tshul la 'jug pa'i mdo.*

If synthesized, when the nondual nature of the equanimity
of all phenomena is realized,
Then compassion is not going to decrease, just as with
Buddhas and Bodhisattvas.
From the view of materializing reality,
Then compassion does not increase, just as with the
Hearers and ordinary beings.

Thus, as said, if the essence of the compassionate nature of emptiness is recognized to be the awareness mind of enlightenment, then if the manifestation is perfected and confidence is reached, because dualistic mind that is the cause of suffering and the basis of delusion is purified, not even the name of samsara is left. This is like a poor person finding a jewel from the depths of the ocean and becoming completely liberated from the suffering of poverty. Dharmakaya is not contrived or created by anyone, including Buddhas and sentient beings.

Furthermore, one may wonder what the difference is between awareness mind and clear light. Awareness mind and clear light are insubstantial. Therefore, essentially, nothing at all can be distinguished between awareness mind and clear light. If the aspects of their qualities are defined, awareness mind is completely free from all obscurations, and the completely nonignorant qualities of the knower are unobstructed and have the aspect of clear light body and wisdom appearance. One should not think that what is called clear light is like any ordinary light that occurs from cause and circumstance, like the brightness of a burning butter lamp or the light emitted from an electrical fixture. Also, one should not think that awareness mind is like the sixth sense of the consciousness of mind that enters conceptions and engages with objects as positive and negative through the consciousness of the eyes, ears, nose, tongue, and body and their objects of form, sound, smell, taste, and touch. Also, one should not think that awareness mind is like worldly expressions of samsaric keen awareness, clear intelligence, great powers of discrimination, and so on, which come from samsara. It is impossible for there to be darkness at dawn. This is the meaning of wisdom awareness. The aspect of the appearance of awareness is actually great uncompounded clarity, free from boundary or center. Sublime beings are discerned by the uncompounded, as was explained earlier. Furthermore, our supreme guide, the incomparable Lord Buddha Shakyamuni, just after attaining perfectly enlightened Buddhahood, said:

> Profound peace, free from fabrication, is uncompounded clear light.
> This Dharma that I have found is just like nectar.

Also, Glorious Renowned Dharma[242] said:

> The net of conceptions cleansed,
> Having a wisdom body of profound expanse,
> Light rays of Kuntuzangpo,
> To the always emanating, I give homage.

From *The Exalted Eight Thousand Stanzas:*[243]

> Because the mind has no mind, the mind's nature is clear light.

Saying that the mind has no mind means that the mind's nature has no basis or root because of being completely free from all elaboration of substance and nonsubstance. This empty essence is wisdom Dharmakaya. The mind's nature as clear light means that the aspect of the appearance of the empty essence of wisdom is unobstructed as the natural clarity of the appearance of the basis. This is how the qualities of wisdom Rupakaya are manifested, so all of this is self-occurring wisdom. From *The Tantra of the Great Perfection:* [244]

> Self-occurring wisdom occurs without relying on root and contributing circumstances.
> Unobstructed wisdom is clarity.

Thus, as said, this is the great union of the clear light of empty awareness. The meaning of the union of awareness and emptiness is not like two strings that have become intertwined to make one. When saying *awareness,* it is not that emptiness is left somewhere to try to find awareness somewhere else. When saying *emptiness,* it is not that awareness is left somewhere to try to find emptiness from somewhere else. From the beginning, there has never been even the subtlest division between the aspects of awareness and emptiness. The empty essence of awareness is Dharmakaya.

242. dpal ldan chos kyi grags pa; Skt. Shri Dharmakirti.
243. *'phags pa brgyad stong pa.*
244. *rdzogs pa chen po'i rgyud.*

The clear aspect of the appearances of emptiness is Rupakaya. The Two Kayas, Dharmakaya and Rupakaya, are always in union, because this is the union of appearance and emptiness, the union of clarity and emptiness, the union of bliss and emptiness, the union of enlightened body and wisdom, the union of enlightened body and purelands, and so on. This is the great, uncompounded union, which is the indivisible vajra centerless center, just like unobscured sky.

From the root tantra of the Great Perfection, *The Reverberation of Sound:*[245]

> In the precious palace of the heart,
> The pure aspect of the essence of original purity,
> The radiance of the body of emptiness and clear light,
> And the perfection of the original youthful wisdom body
> Of the self-light sphere are there,
> And the colors of compassion are clear and manifest.

Thus, the outer luminosity of the appearance of the basis as enlightened body and purelands arises from the presence of the basis, which dwells inwardly as the aspect of inner luminosity. In *The Tantra of the Perfect Skill of the Lion,*[246] it says:

> Actually, it is self-awareness,
> So the sign is obviously manifesting wisdom body.
> The essence of absolute truth does not change.
> Radiant spontaneously present clear light
> Is the actual nature of great bliss.
> This vajra essence is free from cause and circumstance,
> And without deviating from the meaning of perfection,
> The wisdom of skillful means is always abiding in great shunyata.

Thus, the inner luminosity of enlightened body and wisdom purelands appears as the outer luminosity of the conspicuous manifestation of enlightened body and wisdom purelands. This is the sole quality of spontaneously present uncompounded great clear light. In order for these qualities

245. *sgra thal 'gyur.*
246. *rgyud seng ge rtsal rdzogs.*

to actually manifest, there is the practice of passing simultaneously to the direct clear light manifestation of Buddhas (thögal).

There are some who lack understanding of the view of the Great Perfection because they have no experience or realization. They then disparage the teachings of the Great Perfection, especially about passing simultaneously, which they claim is like some eternalist traditions of watching the sun. Without question, not only do they lack realization or experience, they do not even understand these teachings intellectually. In order for beings to perceive the limitless qualities of all the enlightened bodies, purelands, and wisdom activities of Buddhas and Bodhisattvas, there are countless metaphors and similes in Buddha's teachings and the enlightened commentaries that will continue to occur, like examples of the sun, moon, lights, mountains, oceans, and others, in order to connect to the meaning. In the ineffable accomplishment practices of the tantric categories of the New and Old schools, the seat of the sun and moon upon a lotus is continually mentioned in sadhana practices. Extremely sectarian people should not search for contradictions between the view that is held about the sun and the moon in the practice of passing simultaneously, and the view that is held during their own visualizations of the sun and moon disks on which deities are seated during developing stage practice. There is no logic to this abuse because it is the same sun and moon. The Great Perfection view of passing simultaneously is unrelated to the view of some eternalists who pray with reverence and respect to the sun and moon as gods. The practice of passing simultaneously temporarily uses the light of the sun and moon as a method, just as a support, in order for the inner radiance of wisdom body to become outwardly apparent. This view does not consider the sun and moon to be actual gods. Whenever the four visions of the appearances of qualities of the path are fully perfected, then there will be no sun and there will be no darkness. There will be no watcher of the rays of the sun and moon. There will be no paths or stages. These are the signs that will occur when all phenomena are exhausted in the space of stainless Dharmakaya. Without understanding the pith of this meaning, the faults of expressing many words is as Lord Maitreya said:

> Those who are interested in a lower level of teaching
>   have extremely low faculties.
> Surrounding themselves with companions of lower faculties,
> It is possible that they will have no desire
> To accomplish the excellent teaching of the profound and vast.

And Shantideva said:

> The world is seen in two ways by practitioners and ordinary people. Practitioners have a view that disproves the view of ordinary people of the world. Even among practitioners of different faculties, the views of those who are higher disprove the views of those below. Since both believe in substance, they cannot discern the ultimate result. By worldly beings seeing the world as real and not like magic, therefore, that which is pure becomes conceptualized. Without the view of the magical nature, both practitioners and ordinary people argue.

Thus, as said, in debates among intellectuals, whether they agree or have differences, since they rely on complementary conceptual theories, they support and protect each other just like trees in a forest that protect each other from harmful winds. If those who rely on conceptual theories, no matter how profound, extensive, and detailed, meet with teachings that rely on wisdom from the beginning, those who rely on conceptual theories will destroy themselves; just as, when there is a forest fire, the trees that had once protected each other can instantly become each other's enemies, causing more burning, so there is the danger that all can be destroyed without anything remaining. Those who constantly rely only on conceptualization as the source of their worldly intellectual materialist logic and criticize the Dharma of the Great Perfection that takes wisdom as the path will inevitably disprove their own logic by revealing its superficiality and limitations. Since they will only bring about their own destruction, it is not even necessary for those who hold the view of the Great Perfection to give any answer. As it says in *The Sutra of the Adornment of Stalks:*[247]

> There are so many different realms.
> Some of them are burned unbelievably,
> But the sky will not burn forever.
> Self-occurring wisdom is like that.

Also, Chog-kyi Langpo said:

247. *sdong pos brgyan pa'i mdo.*

Since the paths of reverse views are limitless,
There is no need to explain them here.

Also, Buddha said:

The world argues with me,
But I never argue with the world.

Thus, following these words, only scattering flowers of rejoicing is supremely valuable.

Furthermore, even though the sun and moon are the same, there are many different theories about them, such as those of non-Buddhists who worship the sun and moon as gods, or teachings found in the great tantric categories of the New School that explain how the sun, moon, planets, stars, and so on, are established as the mandalas of deities. So, whatever others think, it is unnecessary to abuse their theories. According to ordinary worldly phenomena, the shimmering brightness of the light of the sun, moon, planets, and stars is what they all have in common based on substance phenomena. As is said:

Whether it is one's own philosophy or that of another,
Disparaging the Dharma is the sixth root fault.
If this fault occurs, it must be confessed.

Remembering this, there is really no reason to abuse even eternalist theories. Furthermore, as the female demon of the rock said to Milarepa:

Above in the center of the blue sky
Is the rich brilliance of the clear light of the sun and moon.
That is the wondrous, immeasurable celestial palace of deities,
For it is said to illuminate the darkness of the four continents.

Thus, singing in response, Jetsun Milarepa replied from his hymns of the eight examples of mindfulness:

By looking up into the center of the blue sky,
I am clearly reminded of the nature of dharmata.
I have no fear of substantial phenomena.

By looking over there at the sun and moon,
I am clearly reminded of the clear light nature of mind.
I have no fear of elation or dullness.

Thus, it is necessary to bring these teachings to mind. From the sutra *Gone to Lanka:*

Similar to when seeing light, a lotus, and a rainbow drawn in the sky,
All of these various signs may lead to the path of non-Buddhism.

So therefore, the great scholars and realized masters of the past have always said:

If one does not directly cut through all substantial and insubstantial phenomena to Dharmakaya, then the natural revelation of passing simultaneously to the direct, clear light manifestation of Buddhas can be the cause of delusion.

Thus, the reason they have said this is that if the phenomena of samsara, enlightenment, and the path, these three, are not brought into the three entrances to liberation,[248] then maintaining phenomena as separate and real, and materializing and binding the mind to substance, make it possible to enter a non-Buddhist path that establishes the root of delusion. Thus it is said to be so.

It has never been said that the manifestation of the spontaneously present from the beginning, uncompounded, perfectly natural, pure clear light of wisdom is like the beliefs of non-Buddhists. As previously mentioned, "Profound peace, free from fabrication, is uncompounded clear light. This Dharma that I have found is just like nectar." One should understand this, as this quotation of Buddha says. If one is unable to contain this within one's mind due to the intensity of clinging to appearances as truly materialized and characterized, then it is as quoted earlier, "On one particle, there are immeasurable particles that have inconceivable Buddhas and purelands. All Buddhas are abiding in the center of all wisdom Bodhisattvas. The Bodhisattvas are looking at all these immeasurable purelands and how

248. The three entrances to liberation are rnam thar sgo gsum, which are emptiness, nonwishing, and characteristiclessness.

they can pass beyond their activity to attain enlightenment." Thus, particles do not become bigger and purelands do not become smaller in order for this to be possible. Concerning this prayer from the Mahayana, for some, just hearing these words fills them with great fear and paranoia, without even considering cultivating this as an aspiration or actually reciting the verses. If one wonders why this is so, it is because this is in complete opposition to ordinary-minded worldly beings.

It is extremely meaningful to try to understand these teachings. As it says:

> This Mahayana vehicle is a great, immeasurable
> celestial palace, like sky.

It is important to try to turn one's mind in this direction. It is as the Mahasiddha Tilopa said:

> Son, appearances do not bind; attachment binds.
> Cut attachment, Naropa!

So therefore, if one is inspired by these pith instructions, then by practicing the fearless conduct that has no attachment to any appearances, one will proceed on the path that leads to the state of perfectly enlightened Buddhahood. This point alone is the most profound.

Here, in connection with Guru Yoga, to self-sustain the unconditioned state of awareness, the upadesha teachings of cutting through (trekchö) are indispensable. Therefore, everything that has been said here is logically appropriate. But some practitioners may think that this is not necessarily the time to discuss the subject of passing simultaneously (thögal). In general, thögal was not explained here particularly. Whether one is able to practice thögal or not, however, the basis of the unconditioned state of clear light abides from the beginning. Those who are inspired to practice thögal must establish the connection between primordially pure great emptiness and self-accomplishing clear light. Those who are unable to practice thögal particularly still may be able to realize that emptiness and luminosity are naturally in union without each being separate. These words that supplement the main meaning have been spoken in order to uplift and inspire toward practice. In no way does this present any contradiction, while at the same time it is extremely sensible, reasonable, and suitable.

When saying "emptiness," this is the essence of awareness where time, direction, color, substance, nonsubstance, and so on, do not exist. Since there is nothing that exists materially, it is impossible for causes and circumstances that produce suffering and happiness to exist. Therefore, this is flawless Dharmakaya. This great, empty Dharmakaya is not like being in an indifferent stupor or the vacuity of nothingness. It is the basis for the qualities that are the aspect of the appearance of enlightened body and wisdom manifesting. This essence is the great wisdom mind that cannot be identified, because it is free from the three states of being born, ceasing, and remaining. This, the enlightened mind where nothing is conceptual, is described by the great Omniscient Rongzom, who said:

> Enlightened mind has no conditions such as cause and effect, so there is no essence of being born and ceasing.
> The essence is never born and never ceases,
> So there is no chance for conceptions to arise,
> So it is called the wisdom of no thought of anything.

Thus it is as said.

The meaning of **the absolute Lama** is as follows. Generally, concerning all Dharma, at the time of hearing and contemplating, if there is no description of the distinctions between the basis, path, and result, then the way to practice will not be understood. Therefore, there are distinctions of the basis, path, and result explained as the Three Kayas of the Lama and the basis Lama, path Lama, and result Lama. Here, however, it is necessary to understand that the absolute Guru of empty awareness is the Guru of the great indivisible evenness of the basis and the result. As it says in the Great Vidyadhara Jigdral Yeshe Dorje's *Calling the Lama from Afar:*[249]

> Radiance with nothing to recognize,
> Free from conception, uncontrived empty awareness,
> This is the absolute Lama,
> This is recognizing wisdom vajra.[250]

Thus it is said.

249. *bla ma rgyang 'bod.*
250. ye shes rdo rje.

Abide in indivisible awareness and emptiness, which is the face of the absolute Lama, is not to be understood as a subject that looks at an object with form. It is also not to be understood, according to Kriya Tantra, Upa Tantra, and others, as visualizing oneself as the samayasattva and visualizing the jnanasattva in front of oneself as the source through which siddhi is received. Free from all faults of fabrication of subject and object, the object to be observed and the observer are great indivisible sole awareness. Not seeing anything is the great seeing, which is like stainless sky. Although pervading everywhere, it never appears anywhere,[251] abiding as the nature of the extremely pure dustless space of phenomena. This is the same meaning that is in *Guhyagarbha:*

> The enlightened body, free from front or back,
> Always sees all directions clearly.

Thus it is said.

The absolute Lama of empty awareness is also the wisdom Lama. The reason is that wisdom is never affected by the obscuration of conception. Uncompounded clear light is the purest holy wisdom that is naturally indwelling from the beginning. In that state, whatever appearances arise are from completion to completion the ornament of manifestation, so that a basis for restriction does not exist, so it is liberation from the beginning.[252] Therefore, no matter what arises, never needing to abandon or accept is natural liberation.[253] Since this aspect of knowing is not hidden from one's own self-manifesting wisdom awareness, it is naked liberation.[254] Omniscient Longchenpa said:

> Since all phenomena are liberated from the beginning
> in enlightened mind,
> There has never been one phenomenon that is not liberated.
> Samsara is from the beginning liberated and in the
> beginning pure.

251. One cannot point to it, hold it, see it, or catch it forever, but it penetrates everywhere. There is not a single phenomenon without sky. Although it is everywhere, it cannot be found.
252. ye grol.
253. rang grol.
254. cer grol.

Enlightenment is liberation from the beginning, self-liberated
in perfection.

Thus, as said, since the dualistic mind of samsara and enlightenment is completely pure from the beginning, it is fully liberated.[255] In order to attain the depth of the confidence of liberation in these four great ways of liberating, relying on the upadesha of Garab Dorje known as *The Precious Three Words That Strike the Essence*[256] will assure the ability to attain the citadel of the always sublime Vajradhara. Uniting with all Buddhas evenly is, as Paltrul Rinpoche said:

Listen to me. The doctrines of the three teachings[257] and
the nine vehicles
Were predominantly taught for those with great diligence.
So therefore,
It is said that one must meditate and practice with diligent effort,
and then one will be liberated. By doing this, however,
That wisdom free from being dispelled or sustained is
never going to be seen.
Now, in this effortless vajra peak beyond conception,
Which is, without meditating, enlightening in the uncontrived
expanse of empty awareness,
Even lazy people can be introduced to this present Dharmakaya,
Which is free from attachment to meditation, practice, and
the mind of effort.
Even among the gods and those of this world, there is
no Lama who reveals this path
Except for the Omniscient Lama Longchenpa,
the sole Dharmakaya.

Thus, one will come to know this.

Like that, to make apparent the wisdom mind of the Great Perfection that is effortless and beyond the intellect, there is no elaboration of practices such as abiding in evenness, after abiding in evenness, tranquil stillness, true seeing, or any other separate distinctions or categorizations. It is

255. yongs grol.
256. *tshig gsum gnad du brdeg pa'i gdams pa.*
257. Tripitaka.

best to decide that one only needs to abide within sole indivisible awareness and emptiness. Sublime Master[258] said:

> Abiding in evenness or not abiding in evenness,
> There is nothing of all of these.
> Abandoning all substance and nonsubstance
> Is union, Buddha said.

And furthermore:

> There is not even anything to purify,
> And there is not even a little bit to leave.
> Whatever is pure, see as pure.
> If purely seen, all is liberated.

Thus it is said.

The great empty essence of awareness, dharmadhatu, dwells as equanimity with no change or transference in all three times. The pain of elaborate fabrications will not even arise, so always abiding in peace is tranquil stillness. Since the aspect of knowing of the great emptiness of dharmadhatu is the sublime seeing of the luminosity of awareness, the indivisibility of tranquil stillness and true seeing is the great, vast wisdom mind of Buddha. Omniscient Longchenpa said:

> Profound openness, profound openness, in the nature
> of profound great openness,
> Longchen Rabjam is abiding in the expanse of profound light.
> The exaltation of the profound, sole, nondual expanse is whirling,
> Self-liberating all variations, arrived in the exhaustion
> of dharmata,
> At the unchangeable, self-accomplished, wish-fulfilling most
> supreme pinnacle,
> Like this, may my followers and all other beings be integrated
> in the sole oneness of the beginningless, pervasive, great expanse,
> Having arrived at the firm basis of the impenetrable wisdom
> citadel of Samantabhadra.

258. slob dpon 'phags pa; Skt. Arya Deva.

Thus he said.

In *Rosary of the View Commentary*[259] by Great Omniscient Rongzom, it says:[260]

> If it is explained here, the nature of Vajra Kuntuzangpo
> is the enlightened mind.
> The nature of mind is enlightened, so it is vajra.
> So therefore, from all to all, there are no phenomena
> to abandon or throw away,
> So it is always noble. That is why it is called Kuntuzangpo.

From *The Tantra of Victorious Wisdom of the Three Realms:*[261]

> Realizing the discerning nature of one's own mind
> Is fully enlightened Buddhahood.
> The three realms of existence are also this.
> All the great elements are also this.

"The three realms" means all sentient beings of the three realms of existence. "The great elements" are the immeasurable elements of the three realms of existence.

Thus, as said, that which is called the discerning wisdom of one's mind is unmistakably knowing the nature of mind. Also, it is said:

> When the mind is deluded, that is cyclic existence.
> If the mind is undeluded, that is called enlightenment.

This explanation is not the teachings of Dzogpa Chenpo or Mahasandhi, because it is the belief of all the lower vehicles. So therefore, here, according to the view of Dzogpa Chenpo, even though all phenomena are appearing in the mind, it must be decided that appearance itself is naturally enlightened Buddha. Furthermore, it also says in *The Secret Gathering:*[262]

259. *lta phreng 'grel pa.*
260. This is Kunkhyen Rongzompa's explanation of Guru Rinpoche's commentary on *The Secret Essence Tantra (Guhyagarbha)*, called *The Upadesha Moon Rosary* (*man ngag zla ba'i phreng ba*).
261. *khams gsum rnam par rgyal ba'i rtog pa.*
262. *gsang ba 'dus pa.*

All phenomena are abiding in mind.
Mind is abiding in sky.
Sky is not abiding anywhere.

Thus it says. The meaning is that all phenomena are contained in the mind, and the nature of mind has no characteristics. Thus, this is the meaning.

When abiding in the equanimity of the self-awareness luminosity of the Great Perfection, even if one tries to find any self-characterized passions, they cannot be found, so it is not necessary to rely on an antidote for the passions, as it is said in *The Sutra Revealing Stainless Renown:*

Is perfect liberation not the abandonment of desire, anger, ignorance, and all passions in order to be liberated?
Those who think that perfect liberation is having abandoned desire, anger, and ignorance are those with pride.
Whoever has no self will naturally liberate desire, anger, and ignorance.

Likewise, when abiding in inseparable evenness and after-evenness, stainless virtue will naturally occur, so one does not need to try to increase virtue with stains. It is important not to become attached to the forms of elaborate practices such as prayers, mantras, prostrations, circumambulating, and others. This is pointed out in *The Secret Gathering Tantra:*

If one hopes to attain the supreme state of enlightenment,
Then do not read the scriptures and do not circumambulate stupas.
If one does, enlightenment will not be attained.

The great Lord of Accomplishment Milarepa said:

My son, at the time of meditating on Mahamudra,
Do not persevere in the accumulation of virtue through the body and speech.
This may cause conceptionless wisdom to disappear.

Also, it is said in *Jewel Treasure of the Dharmadhatu:*

In brief, appearance and all phenomena of existence,
Any kind of phenomena of non-appearance and non-existence,
Are all liberated in space from the beginning.
There is no need for anyone to be liberated by effort later.
Even making effort, there is no meaning,
So do not make effort, do not make effort, do not make effort for accomplishment.
Do not watch, do not watch, do not watch the phenomena of contrived mind.
Do not meditate, do not meditate, do not meditate with a contrived mind.
Do not examine, do not examine, do not examine after object and subject.
Do not accomplish, do not accomplish, do not accomplish the result of hope and fear.[263]

Thus, as this says, whatever appearances arise, if one can abide without partiality in great equanimity, it is the supreme samaya.

From *The Secret Essence Tantra:*

Evenness joins evenness.
If one keeps the samaya of evenness,
The great perfection of evenness will be accomplished.

Thus, here, there is no description of stages and paths. As it says in the sutras:

The state of unsurpassed enlightenment cannot be categorized.

Also, in *The Tantra of the Perfect Skill of the Lion:*

The self-sounding awareness of the Great Perfection
Is beyond phenomena and emptiness,
Beyond the phenomena of mind and consciousness,
Beyond both being and not being.

263. The meaning of this quotation is for those who can truly abide in samadhi, not for those who want to use it as an excuse for being lazy.

There is no point of view of good or bad.
There is no meditating or not meditating.

Thus, only sustaining the unending nature of dharmata, and without the distinction of evenness and after-evenness, is as Paltrul Rinpoche said:

There is no distinction between evenness and after-evenness.
There is no distinction between meditation and the cessation of meditation.

Thus, whatever conceptions arise are the self-manifestation of pure primordial wisdom arising. No matter how one is abiding, it is the natural beginningless abiding in the nature of dharmata. Even though it may appear that there is a new liberation, actually, from the beginning, nothing was bound, so it is the great liberation from beginninglessness. As *The Secret Essence Tantra* says:

Unbound from the beginning, so there is no new liberation,
Buddha's phenomena are perfectly accomplished from the beginning.

Also, in *Jewel Treasure of the Dharmadhatu:*

In unchangeable awareness, free from fabrication,
Whatever arises is just coming from the beginningless state; whatever is abiding is just abiding in the beginningless state;
Whatever is liberated is just liberated in the beginningless state, like the nature of stainless sky.
Arising, abiding, and liberation, all these three are coming from unending Dharmakaya, so there is no cessation of arising and liberation.
Since there is no cessation, there is no way for cause and result to interrupt.
Since there is no cause and result, the cliffs of samsara cease.
Since there are no cliffs, where is the state of error?
In the unchanging, beginningless expanse of Kuntuzangpo,
In the transitionless expanse of Vajrasattva,

> Just recognizing one's own unconditioned stainless wisdom mind
> Is thus named Buddha.
> By realizing this, there is no Dharma to accept or throw away.
> All phenomena pervade in the sole oneness of dharmata.
> There is nothing to discriminate, like an island full of gold.

Thus it is said.

Well, then, in order to sustain the wisdom mind of the Great Perfection, if one wonders how body, speech, and mind are directed to engage in this practice, it is as follows. For beginners, in order to purify the flow of karmic energies so that they enter the space of the central energy channel, the body must be straight. If the body is straight, the channels are straight. If the channels are straight, the vital energies can flow. If the vital energies can flow, awareness becomes clear. Whenever awareness becomes clear, the pure essential nature of mind becomes apparent, free from clearing away or keeping.

In order for that to occur, in the seven-point vajra posture, the legs are crossed, the hands are in the gesture of evenness, the stomach is pulled back toward the spine, the chin is slightly lowered, the shoulders are open like a condor's wings, the tongue is touching the palate, and the eyes are looking out over the tip of the nose like a tiger, directly into space. Various methods increase and enhance samadhi, including the vajra recitation with the movement of breath by inhaling with the syllable OM, letting the breath remain with the syllable AH, and exhaling with the syllable HUNG; and samadhi with emanating and drawing in, and so on. These are all important to rely on in order to increase stability in samadhi. According to the wisdom mind of the extraordinary Great Perfection, however, if one is a great practitioner of sustaining self-nature as the sole essence of awareness, then all phenomena are synthesized as wisdom appearances, sound, and awareness. Only knowing that the self-nature of one's own mind is the Three Kayas and never wavers from dharmadhatu, there is nothing other than the uncontrived natural abiding of body, speech, and mind, so it is absolutely unnecessary to apply effort to fixating on accepting and rejecting.

The precious Vajra Master Guru Rinpoche said to his consort, Khandro Yeshe Tsogyal, in *The Essence of Butter Pith Instructions:*[264]

264. *gdams ngag mar gyi yang zhun.*

> Devoted consort, listen to me. Even though there are many profound pith instructions for the body, just leave the body comfortably at ease. Everything is contained in that. Even though there are many pith instructions for controlling the vital energies, such as mantra recitation and others, be like a mute free from speaking. Everything is contained in that. Even though there are many pith instructions for the mind such as holding, loosening, creating, gathering, drawing in, and others, in the ease of one's own uncontrived nature that settles naturally, everything is contained in that.

Thus it says.

From Omniscient Longchenpa:

> With relaxed body and mind, in the mind's bed of tranquillity,
> Like a person with a mind free from engagement who has
> nothing to do,
> Without being rigid or careless, leave the body and
> mind comfortable.
> However one stays, stay in one's pure nature.
> However one abides, abide in one's pure nature.
> However one goes, go in one's pure nature.
> In the space of enlightenment, there is naturally no going or coming.
> Not going and not coming is the wisdom body of all
> the Victorious Ones.
> Whatever one says, say in one's pure nature.
> Whatever one speaks, speak in one's pure nature.
> In enlightened mind, there is naturally no saying and speaking.
> Free from saying and speaking is the speech of all
> the Victorious Ones of the three times.
> Whatever one thinks, think in one's pure nature.
> Whatever one considers, consider in one's pure nature.
> From the beginning, there is no thinker or considerer.
> Free from thinking and considering is the wisdom heart
> of the Victorious Ones of the three times.
> From nonsubstantiality, everything that manifests
> is Nirmanakaya.
> Pure appearance of self-sustaining inconceivability
> is Sambhogakaya.

> The state of no original substance is stainless Dharmakaya.
> The Three Kayas' result is simultaneously accomplished
> in the inconceivable state.

Thus, as he says, this must be realized.

To synthesize all of this, the essential meaning of the wisdom of the Great Perfection is explained through the ways of placing the mind in the five states of greatness. In one body and in a single lifetime, without hardships, there can be the great ascendancy over the domain of the Original Protector. This is so because of the greatness of obviously apparent fully enlightened Buddhahood. In the causal vehicle, effort is made to purify obscurations and accumulate merit over a period of many eons, and after an extended period of time, the state of the result of Buddhahood is still not apparent. This is not like that. This is directly being introduced to self-awareness as the nature of the Three Kayas. Then, by staying in that state, Buddha is just now. This is called the greatness of obviously apparent fully enlightened Buddhahood. From this, the lower views are conquered with splendor.

Freely conquering all the immeasurable phenomena of samsara and enlightenment is called the greatness of being a great wisdom ruler. As Glorious Saraha said:

> Since sole mind is the seed of everything,
> Whoever aspires to transcend samsara and enlightenment
> Is granted the fruit of their wishes.
> I prostrate to mind, like a wish-fulfilling jewel.

Thus it is like this. The mind has the natural ability to completely control all the phenomena of samsara and enlightenment. From this, the view of nihilism is conquered with splendor.

The greatness of perfect enlightenment in dharmadhatu is as said earlier in *The Extremely Extensive Tantra:*

> Not the basis of all conception,
> Natural non-existence is the basis of absolute truth.
> It is called dharmadhatu.
> That is wisdom as it is.

Thus, as said, since there is no basis of indifferent stupor or conception, it is impossible for dualistic mind to exist. So, whatever appearances arise, there is no attachment or obstruction. From this, the view of materializing is conquered with splendor.

The greatness of Buddha as only one's own mind of enlightened awareness means attaining confidence. As said in a hymn from the great saint Saraha:

> If there is recognition, everything is included there.
> No one has known anything other than that.

Thus, this is the same meaning. From this, doubt is conquered with splendor.

The greatness of nothing whatsoever that has become Buddha from all to all is that one's own awareness is the Buddha of primordial purity from the beginning. Knowing that this is Dharmakaya, then whatever arises from that state as emanation is always sole enlightened body and wisdom manifestation. Never departing from this is Buddha purified of temporary obscurations. The high tantric upadesha term of the two purities[265] is only for Buddhas, but Buddhas are not thinking of these two purities. We followers have to see the qualities of the two purities of Buddhas. The two purities are the purity that is essentially pure from the beginning, and the purity of having purified all temporary obscurations. All sentient beings are essentially pure from the beginning because they have inherent Buddha nature that is indivisible with mind, but from lack of recognition of this purity, they still have deluded phenomena. The manifestation of the beginningless purity of Buddha is undeluded wisdom qualities. Sentient beings have not purified temporary obscurations of ordinary dualistic mind's subject and object, which causes desire, hatred, and ignorance, and creates all passions and karma. Although those passions and karma do not exist independently, beings are hypnotized from the lack of recognition of their own manifestation, so many obscurations are created that are not purified because of ignorance and thick habit. Thinking that these are reality is called temporary obscurations.

So, the difference between Buddhas and sentient beings is that Buddhas are holders of the two purities,[266] and sentient beings have not cleaned temporary obscurations and are wandering in samsara. Temporary does

265. dag pa gnyis.
266. dag pa gnyis ldan.

not mean a minute, day, month, or certain duration. Temporary means that the nature of manifestation, which is always unobstructed, is changing like magic from dualistic mind. Unless dualistic mind is purified through stainless meditation, all these phenomena will always be coming and going, being born, ceasing, and remaining, disappearing and occurring, so they are uncertain. This is why they are called temporary obscurations, because by thinking of all of these as reality, samsaric phenomena are caused. Temporary means that since the essence of Buddha nature is always pure, these obscurations can only be temporary. Whenever the purity that is essentially pure from the beginning is realized, by always abiding in that state, temporary obscurations are naturally purified, becoming the same as the wisdom manifestation of Buddha, the holder of the two purities.

For the holders of the two states of purity, the way of naturally abiding is as said by Great Omniscient Longchen Rabjam:

> Since everything is the great spontaneous presence of Kuntuzangpo,
> There never was delusion, there never is delusion, and there never will be delusion.
> This is beyond the limit of just naming or not naming cyclic existence. No one was ever deluded anywhere in the past,
> No one is deluded now, and no one will be deluded in the future.
> This is the stainless emptiness wisdom mind of the three realms of existence, great stainless purity from the beginning.
> Since there is no delusion, there are no undeluded phenomena.
> Original spontaneity is great self-occurring awareness.
> There never was liberation, there is not liberation now, and there never will be liberation.
> Enlightenment is just a name, so no one has ever been liberated.
> There will be no liberation because from the beginning, nothing is bound.
> Like sky, free from distinctions, limitations, and directions, perfectly pure,
> This is complete liberation, the wisdom mind of great stainless purity from the beginning.

Thus it is said.

Therefore, this is called Buddha. Buddha does not mean discovering an ordinary self-characterized noble person from another country. So, this is the greatness of nothing whatsoever that has become Buddha from all to all. From this, accomplishment based on effort is conquered with splendor.

There are many people who have not realized their Buddha nature from lack of faith, belief, and the guidance of a teacher, yet they still say that they are Buddhas. With no recognition of awareness mind, just saying that they think they are Buddhas becomes an enormous obstacle because they do not practice and meditate in order to purify obscurations and accumulate merit to attain fully enlightened Buddhahood. They lose the meaning of their precious human lives, becoming like feathers in the winds of their karma, following after the habits of wherever they are attached and the karmic results of whatever they did before. If they have no faith and are not praying, visualizing, practicing, and meditating in this precious human life, they cannot reach the confidence of abiding in wisdom, so they have no control over being lured by the phenomena of this world for their very momentary lives, meaninglessly.

Great Omniscient Rongzompa said:

> Greatness means that which conquers all that is below it with splendor, so this is called greatness. Also, it was said that since this vast and open-minded view has the power to conquer with splendor all those minds of the lesser vehicles tainted by the stain of holding to characteristics, it is called great. In the essential nature as it is, if there were a mind holding to the distinctions of greater or lesser, this would not be acceptable as the self-nature of greatness. It is said that this nature is free from conceptualizing distinctions of greater or lesser.

Thus it is said.

If all of this is synthesized, as it says in *The Vajra Words of the Wisdom Realization of Kuntuzangpo:*[267]

> KYE HO! Hear me! My natural Great Perfection
> Is where all the phenomena of samsara and enlightenment
>   are complete, free from accepting and rejecting.
> The pith of precious teachings is complete within natural
>   self-liberation.

267. *kun tu bzang po'i dgongs nyams rdo rje'i tshig.*

The pith of all views is complete without either eternalism
or nihilism.
The pith of all meditations is complete without effort.
The pith of all activity is complete without permission
or restriction.
The pith of all results is complete, free from yearning.
Even that which is called complete is just a thought.
The essential nature of all phenomena is enlightened mind.
The mind of all Buddhas is also enlightened mind.
The life of all sentient beings is also enlightened mind.
In enlightened mind, there is nothing relative or absolute.
By saying it is non-existent, do not make it just empty.
By saying it is existent, do not hold to it with the mind and
create it as permanent.
Without holding, without discarding, this is space as it is that
transcends the mind.
This expanse is free from all elaborate objective considerations.
Since I am uncontrived and have no conceptions,
The causes and results of virtue and nonvirtue are permanently
exhausted.
Why should I engage in deity, mantra, and samadhi practice?
To practice and become Buddha is not who I am.
I am the great nature that encompasses everything.
By crossing over the stages and paths, how can I be seen?
Therefore, do not be bound by the tension and contrivance
of hope and fear.
Stay away from the pride of an excellent view.
Stay out of the sheath of superb meditation.
Destroy the self-promoting confines of artificial conduct.
Leave behind the hope and fear of great results.
In the mindfulness that transcends meditation and
nonmeditation,
Calculating activity and nonactivity dissolve in space.
Enlightened mind transcends emptiness and non-emptiness.
The directions of existence and non-existence fall away in
unending profound space.
In inexpressible, inconceivable, unspoken awareness, there is
no grasping mind,

So there is no antidote,[268] which is the immortal tree of awareness.
This fresh nature of self-liberation that is naked and firm
Is the expanse free from all elaboration and effort.
Abide within the unfabricated nature that is free from increase
and decrease in the three times.

Thus, this is the only teaching to decide on.

Transference of Consciousness

The sixth is phowa,[269] the transference of consciousness. The general meaning of phowa is not to remain in one place but to transfer from one place to another. For whoever has not attained the uncompounded stainless Three Kayas, the wisdom mind of Buddha, which transcends the phenomena of being born, ceasing, and remaining, there is dualistic mind, which creates the habits of deluded appearances. All sentient beings rely on these appearances of direction, place, time, being born, ceasing, and remaining. Therefore, it is as said in *The Great Perfection Tantra Containing the Absolute Meaning:*[270]

Since the mind experiences the three times,
The lives of the past, present, and future will occur.
Since the mind changes and transfers,
That is why the body is born and dies.
Since illness, happiness, suffering, and so on,
Are one's mind, this ripens as samsara.

Thus it is said. So therefore, the unborn wisdom mind of Dharmakaya, the unobstructed wisdom mind of Sambhogakaya, and the non-abiding wisdom mind of Nirmanakaya are natural self-awareness, free from the limitation of eternalism and nihilism. Through perfectly realizing the meaning of the basic nature, as it is, of unending awareness, free from all change and transference in the three times, then if one attains the depth of confidence in that state, all appearances of phenomenal existence will arise only as sublime, permanent enlightened bodies and purelands. Without falling to the extreme direction of phenomena flawed by materializing

268. If there is no grasping, there is no need for an antidote.
269. 'pho ba, transference of consciousness.
270. *rdzogs chen nges don 'dus pa'i rgyud.*

characteristics such as direction, time, and place, the subject of the mind that will be transferred, the one by whom the transference is made, and the object of the place to which the transference is made never exist as reality. So, it says in *The Sutra of the Stainless Moon:*[271]

> All those phenomena are like sky.
> Nothing whatsoever is born and no one at all dies.
> Even though there is transference to other existences,
> The beings who are born and appearances of death
> Are like a dream. The essence is empty.
> But by grasping at a self, childish beings become ignorant.

Thus, that is said, and in the *Prajnaparamita*, it says:

> There is no transference of the form of the body, so there is no rejoining,[272]
> Because the form of the body is perfectly pure.
> Likewise, there is no transference of feeling, perception, intention, and consciousness,
> So there is not even a trace of rejoining, since they are all perfectly pure.[273]

Thus it is said.

In the tantras, it says:

> From the beginning unborn,
> The great clear light of the radiance of awareness
> Does not have even an instant of the compounded continuity of birth and death.
> There is only the nature of equanimity in the three times.
> There are no conceptions or elaborate characteristics whatsoever.
> Therefore, throughout the three times,
> There is no transference or change.

271. *zla ba dri ma med pa'i mdo.*

272. There is no rejoining with the skandhas in the next life, because there are no karmic body phenomena.

273. Perfectly pure means that all is empty wisdom. There is no true karmic body, only stainless emptiness wisdom body.

Abiding from the beginning like stainless sky,
It is called by the name of unending mind.[274]

Thus it is said.

The Great Omniscient Longchenpa said:

The nature of enlightened mind
Is like stainless sky, so it has no birth, death, happiness, or suffering.

Thus it is said.

Also, the King of Vidyadharas Jigdral Yeshe Dorje said in his *Unending Manifestation of the Song and Dance of Sublime Aspirations:*[275]

AH HO YE! AWE!
In the sacred pureland of Great Bliss
Resides the Dharmakaya Guru, Amitabha.
Look upon me, your son who prays to you, with your
compassionate wisdom.
Grant blessings and confer empowerment.
This awareness that is empty radiance, free from edge and center,
Lord, is this not your wisdom mind?
This basic nature, originally free from change or transference,
Is this not you, the Unchanging Light?[276]
I have never been separate from this for even an instant.
Even though there has never been separation, still, this has
not been recognized.
Now, when I recognize this,
The Buddha of Boundless Light is lost.
The pureland of Great Bliss has disappeared.
The unborn nature of mind is flowing.
There is only the manifestation of the bliss and emptiness
of awareness flowing unceasingly.
Whatever experiences arise are the great limitlessly
emanating Dharmakaya.

274. gnyug ma'i sems.
275. *'dun ma bzang po'i glu bro gnyug ma'i rol rtsed.*
276. Buddha Amitabha, who is not different from one's own wisdom mind.

Grasping toward a pureland is the phenomenon of delusion.
Naming a Buddha is the narrow pass of attachment.
Amitabha is not outside; look within.
Having found that Dharmakaya comes from myself is
the great satisfaction.
This is the wonder of unceasing tranquillity. E MA HO!

Thus, in Lama'i Naljor, after Guru Rinpoche dissolves into oneself, being indivisible, this is the meaning of **abide in indivisible awareness and emptiness, which is the face of the absolute Lama.**

As said, if one attains confidence, then the movement of karmic vital energies is completely exhausted. Therefore, from Tantra:

Since that which is called Buddha free from karmic breath is the
attainment of the power of the unending wisdom of immortality,
There is nothing transferring and there is no need to transfer
anywhere.

According to the capacity of ordinary individuals who gradually progress on the path, however, the verses read, **I pray to the Protector, Amitabha, Buddha of Boundless Light. May you bless me to accomplish the profound path of transference**. Thus, the meaning of these two lines is as follows. As explained before at the time of refuge, bodhichitta, mandala offering, Lama'i Naljor, and so on, Orgyen Padmasambhava is the embodiment of the objects of refuge, which are the Three Jewels. The basis for the arising of the appearance of Great Orgyen is the Buddha of Boundless Light, or the **Protector of Boundless Light**. Therefore, as mentioned in the extensive and concise prayers written by Karma Chagme for rebirth in the pureland of Great Bliss, the actual arrangement of the pureland of Great Bliss should be clearly visualized **in** the mind. Wherever one is born within cyclic existence, whether it is a high or low birth, one must have weariness in thinking that one never departs from suffering. One should therefore **pray** strongly for transference to the pureland of Great Bliss. It says in *The Great Bliss Prayer to Be Reborn in the Pureland of Amitabha:*

The suffering of the lower realms is unbearable;
The happiness and bliss of gods and humans always
become impermanent.

May my mind have fear of this.
From beginningless time until now,
I have wandered in this samsara for so long;
May I have weariness for this.
Even if I am born from one human birth to another
  human birth again and again,
Still, the four great rivers of suffering of birth, aging, sickness,
  and death are experienced in an uncountable way.
In the negative time of degeneracy, there are so many obstacles.
This happiness and bliss of gods and humans
Is like food that is mixed with poison,
So may I not have desire for even one single hair of this.
All relatives, food, wealth, and suitable companions
Are impermanent, like magic and dreams.
May I never have attachment for even one single hair of this.
The land, water, country, mountains, houses, and everything
Are like the land, country, and houses existing in dreams.
May I recognize that they have no reality.
From the inescapable trap of this ocean of existence,
Like a criminal escaping from prison,
May I escape to the pureland of Great Bliss
Without ever looking back.

Thus, just like that, by remembering the meaning, pray to accomplish transference.

Also, the Copper-Colored Mountain is perfectly adorned with the purelands of the Three Kayas. For example, at the highest point is the pureland palace of the Dharmakaya Amitabha. In the center is the palace of the Sambhogakaya Avalokiteshvara. In the palace below is Padmasambhava, the Lotus-Born. By visualizing Great Orgyen with his entire retinue and continuously repeating the prayer to be reborn there, pray, **may you bless me to accomplish the profound path of transference** (phowa).

In general, there are five different categories of phowa. *The most advanced phowa pervaded by the view of Dharmakaya* is, for example, as said in *The Prayer to Accomplish the Pureland of the Three Kayas:*[277]

277. *sku gsum zhing khams sbyong ba'i smon lam.*

Unobstructed clarity like the sky in autumn,
Abiding as empty clarity without the veil of obscurations,
Is the present time of the pure Dharmakaya of stainless space, free from conception from the beginning.
In immaculate ordinary awareness, free from boundaries,
From the strength of equanimity, one finds with certainty
The secret nature of the inner clarity of the original basis of space.
In the expanse of the wisdom mind of Samantabhadra, having the six supreme qualities,[278]
May I instantly attain the changeless place of abiding.

Thus, in accordance with these words, immediately after the final breath, the immutable citadel is found as timelessly pure Dharmakaya.

Although ordinary mind[279] is explained in many ways, it can be synthesized into three definitions. The ordinary mind that is continuously distracted in delusion is basic delusion that is totally engaged in dualistic mind. Sentient beings hold to existence as self-characterized, so this kind of ordinary mind is only an object of purification. Ordinary mind experienced by practitioners on the path occurs when, for example, any conceptions that arise are instantly identified so that both mindfulness and conception are objectless and pure in natural clarity. This is called the ordinary mind of experience,[280] which is not totally ordinary. The ordinary mind of realization[281] is as previously mentioned by the saint Arrow Shooter:[282]

If there is recognition, everything is included there.
No one has known anything other than that.

Thus, as said, in the basic nature of wisdom mind that is originally perfectly pure and transcends all effort, by not engaging in any attempt to change, modify, abandon, or accept, present awareness is only wisdom that has never known delusion. Since this is ordinary awareness that realizes the unending nature, it is not at all necessary to grasp mindfulness. This is the

278. khyad chos drug. These are the six supreme qualities mentioned before in the explanation of how sentient beings started to wander in samsara and how Kuntuzangpo excels in Dharmakaya from these six most exalted aspects.
279. tha mal gyi shes pa.
280. nyams kyi tha mal gyi shes pa.
281. rtogs pa'i tha mal gyi shes pa.
282. mda' snun, an epithet for Saraha.

ordinary awareness of realization, and this alone one should affirm that one will realize. At the time of death, when the sounds, forms, lights, and especially the appearances of the peaceful and wrathful deities of the bardo of dharmata dawn, for all those who have attained confidence in the developing and completion stages, it will be as it is said in *The Essence of Butter Pith Instructions:*

> All appearances of rainbow light are the natural clarity of
> one's own awareness.
> All appearances of the manifestations of peaceful and wrathful
> wisdom deities are the natural form of one's own awareness.
> All sounds are one's own sound.
> All light is one's own light.
> Have no doubt or second thoughts about this.
> If doubt arises, one will be thrown into cyclic existence.
> If one decides that these are self-manifesting appearances, not
> wavering from clear emptiness,
> The Three Kayas will be attained, and that right there is
> Buddhahood.
> Even if one is thrown into cyclic existence, one will
> definitely not go there.

Thus, as it is said, the way of attaining liberation for practitioners of middling capacity occurs by recognizing the self-manifesting appearances of *the Sambhogakaya phowa of clear light union.*

Then, according to the practitioner's confidence, there is *the Nirmanakaya phowa of immeasurable compassion,* which relies on the ripening and liberating blessings of the Lama's precious teachings. This occurs by not becoming distracted during the appearances of the bardo of becoming and by focusing on pureland single-pointedly. The fourth phowa is perceiving the central energy channel as the path, consciousness as the traveler, and the pureland as one's own home. This is *the phowa of the three perceptions of ordinary beings.*

If a person performing phowa has sublime realization and the ability to know and understand where sentient beings are wandering in the bardo, as well as the ability to lead beings from whatever state they are in, this is the fifth phowa. It is called *the phowa of guiding the dead with the hook of compassion.* This phowa is as said in *The Tantra of Stainless Confession:*

> At the moment of death, the sphere of light is transferred through sound.

Thus, these words illuminate the same meaning.

Also, concerning this last phowa for ordinary sentient beings, it is unacceptable for ordinary people who do not have realization to attempt to perform phowa for those who have reached higher stages on the path. In particular, no matter how good or seemingly advanced a disciple may be, it is totally unacceptable to ever attempt to perform phowa for one's own root Lama, and not only that, it is also unacceptable to recite prayers to guard the consciousness throughout the weeks of the forty-nine-day period. This is because at all times and in all situations, one has already seen the root Lama as the actual Buddha or inseparable from Vajradhara. Knowing that it is clearly said throughout all the sutras and tantras that the root Lama is inseparable from Buddha or Vajradhara, one sees the Lama while alive as the most supreme guide and shows great respect. Once the Lama passes on, to then elevate oneself up to the level of the Lama and drag the Lama down to the level of an ordinary sentient being traveling in the bardo, and to go on to perform purification rites and rituals for forty-nine days and so on, is, to put it nicely, the despicable activity of the darkness of total delusion. It is for this reason that I ask the knowledgeable disciples of future generations not to engage in or attempt to follow this shameless behavior with a wrong point of view.

If there are some accounts of names and dedication prayers for those with connections to a particular Lama that were left unfulfilled because the Lama passed away before being able to complete these activities, and if it is said that it is customary for disciples to perform these ceremonies of guiding the dead, along with the ceremony of offering that is performed, when the Lama passes away, it seems lately that the motivation for this is strongly coveting the wealth and belongings of the dead by disciples without realization or wisdom. Disciples must know how important it is to eradicate such attachment. One will never find a basis for this in Buddha's teachings or logically. It is also illogical to think that the Lama did not complete or forgot certain prayers. One is supposed to see or think that the Lama is Buddha or Vajradhara, which means with wisdom mind, with nothing forgotten. So, if disciples think they must complete the Lama's activities, it means that while the Lama is living, one thinks that the Lama does not forget anything, and when the Lama passes away, one thinks the Lama was forgetful. Without logic or discernment, one is not supposed to have those conceptions. Whether the Lama has passed away or is living, one has to see the Lama in the same way, always in deathless Dharmakaya. Praying to and worshiping the Lama is always the accumulation of virtue.

At the time of practicing phowa, once receiving the commentary from one's teacher on either the extensive or the concise phowa, the practice is maintained until a sign of accomplishment occurs. After the sign of accomplishment occurs, it is inappropriate to continue training. In the tantras, it says:

> Since phowa is an activity that is based on the correct time,
> If the time is incorrect, it can turn into the killing of deities.[283]

Thus it is said.

When practicing phowa during one's life, visualizing the Buddha such as Amitabha in the space above, one ejects the light sphere of consciousness to either the Buddha's feet or Buddha's heart when saying HIC, and then slowly chanting KA, one brings the white sphere of consciousness back down to one's own heart. One must train alone in a solitary place, one's own house, or a quiet place, until signs are conspicuous, such as an opening in the crown chakra. Then, in each practice session, one has to bring the sphere of consciousness back down through one's own crown chakra and think that it is in one's heart, staying there for one's long life. Until the sign of accomplishment occurs, at the close of each session, Buddha Amitabha is transformed into Buddha Amitayus abiding in one's heart, and one recites the mantra of Buddha Amitayus. This is the practice during one's life. In the actual phowa that is done at death, one does not bring back the white sphere of consciousness to one's heart, but keeps elevating it with the sound of HIC, ejecting it into the heart of Buddha Amitabha or Guru Rinpoche without bringing it back, continuing to lift it up until fainting, touching the wisdom heart of Buddha Amitabha, thinking that this sphere dissolves into the wisdom heart of Buddha Amitabha, and abiding in that state. Then, when completely separate and free from the body and breath, enlightenment is attained.

Whenever the time is correct to do phowa, it can be accomplished. The Lama who performs phowa for someone else must in the best way see the truth of the basic nature. At least, it is absolutely necessary that this Lama

283. Of course it is impossible to kill wisdom deities. This is said because yogis and yoginis are practicing to accomplish wisdom deity, so practicing phowa at the incorrect time would stop this.

have certain experience in the meditations of the developing and completion stages.

If the time to act arrives, if strong signs of death come, or if there are signs in the dream state, so that no matter what medical help and ceremonies are performed, they are ineffective and death is imminent, then it is time to do as one had previously practiced. Visualize that the consciousness is a sphere of light, and with the sound of HIC, send the consciousness up and into either the feet or the heart of the Buddha who is the embodiment of all Buddha families. Do not let it descend back down. During the stages of the dissolution of the four elements and the decline of the five sense organs, if the white, red, and black appearances, and so on, of the stages of dissolution occur, strongly knowing that Guru Amitabha or Padmasambhava is actually present in the space directly above the crown of one's head, send the consciousness as a sphere of light directly into the heart of the Buddha who is the embodiment of all Buddha families. Think single-pointedly that one's consciousness dissolves there. Immediately after the final breath, there will be no doubt about the great confirmation of entering pureland.

In general, if the time to use the practice has arrived and the dying individual is young in years, since the strength of the energy channels, airs, and essential fluid has not declined, it may be more difficult to actually transfer the individual's consciousness. If it is someone who has been suffering from an illness for a long time, whose strength of the four elements is exhausted, whose time of death has arrived, or who is elderly with declining elements, then phowa will be easier for that individual. It is like the example of berries and fruits on trees in summer, which are hard to pick before they have ripened. During autumn, the fruits are ripe and ready to fall, so that just by brushing them with one's clothing, they easily drop. As mentioned before, until the actual time for transference arrives, even if the individual has the confidence of accomplishment, never perform phowa. It is acceptable, however, to bring the pureland continuously to mind.

Most importantly, depending on Great Orgyen, in order for life and practice to reach completion, and to serve the teachings of Buddha and all sentient beings in whatever way is necessary, it is important to always perform a regular long-life practice. It is as said in *The Vajrakilaya Long-Life Transmission:*[284]

284. *rdo rje gzhon nu tshe'i lung.*

> There are three aspects to life: the life of the movement of tig-le allowing transference, the life of the vital energies that come and go, and the indestructible unending life.

Thus, as said, the movement that allows for transference, or the support for the increase and decline of the four elements, is the relative causal bodhichitta. If this does not diminish, it is beneficial for increasing the pure elements of the body and maintaining awareness. Since it is the ultimate bodhichitta that supports enlightened body and wisdom, it is necessary that it be maintained just as it is. The life of the vital energies that come and go is the inner five elements' vital energies. When all of those are pure, the vital energies are the five wisdom energies. When the pure inseparability of the coarse relative causal tig-le and the subtle absolute tig-le occurs, coarse karmic energies are purified as the subtle wisdom energies and, like Great Orgyen and others who are indestructible, the great unending life becomes the essential nature of deity.

Generosity of Giving One's Body and the Dedication of Merit

Seventh, the offering of the body, dedication, and aspiration prayers are as follows.

Now, my body, wealth, and the source of my virtue of all my lives I give without clinging to all sentient beings, who have all been my mother. May great waves of benefit be accomplished without obstacle for all sentient beings. Thus, these three lines illuminate the meaning that from beginningless lives until the present lifetime, although innumerable bodies have been taken, they have all only added to the causes and results of further suffering. Moreover, there has not been benefit, even of the size of a sesame seed. Therefore, **now**, in order to make this cherished precious **body** meaningful, one should imagine that inexhaustible clouds of offerings radiate from one's body, upwardly presenting offerings to the exalted guests, who are the Three Jewels and the Protectors of Qualities. Generosity is presented as clouds of gifts to the lower guests of compassion, the sentient beings of the six realms and the guests who are owed unpaid karmic debts. Not only that, whatever is owned, including all of one's possessions and **wealth**, as well as the **root** of all **virtue** accumulated throughout the three times, is **given without clinging to all** kind parent **sentient beings** who **have been** my

mother. All sentient beings are placed in the state of gods or human beings as the support for the stages of the path and are led to holy Dharma, and that path to liberation is according to their energy and faculties. The result of the path is to be placed in the state of enlightenment. Then, just as previous Buddhas and Bodhisattvas of the past have accomplished **great waves of benefit** for all **sentient beings**, likewise, in accord with their activities, "I wish and pray to **accomplish** just like Buddhas who have the ten powers. Help me accomplish **unobstructed** benefit by following your example, fulfilling the aims and desires of all beings."

Finally, just like stainless sky, without any attachment or attempt to abandon or accept anything, the dedication of the perfectly pure three circles as the nature of dharmadhatu is as follows. As it says in *The Great Sky of Vajrasattva:*[285]

> Conceptions of the sky are unborn,
> So conception is just like stainless sky.
> Whoever is without attachment just dedicates in the sky.[286]
> By attaining the state of Dharmakaya, great benefit will
> occur, like sky.

Thus, in the same way, abide in the equanimity of dharmadhatu. At night, when it is time to sleep, visualize that one's heart is a red lotus with four or eight petals. On the pollen heart of the lotus abides the embodiment of all Buddhas as the Guru and Consort, abiding in the nature of flawless great bliss. Sleep in this serene awareness without grasping. It is also acceptable to meditate without visualization. Falling asleep with devotion from the heart is an extremely important way to recognize clear light.

Also, in the direct teachings by voice of previous Vidyadharas, it is said, the inner clarity of wisdom is dissolved yet unobscured.[287] This means to dissolve inward, without allowing one's mind to be overcome by the delusion of distraction toward the external objects of the six senses, and is the meaning of awareness contained in dharmadhatu. The inner mind should not be understood as something separate or distinct by separating the mind into outer and inner distinctions. Mind cannot be made into outer and inner distinctions. It is the nature just as it is, which is undistorted. In order

285. *rdo rje sems dpa' nam mkha' che.*
286. Sky means inconceivable, stainless empty awareness.
287. nang gsal thim la ma rmugs pa.

to understand this meaning, it is necessary to abide in the uncontrived basic nature of clear light. If so, when the time of death arrives, if this clear light is recognized, then like a child joining with the mother's lap, there will be recognition and liberation, or there will be no doubt that the state of the Copper-Colored Mountain will be attained.

If perhaps daytime appearances or the dormant habits of previous lifetimes arise, then during one's dreams, if one has a nightmare or a disturbing dream, one can recognize that the nature of the dream is that it does not have even a particle of true existence. Since the fear, sadness, and so on, of the dream are not true, then no matter what dream may have occurred, do not attempt to examine it or continue the connection with it. Instead, at that very moment, bring the nature of the flawless great bliss embodiment of all Buddhas, the Guru and Consort in union, clearly to one's mind. Through sustaining the essential nature of unveiled fresh awareness, one will arrive in the all-pervasive empty essence of the unconditioned nature of mind, which will purify all previous habits of daytime or dream appearances. Just as it is impossible to know how to sow a seed in the sky, likewise this is supremely beneficial for not allowing new seeds of samsara to be sown in the mind for the future.

Also, if one is dreaming of seeing wisdom deities and Lamas, enjoying the company of best friends, and so on, and the feeling of joy arises, immediately visualize this as inconceivable clouds of offerings, all of which are offered to the Three Jewels. By sustaining the essence of the feeling of joy, realizing that appearances are the appearance of bliss whose essence is naturally empty, there will be no attachment to the feeling of bliss. With all appearances of phenomenal existence as the empty bliss of self-awareness, Vajrasattva is naturally accomplished. Through sustaining awareness, sleep becomes lighter. The reason is that by sustaining the unobscured nature during daytime appearances, the power of this affects the mind. The mind and the gross or heavy energy that originates from the mind become clearer and more refined. The first sign of this is that the mind gradually becomes purified in the self-awareness wisdom energy of the space of clear light. Then, at some point, when recognition turns into confidence, all of the conceptual obscurations of daytime and dream appearances and the appearances of past and future lifetimes are purified without anything remaining. Everything becomes the great all-pervasive sole nature of clear light.

At night, just before one is about to fall asleep, direct one's awareness to the unceasing continuity of appearances as the wisdom deity Lama and sleep in this way, or fall asleep in the awareness that the essence of the wisdom deity Lama is self-awareness, free from fabrication, which is the great clear light of Dharmakaya. Sleeping in these ways is extremely important. Whenever one is dreaming positive dreams, by sustaining awareness, then awakening becomes not just awakening from a dream, but uninterrupted continuity, and positive dream and daytime phenomena will naturally join. When the time comes that the appearances of this life are exhausted and the moment of death occurs, there is no doubt that the sacred appearance of deathless, permanent Dharmakaya will manifest. The reason for this is:

> Death is not death.
> For practitioners, it is enlightening.

Thus it is said.

At the time of eating and drinking, no matter what amount is being consumed, without grasping, think that the food and drink contain all desirable, flawless qualities of samsara and enlightenment, pure and perfectly complete. Dedicate and offer unceasing vast and immeasurable offerings to the Three Jewels. Think that one then receives the food and drink as a blessing from the Three Jewels. In this way, not only will there be no stain from consuming offerings, but merit will be accumulated as well. Whenever one wears new clothing, without grasping, think:

> Having beautiful colors, they are soft, delicate, light, and have a variety of qualities, including hundreds of supreme ornaments presented as offerings.

Thus, as said, by visualizing an inconceivable array of excellent garments, offer them all to the Three Jewels.

In whatever direction one is going, keep the perception that one is going to the purelands of the Buddhas. If so, all activities such as eating, sleeping, staying, and going will be always meaningful.

Thus, these are the concise preliminary practices from the Dharma section of *The Infinity of Pure Wisdom Phenomena*[288] of Tragtung Düdjom Lingpa. The Lord Father, Great Treasure Revealer, Dharma King Jigdral Yeshe

288. *dag snang ye shes drva ba.*

Dorje, directly from his voice, to make a Dharma connection for countless people of different races who live in the Eastern and Western countries of this world, chose to teach this as a main convenient daily practice. Many faithful disciples requested again and again that I write a commentary on this practice. This became the root cause. Many years ago in the land of Tibet between Kongpo and Lhasa, the nun Samten, from the small valley called Tsomo Rak; Rigdzin Drolma, the consort of the late Lama Dornam; several Lamas and Tulkus from Golok; the practitioner of the profound two stages, Lama Tsedrub Tharchin; and others who see me with the pure view that sees brass as gold incessantly requested that I compose my own Guru Yoga practice. This contributing circumstance was so tenacious that the auricles of my ears were continuously pestered. Since my own qualities in scholarship and practice are completely lacking, I had no confidence to write a Guru Yoga practice with myself as the support. Instead, I felt that if there was a commentary written based on this concise preliminary practice, it would surely benefit many beings. Therefore, inspired by and in keeping with the tradition of the direct teachings and transmissions of the Buddhas and Bodhisattvas of the past, I wrote this down in Tibetan cursive handwriting.

It is ideal if all those who possess the fortune of intelligence can rely on the speech of Jigme Gyalwa'i Nyugu written by Paltrul Rinpoche, *The Voice of My Root Guru Samantabhadra,* and my Lord Father's extensive New Treasure Commentary called *The Lamp Illuminating the Path of Liberation,* as well as the other great preliminary practice commentaries that exist. This is written for those who pursue objective appearances as ordinary beings or those who gradually progress along the path. In order for their practice to advance, among the six paramitas, at the time of practicing samadhi, terms such as tranquil stillness, true seeing, abiding in evenness, after abiding in evenness, dispelling obstacles, developing advantageous conditions, the qualities of the stages and paths, definitions, and so on, are synthesized into the essence of their meaning. As Paltrul Rinpoche said:

> In order to benefit practitioners who are willingly
> engaged in practice,
> Unlike philosophical texts written in a structured,
> scholarly way with poetry,
> The perfect path of common and village words
> Is the well-chosen specialty of sublime beings.

Thus, in following this teaching as my main intention, emphasis on multiple categories, sentence structure, metrical distinctions, poetic phrasing, and other such elaborations are avoided. Whatever spontaneously and naturally came to my mind on its own was written down here.

At the insistent request of Lama Orgyen Thinley Kunkhyab, the instructions on the meaning of the view, meditation, and activity, as well as the inseparable basis, path, and result as the view, have been openly explained. This is especially to refresh the memory of those practitioners who have awareness of self-manifesting appearances, or those who may possibly be instantaneous developers of keenest faculties.

As in Guru Yoga: **The Lama dissolves into light and is absorbed into oneself. Abide in indivisible emptiness and awareness, which is the face of the absolute Lama**. Thus, just as the profound precious teachings on the Great Perfection's cutting through have been taught, I have attempted to write this with open directness that is free from the restrictive net of elaboration. Still, by sitting at the feet of and fully relying on a qualified Lama who has deep confidence in the view and holds the blessings of the wisdom lineage, one who has irreversible faith will recognize the nature of self-awareness. This is because the energy of wisdom awareness is perfectly pure from the beginning. Even now, the nature of one's mind will never become something other than that, even if one tries to find this nature elsewhere for countless eons of time. From many previous lifetimes, by the strength of the habit of non-existent dualistic appearances, the nature of this mind, which is actually easy to realize, has been turned into a secret that has become extremely difficult to realize. That is why it says in *The Mahasandhi Prayer of Manjushri:* [289]

> Because it is so easy, it is not trusted and remains the secret of the mind. May it be seen through the strength of the Lama's precious teachings.

Thus, it is very important to have the single-pointed wish to follow what is said in this prayer.

Whatever the case, although I do not have the strength or depth of the exalted view, just by hearing the words of the liberating doctrine of the

289. *'jam dpal rdzogs pa chen po'i smon lam.*

Great Perfection, those who have great fortune will only receive the great benefit of the blessings of this level of Dharma. They will certainly never be harmed. As Omniscient Rongzompa said:

> Even if the words of the Great Perfection are spoken
> as loudly and abruptly as possible,
> They are always refined and serene because they are like sky.
> Even if the words of the lower vehicles are spoken
> with refinement and serenity,
> They are coarse and substantial, just like a pile of dust.
> So, therefore, it is necessary to examine and see the
> way in which the Great Perfection is vastly open,
> profound, and refined.

And he continues:

> All those who are attached to commentaries on language and logic feel convinced that their own philosophies are flawlessly established and accepted. Since the way of the Great Perfection can never be established through logic such as this, without thinking that it is something to be abandoned, enter this path with faith. If one does not, then one will become full of the pride of self-respect.

Thus it is as said. Also, Vasubhandu said:

> Whoever is only in accord with the doctrine of the Victorious Ones
> Will teach without mental distraction.
> Since this is in harmony with the path to liberation,
> Like the speech of the Sage, we can place it on our crown.

Thus it is said. If one's lotus of intelligence is not blooming by following these words, still, as Paltrul Rinpoche said:

> If a person is ignoble and vulgar with a hundred faults,
> But has one single good quality of knowledge,
> Then do not think of those faults, but accept that
> single positive quality,

And like a swan extracting milk from water,
Accept it voluntarily and willingly for one's benefit.

Thus, rejoicing in these words is positive virtue.

. . . ——————— *This was written by Thinley Norbu.* ——————— . . .

A Commentary on the Meaning of

"The Continuously Blossoming Rosary of the

Lotus Assembly Palace" Called

The Light Rays of the Youthful Sun

Prostrations to the Lotus-Born Fully Enlightened Buddha.

AH is Vairochana;[1] 'A is Akshobhya;[2] the NARO[3] is Ratnasambhava;[4] the crescent moon-shaped DA-TSE[5] is Amitabha;[6] and the sole sign TIG-LE[7] is Amoghasiddhi.[8]

Thus, whether OM,[9] HUNG,[10] HRI, or others, whether the sound of mantra is a single sound or whether it is many, whether the deity of the mandala is peaceful or wrathful, male or female, the principal deity or the retinue, and so on, whatever mantra is explained, it comes from the self-sound of dharmata.

It is the characteristic of dharmata not to possess even a subtle particle of material substance. Since nothing substantial exists, because there is no root or contributing circumstance, it is absolutely impossible for the root circumstance of suffering to occur later. This is because there is only stainless perfection. Therefore, because dharmata is always unchanging,[11]

> As it was from the beginning, it will be in the future.
> That which is unchangeable is dharmata.

1. rnam par snang mdzad.
2. mi bskyod pa.
3. The Tibetan vowel corresponding to the English *o*.
4. rin chen 'byung ldan.
5. zla tshes.
6. snang ba mtha' yas.
7. thig le.
8. don yod grub pa.
9. OM is composed of these five syllables, each of which is the syllable of one of the five Buddha families. OM is the syllable of the wisdom body of all immeasurable five Buddha families.
10. HUNG, like vajra, is the syllable of the wisdom mind of all immeasurable Buddhas.
11. From *rgyud bla ma,* the *Uttara Tantra.*

Thus it is said.

This dharmata is absolutely uncreated, yet it is known as everything that appears through the unobstructed aspect of omniscience. In dharmata, whatever arises, there is no conception of grasping to good or bad, so sound is self-occurring and self-arising. It is said:

> Just as the sound of a guitar
> Comes from the relative aspect of awareness,
> But that sound is not remaining outside or inside,
> Likewise, the enlightened speech of the Tathagatas
> Is not remaining outside or inside.

Thus, at the time of the vehicle of cause and result in which all phenomena are said to depend on root and contributing circumstances, the sound of a guitar arises from the relative aspect of awareness. Even so, enlightened speech of Tathagatas does not remain outside or inside with root and contributing circumstances. It is necessary to realize that the enlightened speech of Buddhas is itself inconceivably secret. Not remaining anywhere outside or inside and not finding anything substantial anywhere outside or inside are themselves the sounds and words that can arise anywhere of all aspects of enlightened speech, called the self-sounding of dharmata.

When the natural sound of dharmata, unborn and free from root or contributing circumstances, is objectified by all sentient beings, delusion occurs. From that circumstance, sentient beings rely on the many sounds and words of attachment and aversion that depend only on root and contributing circumstances. Therefore, Sakya Panchen said:

> Until the stick beats the drum,
> The sound of the drum will not occur.

As it is said, all sound is impermanent that occurs only by depending on root circumstances, such as a drum, and contributing circumstances, such as beating it, so that when root and contributing circumstances connect, there is sound. Whatever the case, according to practitioners on the path, Paltrul Rinpoche said:

> No matter how much is said, speech will never end.
> If you realize speechlessness, that is the origin of all speech.

As it is said, by relying on the kindness of a sublime Lama and realizing the meaning of the perfectly pure inexpressible nature of dharmata just as it is, the sounds and words of all expressible phenomena are heard as naturally arising, self-occurring sound. In this case, HRI is the seed syllable of the Lotus family of the immeasurable power of speech and the absolute lord of all Buddha families. From *The Spontaneous Fulfillment of Wishes:*

> Wondrous! In the western pureland of Great Exaltation,
> By the movement of the compassionate blessings of
> Buddha Amitabha,
> The Nirmanakaya Padma Jungne[12] manifested
> And came to this world for the benefit of all beings,
> Compassionate One who benefits beings unceasingly.

As this says, Orgyen Rinpoche is the manifestation of Buddha Amitabha and the embodiment of enlightened body and wisdom qualities. This is why the prayer begins by saying HRI, the essence mantra of Guru Rinpoche.

Whenever immeasurable Rupakaya appearances arise from stainless Dharmakaya emptiness, all of its forms are enlightened form, which means they can be anything. The Rupakaya forms of the Buddha families are representative of the body of all Buddhas. This is not made up; it is unobstructed appearance. Whenever a sadhana is practiced, there is first a syllable to visualize, such as the syllable HUNG of the Vajra family, which is the syllable of Vajrasattva, but all immeasurable Buddhas are contained in the one enlightened body of Vajrasattva, and also in wrathful aspects of the Vajra family, such as Vajrakilaya. Likewise, Padmasambhava of the Lotus family contains all immeasurable Buddhas indivisibly. These variations in the aspects of appearance are only revelations of the quality of unobstructedness. All inconceivable qualities of Buddhas are contained in each Buddha, not in a material way, and each Buddha family is undivided from any other Buddha family. One cannot materialize Buddhas as having only one certain aspect. The visualization of a mandala depends on the individual and the particular sadhana and mandala that are practiced, so the directions of the five Buddha families can change or transform. So, one cannot materialize the syllables and Buddhas here in an exact way, because all of the five Buddha families are based on Dharmakaya, and Dharmakaya is indivisible pervasiveness and openness that cannot be conceptualized and materialized.

12. The Lotus-Born.

The syllable HRI is the origin of the enlightened essence of sound of the Padma family, which contains all immeasurable aspects of Buddhas. There are many different explanations of the meaning of HRI, but in synthesis, the syllable AH is unborn, formless, stainless Dharmakaya, the origin of all immeasurable Buddhas. This essence of Dharmakaya is indivisible from the immeasurable aspect of Buddhas' qualities and inconceivable manifestations of infinite purelands; it is the essence of Buddha Vairochana. The syllable HA is whatever qualities arise that cannot be divided with material conception, impenetrably uninfluenced by the negative phenomena of samsara or the positive phenomena of enlightenment, so therefore they are indestructible forever; it is the essence syllable of Buddha Akshobya. The syllable RA is all of the inexhaustible aspects of Buddha's wisdom body, wisdom speech, wisdom mind, wisdom qualities, and wisdom activity; it is the essence syllable of Buddha Ratnasambhava. The syllable 'A is the aspect of never clinging to whatever arises of the qualities of samsara or the purelands of enlightenment; it is the essence syllable of the lotus family of Buddha Amitabha. Never remaining in samsara and never having attachment to enlightenment is desirelessness. Because nondualistic wisdom has no dualistic clinging, it always benefits pitiful samsaric beings, holding them with immeasurable compassion, and at the same time always abides with all immeasurable Buddhas indivisibly. This is the greatest nonattachment, like a lotus born from mud without being affected by it, its beautiful form blossoming with exquisite colorful qualities. The GIGU[13] is all qualities effortlessly self-accomplished; it is the essence syllable of Buddha Amoghasiddhi. Also, HRI contains the five Dakinis, including empty space, the essence of Buddha Dakini, which is the basis of all wisdom Dakinis and can manifest immeasurable Dakinis without contradiction; HA, which is Vajra Dakini; RA, which is Ratna Dakini; 'A, which is Padma Dakini; and GIGU, which is Karma Dakini.

The meaning of the first line, **In the assembly palace of great exaltation, Radiant Lotus Light,** is as follows.

In general, the meaning of *tsok*[14] is a gathering or heap of uncountable varieties of offerings of compounded substances, such as beautiful, splendid forms, pleasing sounds, delightful smells, delicious flavors, soothing feelings, and so on. So, first, the object to which offerings are made is the pureland of Guru Rinpoche. All immeasurable Buddhas of the victorious Three Kayas mandala are contained in the pureland of Guru Rinpoche, as

13. The Tibetan vowel corresponding to the English *i*.
14. tshogs.

evenly and inconceivably pervasive as dharmadhatu, in the manner of being free from gathering and separating from the beginning as the assembly of the pureland of Lotus Light, with a celestial palace adorned and arrayed with all limitless qualities of perfection. All directions are completely ornamented with blooming lotus flowers. Abiding within the upper Dharmakaya palace is limitless pure light phenomena, Buddha Amitabha. In the middle Sambhogakaya palace is the Great Compassionate One, Avalokiteshvara, with his immeasurable self-manifesting retinue, including the Eight Bodhisattvas. Below in the Nirmanakaya palace is Orgyen Padma Jungne with his immeasurable self-manifesting retinue, including the skull rosary of five wisdom families, eight manifestations, and many wisdom Dakinis, including Yeshe Tsogyal and Mandarava. Also, as the emanation of the great discerning wisdom of the three principal Buddhas, there are the sublime male and female Vidyadharas, Dakas and Dakinis, Yidam,[15] and Dharmapalas.[16] All of them are unlike paintings or statues, because their inconceivable nature is great bliss and their aspect is the luminous quality of natural light. The aspects of the celestial palaces and the assembly of deities and their qualities of enlightened body and purelands are clear and pristine, but their essence is indivisible forever.

Unlike the temporary bliss of the tainted passions that arises from root and contributing circumstances, the taintless great exaltation of the appearance of enlightened body and wisdom is only stainless and unending.

This bliss is not like a state of mind sought through the methods of nihilist psychology and psychiatry, which are always limited because they only switch from one material state to another material state and never go beyond suffering. There is no belief in an uncompounded, immaterial state of Buddha or deity, which always beneficially permeates the material, so there is no way to enter stainless space with a wisdom point of view. Whatever is material, its nature is momentary. By only believing in momentary energy, whatever methods are used only go from material to material, which is always changeable, decreasing, and temporary, so they are actually unable to bring happiness from this life to other lives up to enlightenment due to being nonspiritual. These methods are like drinking and becoming drunk or using drugs and becoming stoned. There is a great difference between trying to cause a state of being comfortable and happy without having any idea that goes beyond temporary materialism or that gives one the capacity

15. Peaceful and wrathful wisdom deities with whom one promises to become one.
16. Dharma Protectors.

to keep and increase continuous soothing energy, and the ecstasy created by spiritual images and methods, which will be continuous throughout one's lives until ordinary vital energy is transformed by attaining fully enlightened flawless ecstasy.

Therefore, the mandala of enlightened body and pureland is described in *The Stages of Vajra Activity:*[17]

> When the deities and samaya holders are all assembled,
> This is called the assembly of great exaltation.

Thus, this is the object to which tsok offerings are made.

Then, **maha-yogis and -yoginis are accomplishing great wisdom exaltation**. The terms *yogi* and *yogini* are *naljorpa (rnal 'byor pa)* and *naljorma (rnal 'byor ma)* in Tibetan. The word *rnal 'byor* cannot be used for Buddha, but refers to those who are practicing to become Buddha. It belongs to the path of practice to reach Dharmakaya, which is beyond the path of practice. *rNal ma* is the pure, uncontrived, fundamental support. *'Byor ba* means to receive those qualities and to attain and abide in that state. Practitioners rely on *rnal 'byor*, such as visualization of the mandalas of deities, in order to recognize the wisdom deity of dharmata.

In general, according to Omniscient Longchenpa, this is the meaning of the term *yoga:*

> The mind abiding in uncontrived, pure dharmata is called yoga.

As it is said, those of keen faculties who have great faith in the Dharma of unsurpassed secret mantra, whoever they are, must first receive ripening empowerment, liberating precious teachings, and supporting transmissions from a fully qualified Lama. Following this, according to developing stage Mahayoga, there is the practice of the yoga of the three mandalas of all appearances as deity, all sound as mantra, and all thought as enlightened mind. According to the transmission lineage of Anuyoga, there is the practice of the yoga of the energy channels as the Nirmanakaya mandala, the vital airs as the Sambhogakaya mandala, and tig-le as the Dharmakaya mandala. As *Guhyagarbha* says:

17. *rdo rje las rim.*

The miraculous cymbals of the wisdom of flawless
exaltation[18] are offered to deities
Who are always sustaining the enjoyment of the
wisdom of flawless exaltation.

The word *rol mo* means cymbals, but it can also have many other meanings, including any occurrence of wisdom mandala, whether in the aspect of form, sound, or thought, with positive energy.

As it is said, whether it is through the method of one's own body or the method of relying on the body of another who is a qualified consort on the path of developing empty bliss, offerings are made to the assembly of the deities of the mandala. According to the upadesha lineage of Mahasandhi,[19] *The Three Verses That Strike the Essence,*[20] the four ways of placement,[21] and other precious instructions on cutting through all substantial and insubstantial phenomena[22] establish the view of Dharmakaya enlightened wisdom. With the three postures[23] and the three ways of gazing, the qualities of the inner luminosity of the essence, nature, and compassion become outwardly clear as the actual appearance of enlightened body and purelands as limitless as the space of sky. By the practice of fully perfecting the qualities of the four visions, the inner luminosity abides again in the manner of the ever-youthful vase body, or arises as the body of the great transference into rainbow light.

In particular, Jigdral Yeshe Dorje, the emanation of Padmasambhava, the second Buddha of Oddiyana, explains in his enlightened mind revelation called *The Wisdom Heart Essence of the Dakini*[24] that the samaya of the vase empowerment of enlightened body, the outer yoga of form, is the support and supporting mandala of the mudra of enlightened form. The samaya of the secret empowerment of enlightened speech is the profound yoga of mantra, which has the practice of the completion stage with characteristics relying on the energy channels and vital airs. The samaya of the empowerment of the enlightened mind of prajna wisdom is the special yoga of bliss that has the practice of the path of heat and the mudra relying on the white and red essential nectars. The samaya of the empowerment of the

18. bde ba'i ye shes rol mo.
19. rdzogs pa chen po.
20. *tshig gsum gnad brdeg.*
21. cog bzhag rnam bzhi.
22. khregs chod.
23. The Dharmakaya posture, Sambhogakaya posture, and Nirmanakaya posture.
24. *mkha' 'gro'i thugs thig.*

precious absolute indication, the nature as it is, is the yoga of the absolute perfection of wisdom. By practicing the completion stage without characteristics, which is the path of cutting through to original purity and passing simultaneously to the direct clear light manifestation of Buddhas,[25] the enlightened great transference body of sublime exaltation is attained. Whatever the general and specific sadhana practices, whichever yoga one relies on, all of them without exception are only for developing the qualities of stainless great exaltation. Therefore, all those who accomplish this are **maha-yogis and -yoginis who are accomplishing great wisdom exaltation.**

Also, if a gathering of yogis and yoginis for tsok is a group of males, it is called a celebration of Dakas. If there is a gathering of females, it is called a celebration of Dakinis. If there is a gathering of yogis and yoginis together, it is therefore said to be supreme. For all of these, the practice that is done must be harmonious with the category of secret Mantrayana Dharma, and the samaya of all practitioners must be only pure. Therefore, from *The Stages of Vajra Activity:*

> A gathering of yogis and yoginis who are all harmonious
> Is called the assembly of yogis and yoginis.

Offering sublime great exaltation amrita. As it is said, the basis below is the mandala of wind. Upon that is the mandala of water. Upon that is the mandala of earth, which is the greatly powerful golden ground. These three supporting mandalas support mountains, continents, and oceans. Arising from the center of the great and powerful golden ground of the earth is the king of mountains, Mount Meru. In the four directions are the four continents. To the right and left of each great continent are two subcontinents, totaling eight. Encircling Mount Meru are seven rings of golden mountains, and between each of them are seven delightful lakes.

On the four levels of Mount Meru are the gods of the four kinds of great kings, and at the peak are the thirty-three levels of the gods who have power, like Indra. In the sky above Mount Meru are the sun, moon, planets, and constellations. Similarly, in space beyond Mount Meru are the abodes of the other four classes of gods from the six classes of the gods of desire, which are the abodes of the gods free from battle with the asuras; the gods always in joyfulness; the gods happy with miraculous activity; and the gods sustaining with the miraculous activity of others.[26]

25. thod rgal.
26. These abodes are 'thab bral, dga' ldan, 'phrul dga', and gzhan 'phrul dbang byed.

The first level of the god realm of samadhi is composed of three heavens. These are called the Group of the Pure, the Priests of Brahma, and the Great Pure Ones.[27] The heavens of Light, Measureless Light, and Clear Light are contained in the second level of the god realm of samadhi.[28] The heavens of Virtue, Limitless Virtue, and Flourishing Virtue are in the third level of the god realm of samadhi.[29] The heavens of Cloudlessness, Merit-Born, and Great Result are the three god realms of ordinary individuals.[30] Not Greater Than the God Realm of the Unafflicted, the Unafflicted, Having Abundant Phenomena, Excellent Vision, and the Unsurpassed are the five gods and places of the gods of the class of aryas.[31] Although not possessing an actual form, abiding in the state of formless samadhi is the realm of the four limitations of the sense sources.[32]

This description of the outer and inner universe and its contents is according to the metaphysical category of Abhidharma from the Sutra tradition of Buddhism, which is unlike ordinary nonspiritual descriptions of this world's geography. All sentient beings who are the inhabitants of these realms are subject to the habits of their positive and negative karma. For example, it is similar to the manner in which a dreamer will dream about the various appearances of the world and those within it. If the way the inhabitants of this world perceive the characteristics of their mutual planet were to be explained, there would still be individual descriptions of it as round, flat, various sizes, and so on. Even when using the example of a single substance of water, in the hells, water is fire. In the hungry ghost realm, it is blood and pus. For animals, it is a dwelling place. For sentient beings living on the earth, it is liquid to drink. For human beings, water is distributed over fields to ripen crops, and is also used for medicine, tea, liquor, and many other necessities. For the gods, water is nectar. All Buddhas see water as Dakini Mamaki, and so on. Each sees the same substance differently.

Those who have fallen to the extreme direction of nihilism believe in the view of the reality of existence, only accepting what appears to their own senses and is agreed on by other nihilists. They do not accept that this world and its contents have originated through the increasing strength of the

27. tshangs ris, tshangs pa mdun na 'don, and tshangs chen.
28. 'od chung, tshad med 'od, and 'od gsal.
29. dge chung, tshad med dge, and dge rgyas.
30. sprin med, bsod nams skyes, and 'bras bu che ba.
31. mi che ba, mi gdung ba, gya nom snang ba, shin tu mthong ba, and og min. One can read about these abodes in the sutras to know more about them.
32. skye mched mu bzhi.

habit of mind. They claim that all the substantial reality of this world happens by itself. Without following this, one has to follow the words of truth, the enlightened speech of the Greatest Sage Buddha. Then, there is the benefit of understanding the system of the phenomena of samsara and enlightenment according to the way it is.

Whatever the objective appearances of the five sense organs, however, such as exquisite objects seen by the eyes, pleasing sounds heard by the ears, delicious scents taken in by the nose, sweet tastes experienced by the tongue, soft sensations of touch, and so on, they are the appearance of the five desirable qualities of the senses.

Pure water is offered for the mouth, cleansing water is offered for the hands and feet, flowers are offered for the crown, incense is offered as fragrant smells for the nose, butter lamps are offered for the eyes, scented water is offered for the body, celestial food is offered for the tongue, and music is offered for the ears.

Furthermore, there are the eight auspicious substances, which are the medicinal yellow giwang pigment, the supreme grass durwa, bilwa fruit, the white conch that swirls to the right, red vermilion, white mustard seeds, the mirror, and yogurt. These eight auspicious substances are always used in offerings because, historically, many extraordinary beings made offerings of these substances when Buddha Shakyamuni attained the state of enlightenment.

The white parasol offered for the head, the golden fish for the eyes, the conch for the teeth, the lotus for the tongue, the vase for the neck, the unending knot for the heart, the victory banner for the body, and the wheel for the hands and feet are the eight auspicious symbols.

The precious wheel, the precious jewel, the precious queen, the precious minister, the precious elephant, the precious horse, the precious general: these seven precious offerings of the kingdom, and the great treasure vase, and so on, are the gathering of whatever and wherever perfectly complete substances exist in the three realms that are exceedingly pleasing to behold. These are the common outer offerings.

The uncommon inner offerings are the five kinds of meat, which include human, cow, horse, dog, and elephant meat.

To introduce the meaning of rakta, according to the essence, it is desire. According to substance, it is blood. According to color, it is red. So, in a brief way, whatever is red is a sign of the phenomena of rakta. According to beings in cyclic existence, rakta is the inherent blood of the egg of the mother. According to the basis of existence, it is the element water, or the root causes that settle the outer container of existence and the inner essence of beings, called mula rakta (root rakta). The great result heart blood rakta liberates cruel beings for the benefit of sentient beings. The rakta of the unchanging absolute nature is Amitabha, with immeasurable red light wisdom body. These are the five root raktas.

Also, the rakta of the sublime male consort's right nostril; the secret rakta of the sublime female consort's lotus; blood, which is attachment to existence; and the heart blood of the hero already slain in battle are the four inner root raktas.

The blood of wild animals such as tigers, leopards, and so on; the blood of winged animals such as birds and vultures; the blood of animals with hooves such as horses and mules; and the blood of cloven-hoofed animals such as yaks and others are the four outer root raktas. Together with the four inner root raktas, these make eight.

Along with these are vermilion and others, which are the five raktas of earth. Red sandalwood and others are the five raktas of wood. Rubies and others are the five raktas of stone. The red hollyhock and others are the five raktas of flowers. Ramoshag herb and others are the five raktas of medicine. Grapes and others are the five raktas of fruit. Resin and others are the five raktas of colors. Combined together, these are thirty-five. Furthermore, there are variations concerning these numbers and groupings of rakta taught in the inner tantras of secret mantra.

The amritas are Dharma amrita,[33] absolute amrita, sign amrita, precious substance amrita, and medicinal amrita. Of these five, the first three are naturally contained at the time of practice. The precious substance amrita includes excrement, urine, the white and red bodhichitta substances, and brain or marrow, which are the five basic amritas. The greatest enemy is conception, so in order to destroy conception, whatever is considered to be clean and dirty is made even. That is why these are offering substances, which are to reverse worldly conception. Medicinal amrita is dark red sandalwood, malaputra or manu (elecampane), cloves, juniper, saffron, nutmeg, crystal-like camphor, and cinnamon as the eight basic amritas. Or there are barley, rice, wheat, grapes, sprouts, stalks, branches, leaves, flowers, grains with husks, and so on, that are the basic amrita substances. Also, there are one thousand classes of nonpoisonous medicines. Whatever root sadhana one relies on, as just explained, these eight root and one thousand

33. chos kyi bdud rtsi.

branches possess the four ways to bring liberation through seeing, feeling, tasting, and touching.

The meaning of the word for amrita, *dütsi (bdud rtsi),* is that the demons (*bdud*) of the passions are transformed by the wisdom elixir (*rtsi*) of practice. When the passions that are the root cause of samsara's suffering arise as enlightened body and purelands of great exaltation, this is called wisdom elixir.

Torma[34] is made with the main ingredient of flour from barley, wheat, or other grains mixed with the fine powders of pure medicinal amrita, the medicine of the essence of liquor made of wheat, rice, or whatever is available in the country where one resides, the three white substances of milk, cheese, and yogurt, the three sweet substances of honey, molasses, and sugar, amrita Dharma medicines,[35] and others, which are used to make the individual tormas of the Three Roots, or one torma that represents the synthesis of one hundred deities. These substances or whatever is available can be used for making torma according to one's capacity. The base of the accomplishment torma is the celestial palace. The glorious torma itself is visualized as the assembly of deities of the Three Roots. The offering torma is made in the same shape as the accomplishment torma and placed in front of oneself as the visualized support for immeasurable offerings. At the time of reciting the words of offering in the sadhana, it is sprinkled with offerings of medicine and rakta.

If one intends to entreat wrathful miraculous activity, then the torma is made in the shape of the heart of the rudra surrounded by a retinue,[36] meat, blood, entrails, and other similar substances that adorn it. Likewise, the torma container is visualized as a triangular box, [37] and the torma as the aspect of weapons, surrounded by a retinue of butchers holding knives. The use of wrathful enlightened activity, relying on a wrathful torma, and using wrathful means directed toward the defilements and bad karma of sentient beings in order to liberate them from suffering are special exceptions that are necessary and important during the lower activity of liberating enemies and obstructing forces, only for the benefit of others and never for one's own power. This activity is not to be carried out as a regular practice for any other reason. In order to clean one's own fear, paranoia, and any negativity, this

34. gtor ma.
35. bdud rtsi chos sman.
36. The retinue is represented by small rectangular tormas.
37. hom: a triangular box used for performing wrathful activities.

method of transforming negative energy to positive comes from inner tantric teachings. It has nothing to do with anything in reality. Whoever practices this has to realize that all phenomena are like magic, like a magician who displays magic without believing it is true or that it exists in reality, in order to annihilate reality. It is the practice of transforming one's own previous reality paranoia and negative feeling into wisdom manifestation. New practitioners must understand this; otherwise, from thinking of reality, they can cause misconceptions about tantric teachings. Murders and killing can continuously be seen in reality, and people are interested in watching these on television without any point of view. These precious teachings are not like that, but are to transform negative habit into positive through many skillful means, with point of view, meditation, and activities.

According to the situation of practitioners, due to the greatness of the methods of secret mantra, a single torma at the time of practice is visualized as the deity. At the time of offering, the torma is visualized as all limitless desirable offerings. When receiving spiritual blessings, the torma is visualized as wisdom nectar. In order to reverse forces bringing harm to the teachings of Buddha or sentient beings, the torma is visualized as a magic weapon[38] with great compassion. Of these four ways of understanding the torma, by relying on whichever is the most important support according to circumstances, the purpose will be accomplished.

If one is primarily practicing a sadhana of the extremely vast Mahayoga tantra, then the torma is blessed by relying on the three samadhis. The vessel is visualized as an exceedingly huge skull. Within this are the five meats, the five nectars, and so on, blessed as inconceivable clouds of offerings.

In general, these offerings are neither liked nor disliked by wisdom deities. The significance of these offerings is related to practitioners, who have clean and unclean phenomena from many lives' dualistic habit, so especially if one attains a precious human body, one has more of these dualistic habits with the contradiction of acceptance and rejection because the mind is clearer than in other realms. The five meats and five nectars that are mentioned in inner tantric offerings are objects of rejection, and so in order to change rejection into acceptance, to clean dualistic habit, these kinds of inner offerings occur so negative conception is transformed into positive phenomena.

Buddha's teaching is inconceivably vast. Even though Buddha does not need to teach anything, because Buddha is fully enlightened beyond conception,

38. zor.

beings have different karmic phenomena, so Buddha taught different skillful means for different beings from different vehicles. For example, in the Hinayana, women have to be seen as having nine disgusting attributes in order not to cause the attachment of samsara, to liberate beings to the state of nirvana. All offerings must be considered pure by general human beings, such as clean water for baptism and for drinking, flowers, perfume and incense for the nose, light for the eyes, clean vegetarian food for the tongue, and the sweet sound of music for the ears. In the Mahayana, all phenomena, including women, are magic manifestation, so whatever arises is not reality, and any kind of offerings are like magic. According to inner Vajrayana, phenomena are not seen just as magic phenomena; one is supposed to think of deity and deity phenomena, including all female deities, as the aspect of emptiness wisdom. Always stainless form appears as the manifestation of beauty, and thus one sees any female human beings as wisdom Dakinis. There is no ordinary woman to abstain from until ordinary reality phenomena are transformed to the state of the five Buddha families. Any phenomenon is the manifestation of stainless shunyata, which is the origin of empty wisdom Dakinis, who are its supreme form. So forever, up to enlightenment, women are worshipable. This is the samaya of inner Vajrayana. Likewise, in the many practices from any doctrine below Atiyoga, no matter what kind, the actual characteristic of their theories is:

> Conception is cleaned by conception.

At the time of practicing the profound completion stage Anuyoga with characteristics, it says in *Wisdom Sphere of Oneness:*[39]

> The syllable BHA is the bhaga.
> The syllable LING is the linga.

As said, from the outer point of view, this is the union of the method of phenomena and its emptiness wisdom. From the inner point of view, the male and female white and red nectars gather and join in order to increase and expand flawless wisdom exaltation. From the secret point of view, they are the indivisibility of dharmadhatu and wisdom, as the great wisdom of indivisible great emptiness and wisdom exaltation. Then, from its self-manifestation, the outer container of the elements and inner essence of beings are viewed as torma and

39. *ye shes thig le.*

blessed to become the mandala of deities. From the natural blessing of the torma, all phenomena become absolute wisdom pureland and deities for great yogis and yoginis, so it is called mahabalingta.

Also, in the past, in order for the Great Glorious One(dpal chen po) to slay and liberate the rudra of existence in the place where all wrathful Dakinis gather, he performed the enlightened activity of union. This also is said to be the first teaching of secret mantra, from which it flourished.

> On the peak of the meteorite mountain Malaya,
> The male demon Matram Rudra was annihilated and liberated.
> By performing union with all the wrathful female rakshas,
> The doctrine of secret mantra first occurred.

Thus it is said. In brief, the rudra of the view of self is liberated with the wisdom weapon of selflessness. In the place that is the source of bliss, the bhaga of the vajra queen of great bliss, perfectly sublime great exaltation unites with the stainless sky of dharmadhatu as the offering of union and liberation. Since medicine, rakta, torma, and so on, are the inner offerings of secret mantra, it is not even necessary to say that they are the best offerings to be made by those with keen faculties who have achieved stability in the visualization and completion stage practices, and who have open, vast minds. Even if that is not so, for those who have the karmic connection and gifted minds to have faith in Mantrayana, this practice is suitable. For all those with dull faculties whose minds are small and who curse and slander the tradition of the vehicle of result based on their own wrong material reality point of view, it is necessary to keep this secret so they do not harm themselves through misinterpretation.

Followers of other religions often illogically criticize inner Vajrayana traditions. This criticism does not come from the insight of awakened intelligence, but from excessive sectarianism. It is also generally irrelevant because it is based on misconception and its misinterpretation. For those who want to understand Buddhism clearly, it is necessary to study the Buddhist points of view taught in the Hinayana, Mahayana, and Vajrayana according to their own choice. Whoever studies Buddhism in the right way will not find any faults to criticize, but only the benefit of its great skillful teachings for attaining enlightenment.

It is also unnecessary for followers of the causal yana to misinterpret inner Vajrayana practices, thinking they are wrong. If they truly have faith in Buddha, they should consider the kind of Bodhisattva activity described in causal yana histories that tell how, before enlightenment, the Buddha manifested as Bodhisattvas. These manifestations were sometimes in the form of someone poor, sometimes in the form of a wealthy king or queen, sometimes wrathful, and sometimes lustful, with whatever aspects and activities were necessary to connect with beings according to their faculty and energy in order to guide them. For example, in one well-known history, Buddha manifested as a Bodhisattva in the form of a sea captain who killed a cruel being to prevent him from killing five hundred merchants on his ship who were actually Bodhisattvas. He performed this wrathful activity thinking that if the cruel being killed the precious Bodhisattvas, he would spend many eons in hell. By annihilating him, he saved the cruel being from making negative karma and enduring its results, and the five hundred Bodhisattvas were able to remain to benefit sentient beings.

People worship their gods in different ways according to different traditions, with offerings of different substances such as grains, flowers, fruits, herbs, and incense. In some non-Buddhist traditions, blood and meat are used for offerings, which sometimes require the sacrifice of animals or even the sacrifice of human beings.

Christians receive the substances used in communion with pure perception and devotion. They drink red wine considering it to be the blood of Christ and eat bread considering it to be the body of Christ. As Jesus said, "This is my body; this is my blood." Otherwise, if they did not change their perceptions, whatever they were eating and drinking would be just another snack.

Many eternalist religions have traditions in which substances are blessed and transformed, but even if people do not worship in this way, they normally eat meat without guilt or compassion for the animal. Of course, nihilists do not have the phenomena of gods, but they still unhesitatingly eat meat and drink alcohol for only temporary pleasure, without even one conception of offering to gods or being generous for the benefit of beings. Therefore, when those who are not Buddhists see that there are wine or meat offerings in the traditions of inner Vajrayana practices, it is not necessary for them to judge these traditions from either their nihilist or eternalist non-Buddhist points of view by misconceiving that these offerings are something terrible.

When offerings of meat, red liquids that are a substitute for blood, or other such substances are mentioned in inner Vajrayana sadhanas, it does not mean that anyone is being instructed to slaughter other beings for these substances as those in some other religions sacrifice animals or even human lives. If everyone is honest, they know that for many years until now, people in the same religion kill each other over theoretical disagreements, and people of one religion sacrifice people of different religions. In inner Vajrayana, only the meat of animals that have already been slaughtered without any intention by the practitioner to slaughter them or eat their meat, or the meat of animals that have died as a result of their karmic circumstances, can be used as offerings, which are made for the benefit of the animals themselves as well as for the benefit of all sentient beings. These substances are never obtained through ordering animals to be killed.

Another aspect of inner Vajrayana practice that is frequently misunderstood is the practice of union with a consort. The meaning of Buddhas in union with their consorts is also misunderstood. Beings have extremely contradictory minds. Although everyone likes sex, and whatever expression of sexuality is possible can be found, this precious method of inner Vajrayana, which is natural, and especially which is practiced with a vast point of view and pure intention, which is not illegal, and which is a self-secret inconceivable offering, is thought of as something wrong. Is that not ridiculous? It is extremely unnecessary to misinterpret this. The female consort is actually the manifestation of the empty exaltation of wisdom mind, and the male consort is actually the manifestation of the method of skillful means. The meaning of union is to abide in substanceless nondualistic wisdom, which is named the consort, because it does not cause any samsaric suffering. It does not cause suffering because it does not involve ego. This is called exaltation because emptiness has no conceptualization of substance. Since there is no substance, it does not cause any passions, emotions, or karma, so there are no defilements. Therefore, it is always naturally peace. That is exaltation. In order to abide in that state until fully flawless exaltation is attained, without relying on material energy, one must practice with suitable energy and doubtless faith in wisdom deity, with the correct skillful means according to the path, which is symbolized by the male aspect of method in union with the female aspect of wisdom, the Dakini. Union with a consort is practiced in order to develop the inconceivable secret wisdom Dakini of flawless empty exaltation. Actually accomplishing this depends on the perfect characteristics of the karma mudra Dakini. It does not say in any tantric texts that union can be mispracticed by just using its name.

Those who do not have the capacity to practice in this way because of their ordinary habits accumulated over many lives should not engage in it.

This practice includes extensive visualizations and depends on the capacity and point of view of the practitioner. For example, the linga is seen by inner Vajrayana practitioners as the vajra, which is the indestructibility of enlightenment. However, it is rudra[40] when negative thoughts become reality due to the evil projections of ego being expressed outwardly, which causes suffering without reason.

Sometimes there are signs seen in modern life of this kind of rudra, which misleads beings and results in destruction. For example, when one author's novel filled with his own negative thoughts and projections of a fictional bombing disaster inspired other confused and deranged people who read the book to act out these fictional negative phenomena in reality, the result was that many innocent people were actually harmed. This kind of rudra mind has to be transformed.

All rudras come from beings' attachment to ego, or self, that tries to be self-victorious in the material world, which is the root of all harm and must be annihilated through realization. Then, all harmful phenomena can be purified. In some inner Vajrayana practices, the form of the linga is used as a substitute for the rudra of ego, which is the root cause of all suffering. It is often explained in Buddhism that ordinary ego, which is the cause of samsaric attachment, must be annihilated through the realization of wisdom awareness, so even if many linga are used to represent the enemies of enlightenment, it does not mean these forms are actual enemies or that it is necessary to actually harm anything. This kind of misconception is only the result of the habit and capacity of an individual's mind.

One's own ego is annihilated only through realization and practice. Because samsara is created through attachment to ego, when ego that is the root of suffering is annihilated, samsara is annihilated. The annihilation of samsara is symbolized by drinking the blood of samsara until samsaric suffering is emptied. One becomes Heruka, the one who drinks the blood of suffering, which in Tibetan is called Tragtung *(khrag 'thung).*

If, due to time and place, one is unable to practice using the five meats, five nectars, rakta, and so on, in place of medicine one may use amrita Dharma medicine that has been accomplished by a wisdom-realized Lama. In place of rakta one may use sindhura[41] or blend deep red coloring with Dharma medicine and mix that together with pure water. As a substitute

40. Demon.

41. A nonpoisonous red pigment from special earth, the seashore, or pure trees, or saffron from the pistils of flowers.

for the liquor of the gathering, one may mix Dharma medicine with pure water and, with the purest intention according to the words of the sadhana, make the offering with clear visualization. In this way, all aims will be fulfilled. Also, by arranging a variety of gathering substances such as fruits and many different foods, drinks, and so on, with all outer, inner, and secret offerings, everything is blessed by the manifestation of all form as wisdom deity, all sound as mantra, and all thought as dharmata, or the pure essential nature. This is **offering sublime great exaltation amrita**. Thus it is said. From *The Stages of Vajra Activity:*

> All wealth is perfectly contained.
> That is called the wealth of ecstasy of the great assembly.

This speech is in accord with the root text.

Illuminating clouds of wondrous great exaltation. In this way, the offerings of outer, inner, and secret sacred substances are all blessed by wisdom deity. All practitioners receiving the qualities of the pure uncontrived state who practice the two stages of supreme secret mantra correctly and have achieved the depth of confidence have only stainless perception as the source of appearances. The aspects of appearances are extremely vast, like clouds gathering in the sky. Their essence is natural great exaltation, like the clouds of offerings of Kuntuzangpo, beyond the intellectualizing mind of ordinary individuals, so it is the awe of wondrous qualities being offered, illuminating clouds of wondrous great exaltation. Thus it is said.

Great exaltation queen, Yeshe Tsogyal, and your gathering of Dakinis. As this says, the natural state of the Dakini is perfectly pure from the beginning. In the inconceivable space of dharmadhatu, the qualities of wisdom awareness are great exaltation's natural expression of all unobstructed emanations, which are dharmata. Therefore, all phenomena within samsara and enlightenment arise as the appearance of bliss, so that everything equal to the sphere of limitless space occurs from the five consorts of space of the magical dance of the manifestation of the wisdom of great exaltation wisdom Dakinis. The teachings of secret Mantrayana flourished originally in Oddiyana,[42] and then

42. In general, historically at that time, Oddiyana is considered to have been in Swat Valley, but actually this cannot be materialized. Wherever sublime beings taught and fortunate disciples practiced Vajrayana teachings and had attainment has the secret nature of a secret holy place, so wherever Vajrayana teachings flourish can be called, according to time, Oddiyana. For example, some sublime beings have sometimes called Tibet the country of Oddiyana.

in the second Oddiyana, Tibet, the place where the embodiment of all wisdom Dakinis and all their qualities of wisdom manifested, the queen of all Dakinis, Yeshe Tsogyal. Since she is always surrounded by an inconceivable retinue sustaining in her self-display, **Great exaltation queen, Yeshe Tsogyal, and your gathering of Dakinis, may your great exaltation wisdom Dharmakaya mind be fulfilled.**

Here, it is necessary to understand that to fulfill the unconditioned wishes of Yeshe Tsogyal is to have the intention to accomplish anything that pleases her great exaltation wisdom Dharmakaya mind, in order to please all beings. According to the actual nature of the perfectly pure absolute truth of dharmata, as Omniscient Rongzompa said:

> Since enlightened mind has no root or contributing circumstances, the essence is never born and never ceases.
> In the unborn, unceasing nature, there is no place for conceptions to arise, so there is nothing to be wished.

Thus it is said. Therefore, the enlightened minds of nondual wisdom of all Buddhas are completely fulfilled. It is not as though one were making an ordinary individual happy, but if we consider undeniable interdependent phenomena, then as Rigdzin Jigme Lingpa said:

> Whatever is beneficial for sentient beings is beneficial for the Victorious Ones.
> Whatever harms sentient beings is harmful for the Victorious Ones.
> So, the happiness and suffering of myself and all sentient beings are evenly the same, as the Victorious Ones said.
> By the truth of the purification and realization of the Victorious Ones, may all these beings be protected.

As said, the method of completely fulfilling the Buddhas' heirs, male and female Bodhisattvas, and others will only benefit all sentient beings. Pleasing the enlightened minds of Buddhas relies on the teachings of Buddha flourishing. Therefore, in order to benefit all sentient beings in the present and future, to serve the precious teachings of Buddha in general and the teachings of the clear light Great Perfection in particular, to make the teachings flourish perfectly will fulfill the unconditioned wishes of the enlightened mind of the wisdom Dakini Yeshe Tsogyal in the space of flawless great exaltation. So, the verses say, **May your great exaltation wisdom Dharmakaya mind be fulfilled.**

All-pervading lord, essence of all Buddha families, holder of unchangeable boundless light, Buddha Amitabha, may your unconditioned wishes be fulfilled. As said, in general, all Buddhas have perfectly purified the two obscurations of passions and cognition, including all residual habit, so therefore it is great Dharmakaya. This is not like ordinary sentient beings with passions, karma, male and female, races, ancestors, good and bad, and so on. None of these exist for Buddhas. So therefore, it is said:

> Do not look for a form or characteristic of Buddha.
> Also, do not analyze Buddha by caste, nature, or language.
> This will not become nihilist.
> Also, Buddha is not differentiated by mind and the consciousness of mind.
> Whatever is dharmata, that is Buddha.

Thus it is said. Therefore, "This will not become nihilist" means that vast accumulations of merit are perfected from the beginning. All Rupakaya is the immeasurable appearances of enlightened body and purelands, revealed through the blessing of unobstructed compassion. As said:

> By skillful means of compassion, you were born in the lineage of the Shakyas.
> Always triumphant over others, annihilating demonic forces.
> With a splendid, enlightened body like a mountain of gold,
> King of the Shakyas, Buddha Shakyamuni, at your feet, I make offerings.

Thus, as this quote shows, of the four castes of humans in ancient India, in this case, at that time the Shakya race was considered supreme because of their sublime and noble qualities. So, through the five states of omniscience, Buddha took birth in the family of the kings of Shakya. According to the story of his life, he then performed twelve miraculous deeds for the benefit of sentient beings. Also, the Dharma king, Orgyen, was born from the womb, as well as his wondrous birth from the bud of a lotus, unstained by the womb. According to the faculties and wishes of beings to be subdued, he took rebirth as one enlightened body and eight manifestations with eight names. With twenty emanations and more, his ability to accomplish the benefit of beings was inconceivable. In all directions, times, and situations, there have been and will continue to be immeasurable Nirmanakaya Buddhas. All these Nirmanakaya Buddhas originate from the appearances of the five Sambhogakaya Buddha families' enlightened body and purelands as pervasive as the space of sky. Thus, inconceivable appearances of Sambhogakaya enlightened body and purelands all have as their basis the one who abides in the space of Dharmakaya as the holder of pervasive enlightened qualities of all Buddha families, the protector of unchanging pure appearances of light, Buddha Amitabha.[43]

In general, phenomena mean that the nature of mind is unobstructed. Based on that, according to ordinary sentient beings and practitioners who are engaged on the path of enlightenment, there are self-appearances and other-appearances. There are also distinctions of appearances, the objects of appearances, and so on. Self-appearances are not the common manifesting objective appearances of the outer elements and inner essence of beings, waking and dream appearances of happiness, suffering, and so on, but are anything that appears from the self to the self. Objective appearances are all the temporarily arising common projections of the outer elements and inner essence of beings, happiness, suffering, and so on.

To sentient beings with ordinary deluded mind, appearances are reversed, and also the way of seeing is reversed, which comes from thinking that all phenomena truly exist in reality. Like this, children see a circling torch as a wheel of fire.

To practitioners, appearances are reversed, but the way of seeing is not reversed, which comes from recognizing that all phenomena are unreal and like magic, without true existence. Like this, the wise see a circling torch as what it is.

Whatever the case, to synthesize a description of all appearances into three categories, there are the impure appearances of sentient beings, the appearances of the experience of yogis and yoginis, and the stainless appearances of Buddhas. The reason that the impure appearances of sentient beings occur is by not abandoning ignorance, which becomes the cause perpetuating the appearances of passions, karma, and the suffering of samsara. The reason that the appearances of the experience of practice of yogis and yoginis occur is that by the power of practicing on the path, the habits of mind arise as various visions that are good, bad, variable, and diverse. This is sometimes called the experience of pure worldly wisdom because previous karmic residual habit is not completely purified, which is called worldly, and phenomena that excel beyond that of ordinary beings arise,

43. snang ba mtha' yas (Nangwa Thaye).

which are called pure. If the practitioner has realized pure awareness, then the power of the appearance of the experiences of bliss, clarity, and conceptionlessness will arise free from grasping. Buddha has only pure phenomena. As Panchen Vimalamitra said:

> Having cleansed the stain of dualistic phenomena and having expanded nondualistic wisdom is Buddha.

As said, the appearances of enlightened body and great wisdom free from obscurations always abide in all-encompassing space that is free from decreasing and increasing throughout the three times. For that reason, here in this state, there is only the power of pure appearance, Buddha Amitabha, or Nangwa Thaye, Limitless Wisdom Phenomena. Generally, to fulfill his unconditioned wishes, actual and visualized inconceivable clouds of offerings are presented. Specifically, in the three states of being, which are being Kuntuzangpo, being Kuntuzangmo, and being indivisible, his unconditioned wishes are completely fulfilled by perfectly realizing the enlightened mind of these three states of being. The three states of being are, as Omniscient Rongzompa revealed according to supreme upadesha:

> Whatever appearance arises is conquered in the manifestation of Kuntuzangpo, so therefore it is called being Kuntuzangpo. Although everything appears, a self-essence does not exist anywhere. It is not changing because it is stainless forever and never causes defilements, so therefore it is called being Kuntuzangmo. Two separate characteristics do not exist, so therefore the nature of appearances is unborn. The unborn nature itself arises as various appearances, so therefore it is the unceasing blessing of compassion.

Thus it is said.

Treasure of compassion who subdues all beings, Avalokiteshvara, may your unconditioned wishes be fulfilled. As said, in the tradition of unsurpassed inner secret mantra, according to the natural expression of the unconditioned great loving-kindness of all Buddhas, in the Akanishtha pureland of the Sambhogakaya, the five Buddha families who are the manifestations of Buddha are inseparable with the enlightened awareness of the way in which the Bodhisattvas who have attained the result abide. In this world, the southern continent, with one hundred million realms, for Bodhisattvas who abide up to the tenth level and have compassion that has an object, the illness of the Bodhisattva's compassion will not be cured until the illness of the passions of all sentient beings is finally cured.

As it is said, with the loving-kindness a mother feels toward her only child directed toward all suffering sentient beings, until the three realms of samsara are empty and with miraculous activity that subdues beings in whatever way is necessary, the Bodhisattva's vow endures as a mighty treasure of great compassion. To Avalokiteshvara, the one whose eyes see without partiality, in order to fulfill your unconditioned supremely vast wisdom, in general, may your unconditioned wishes be fulfilled through actually arranged offerings as well as offerings emanated from mind. In particular, may your unconditioned wishes be fulfilled through the offering of the four boundless wishes, the six perfections,[44] and especially by realizing the meaning of emptiness as the essence of compassion.

Conqueror of all samsara and enlightenment who wears a rosary of bone ornaments, Supreme Victorious Lotus Dancer, Padmasambhava, may your unconditioned wisdom heart be fulfilled. Thus, the meaning of this is mentioned by the actual manifestation of Orgyen Padmasambhava, the fearless Vajra Master Düdjom Yeshe Dorje, whose mind revelations include both cycles of the practice sadhanas of yab and yum.[45] The sadhana for the yab includes the four cycles of outer, inner, secret, and essential practices. In the historical scriptural prophecies of the essential cycle of *The Wrathful Compassion of Guru Dorje Drolö*,[46] it says:

> The Nirmanakaya manifestation of Amitabha, I,
> the Indian scholar, the Lotus-Born,
> From the self-blossoming center of a lotus,
> Came to this realm of existence through miraculous powers
> To be the prince of the king of Oddiyana.
> Then, I sustained the kingdom in accordance with Dharma.
> Wandering throughout all directions of India,
> I severed all spiritual doubts without exception.
> Engaging in fearless activity in the eight charnel grounds,

44. As mentioned in the *Düdjom Tersar Ngöndro* commentary, where the four boundless wishes and six paramitas are explained. See the section "Developing Bodhichitta," p.68.
45. Guru and consort.
46. *thugs rje khros pa gu ru rdo rje gro lod.*

I achieved all supreme and common siddhis.
Then, according to the wishes of King Trisong Detsen
And by the power of previous prayers, I journeyed to Tibet.
By subduing the cruel gods, nagas, yakshas, rakshas,
and all spirits who harm beings,
The light of the teachings of secret mantra has been illuminated.
Then, when the time came to depart for the continent of Lanka,
I did so to provide refuge from the fear of rakshas
For all the inhabitants of this world, including Tibet.
I blessed Nirmanakaya emanations to be representatives of my body.
I made sacred treasures as representatives of my holy speech.
I poured enlightened wisdom into the hearts of those
with fortunate karma.
Until samsara is emptied, for the benefit of sentient beings,
I will manifest unceasingly in whatever ways are necessary.
Through profound kindness, I have brought great benefit for all.
If you who are fortunate have the mind of aspiration,
May you pray so that blessings will be received.
All followers, believe in me with determination.
Samaya.

Thus he spoke, and accordingly, from the heart of Buddha Amitabha,[47] light rays of compassion went into the northwestern Dakini land of Orgyen. On the island in Lake Dhanakosha, manifesting upon a lotus, he[48] was born as instantaneous pure awareness. He became the son of Indrabodhi, the king of Orgyen, and learned the ocean of outer and inner doctrines.[49] Abandoning his kingdom, in the eight charnel grounds, he performed fearless activity. He is a fully enlightened Buddha of the two purities who did not need to depend on the path of training to accumulate and purify. Through omniscience, he knew what was necessary for future followers and revealed the way to accomplish common and supreme siddhi. With the dance of compassionate wrath, he annihilated[50] all demons and malevolent spirits, making them his

47. rgyal ba 'od mtshan stong 'bar (Gyalwa Ö Tsen Tong Bar), Buddha Flaming with Thousands of Light Signs. In general, *stong* means a thousand, but it is unnecessary to think that *stong* means only a thousand; it is just used poetically. As one of the names of Amitabha, it is like Nangwa Thaye, which is Boundless Enlightened Phenomena.
48. The Lotus-Born.
49. Non-Buddhist and Buddhist doctrines.
50. Guru Rinpoche annihilated their negative habit and opened their Buddha nature.

followers. In order to fulfill the enlightened wishes of King Trisong Detsen of Tibet, he placed his lotus feet on the land of Tibet and stayed there to build the glorious Akanishtha Wheel of Dharma Beyond Conception, the supreme temple of Samye, and established the traditions of scholarship and accomplishment. His many fortunate disciples included the nine heart sons, the twenty-five sublime disciples, and countless others, all of whom were placed in the kingdom of the union of Vajradhara. Incalculable beings were placed on the great secret path that ripens and liberates.

In essence, in the one hundred million continents of this world system, there are one hundred million manifestations of Orgyen Padma Jungne.[51] He subdues beings according to their faculties through his great merit enlightened body. He subdues beings through his enlightened speech. He subdues beings through his pure awareness mind. He subdues beings through inconceivable miraculous activities. In these four ways of subduing, he blesses beings by placing them in a high-realm body to go from high realms to high realms in order to attain enlightenment. He reveals the path of enlightenment and blesses beings with the result of enlightenment. It is as it says:

51. Padma Jungne is one of the names of Guru Rinpoche, as are Padmakara and Padmasambhava. Some people acknowledge Padmasambhava, who cannot be denied because of historical accounts, but not Guru Rinpoche, which is due to sectarian jealousy. Also, at the time of Padmasambhava, the garments worn by Padmasambhava were those of scholars and monks. Sometimes intellectual scholars and learned ones who are still attached about material aspects of form think that Padma Jungne, who does not wear these same garments, is different from Padmasambhava. Historically, at the time when Buddhism flourished in Tibet with enlightened beings such as Guru Rinpoche and Vimalamitra, some scholars in Indian institutes became jealous and spread much slander in order to cause disturbance by claiming these enlightened beings were not actual saints but phony siddhas, attempting to prevent Vajrayana teachings from flourishing in Tibet. However, in the general Mahayana, and especially in the Vajrayana, the state of enlightenment is the Three Kayas: the Dharmakaya, Sambhogakaya, and Nirmanakaya. Sambhogakaya is always abiding in pure Akanishtha Heaven, the state of fully enlightened Buddhas' phenomena. From that state, in order to benefit beings with many varieties of faculties, Nirmanakaya manifests. The meaning of Nirmanakaya is that there is no reality of birth or death because mind is only wisdom, but Nirmanakaya's aspect can reflect anything according to beings' impure and pure phenomena in order to guide them. So, the aspect of manifestation can reflect anything according to various beings' faculties. There is not an iota of contradiction about the infinite aspects of sublime beings for those who believe in the Mahayana or the Vajrayana; these aspects are just one's choice. Those who follow Guru Rinpoche's teachings pray to Guru Rinpoche with many different names, such as the names given in the Eight Manifestations and in the Barche Lamsel prayer, including Pema Jungne, Tsokye Dorje, and Sangchen Dorje Drakpo Tsal. There are many more manifestations and special names beyond these. Countless manifestations logically exist according to even ordinary beings' phenomena, so different aspects cannot be denied or prevented.

In one particle, there are immeasurable particles with
inconceivable Buddhas and purelands.

Orgyen Padmasambhava is free from being single or many. In all the purelands of the Buddhas, he abides in one taste with the totality of their enlightened awareness. From that unceasing nature and until the realms of beings are emptied, his activity of subduing the objects to be subdued is unsurpassed in place and time.

The meaning of all families of Buddhas can be synthesized into enlightened body, Buddha Vairochana of the Tathagata family; enlightened speech, Buddha Amitabha of the Padma family; enlightened mind, Buddha Akshobhya of the Vajra family; enlightened qualities, Buddha Ratnasambhava of the Ratna family; and enlightened activity, Buddha Amoghasiddhi of the Karma family. The five families and the qualities of their enlightened bodies and purelands are represented by the central Buddha Thötreng Tsal. To the east is Vajra Thötreng Tsal. To the south is Ratna Thötreng Tsal. To the west is Padma Thötreng Tsal. To the north is Karma Thötreng Tsal. The self-manifesting appearance of all enlightened embodiments and purelands synthesized as the nature of self-freedom is the **Conqueror of all samsara and enlightenment who wears a rosary of bone ornaments, Supreme Victorious Lotus Dancer, Padmasambhava, may your unconditioned widom heart be fulfilled.**

Thus as said, as Dharmakaya, the Victorious Wisdom Dancer of the Lotus Family is Amitabha, Limitless Light. As Sambhogakaya, the wrathful manifestation of the compassion of Amitabha appears as Hayagriva and others. As the peaceful manifestation, he is Avalokiteshvara. As Nirmanakaya, he is the pith of one hundred Buddha families contained within the sole wisdom body of the exalted great Orgyen Padmasambhava. An inexhaustible sky treasure of actual and emanated offerings is naturally offered. May the general teachings of all Buddhas, the specific teachings of Vajrayana, and in particular the unsurpassed clear light Mahasandhi teachings flourish according to the pure unconditioned wishes of the enlightened awareness of Guru Rinpoche. By myself and all those who are your followers perfectly accomplishing that which is natural flawless great exaltation, may your wishes be fulfilled!

Supreme queen consort of the mandala, abiding in Dharmakaya, Victorious Ocean of Wisdom, Yeshe Tsogyal, may your unconditioned wishes be fulfilled.

It is not possible to use the great element sky as an example of being like this or like that because it is aspectless, but still, the sky is the basis of all other elements. Likewise, in the space of Dharmakaya is the great Dharmakaya prajnaparamita Dakini, Yeshe Tsogyal, whose aspect cannot be shown because it is stainless Dharmakaya but abides as the absolute basis of all countless mandalas of Buddhas. Aspectless Dharmakaya is the unobscured continuity of great emptiness. The aspects of all Buddhas are coming from that state, going to that state, and abiding in that state, so therefore it is the origin of all Buddhas, like sky. That is why in Dharmakaya, Yeshe Tsogyal is the supreme great wisdom mother, Kuntuzangmo, the absolute source of all mandalas of Buddhas.

Likewise, in the space of Sambhogakaya, Vajra Varahi and others represent the Dakinis of the five families and their mandalas as innumerable as particles. Yeshe Tsogyal abides as the sublime queen with luminous wisdom body, wisdom speech, wisdom mind, wisdom qualities, and wisdom activities, perfectly, forever.

Yeshe Tsogyal abides in the principal Nirmanakaya purelands and, in particular, in the western land of Oddiyana, in Pulliramala, in Ahbhuda, in Dzalandhara, in Dewikotra, in Malawa, in Rameishara, and in Godawari, which are the eight sacred places of the space activity mandala of enlightened mind; in Kalingka, Omtriya, Trishakuni, Kamarupa, Kosala, Lampaka, Kansika, and Himalaya, which are Tsandho and Nyewai Tsandho,[52] and are the eight sacred places of the mandala of enlightened speech; and in Sorakyatra, Grihadewa, Pretapuri, Suwanadipa, which are Duwa and Nyewai Duwa,[53] and in Sindhu, Kuluta, Nagara, and Maru, which are Thungchö and Nyewai Thungchö,[54] and are the eight sacred places of the mandala of enlightened body. In total, these are the twenty-four sacred places. To categorize them in terms of sacred places, six of them are sacred places of activity, fourteen are sacred places of sustaining experience, eight are sacred places sustaining samaya, and four are sacred places of cultivating longing desire. These are the thirty-two sacred places, and so on, which include the eight great charnel grounds.

Wherever a realm exists where the Nirmanakaya is subduing beings, in that particular world system, each of the sentient beings residing there has various individual perceptions based on karma. Like the dissimilarities in the teachings found in the Abhidharma as opposed to the Kalachakra, although there are these holy places and lands, since the channels and elements of the

52. tshan dho and nye ba'i tshan dho.
53. 'du ba and nye ba'i 'du ba, Assembly and Occasional Assembly.
54. 'thung spyod and nye ba'i 'thung spyod.

inner vajra body are different, it is said that the external appearance of the reflection will also be different. This cannot be certain or only one way, like numbers. Those who follow the philosophies and ideologies of nihilistic views about the world do not need to define this as a contradiction.

A place where all Dakas and Dakinis continuously reside is called a holy place.[55] A place where they abide sometimes is called an occasional holy place. A place where desirable qualities are always unceasingly used and enjoyed is called a land.[56] A place where desirable qualities are sometimes enjoyed is called an occasional land. A place where there is constant purification is called a place of continual cleansing,[57] and a place where there is sometimes purification is called a place of occasional cleansing.[58] A place where there is always unceasing activity of conversing in the secret teachings of the holy Dharma of the Dakinis is called a gathering,[59] and a place where there is sometimes the activity of conversing in the secret teachings of the holy Dharma is called an occasional gathering.

The eight great charnel grounds are the great charnel ground of Cool Grove[60] in Magadhaya of the east, Lotus Arrangement[61] in Oddiyana, Expanse of the Cuckoo[62] in the land of Zahor, Perfected in Form[63] in the land of Sen-ge, Play of Great Joy[64] in the land of Persia, Yamakha[65] in the land of Nepal, Display of the Great Secret[66] in the land of Thogar,[67] and Actual Perfection of the World[68] in the land of Li. These are the eight great charnel grounds. This is mentioned in *The Synthesis of the Great Glorious One*.[69] The appearance of the manifestation of dharmata, however, is anything and everything arising. Wherever the feet of all the oceans of countless Buddhas, male and female Bodhisattvas, Mahasiddhas, and Vidyadharas who have come in the past have been present is blessed as a sacred place

55. gnas.
56. zhing.
57. tshan dho.
58. nye ba'i tshan dho.
59. 'du ba.
60. bsil ba tshal.
61. padma brtsegs.
62. khu byug klong.
63. sku la rdzogs.
64. he chen rol.
65. ya ma kha.
66. gsang chen rol.
67. In northwestern India.
68. 'jig rten mngon rdzogs.
69. *dpal chen 'dus pa.*

and land. In this way, the sublime sacred places and lands that exist are inconceivable.

The reason, as just expressed, is that previous sublime beings blessed holy places with the stainless blessings of dharmata in order for those places to bless future practitioners. Therefore, in all of the thirty-two lands, there are Dakinis who are born from purelands, Dakinis who are born from the minds of Mantrayana practitioners, Dakinis who are simultaneously born, and Dakinis who are countless in number. Supreme among them all is the one known as Yeshe Tsogyal. As it says in the sadhana of *The Wisdom Heart Essence of the Dakini:*

> HUNG. Vajra Dakini of great exaltation,
> Perfection of enlightened body, speech, mind,
> and the five wisdoms,
> Queen of all Dakinis,
> Conqueress turning the power of wisdom.

Thus it is said.

Those who subdue by any skillful means with miraculous activities according to the phenomena of sentient beings, all one hundred thousand Dakinis, may your unconditioned wishes be fulfilled. The dancers of magical manifestations of emanations that subdue unobstructedly in whatever way is necessary include, for example, White Tara, whose aspect is extremely peaceful. The goddess Saraswati and others like her are emanations that pacify the fear and dispel the suffering of all sentient beings. The aspect of supreme enrichment is the goddess Vasudhari and others like her who perform the activity of dispelling the poverty of all sentient beings, increasing life and merit. The aspect of sublime desire is Kurukuli and others like her whose emanations bring all sentient beings under their control by transforming desire into great desireless desire. The manifest appearance of wrath as sublime compassion is Krodikali[70] and others like her. Through their emanations and enlightened activity, the conception of self, which is the basis of the suffering of all sentient beings, is severed in the enlightened expanse of selfless Dharmakaya.

In brief, these are the principal Dakinis of the all-encompassing Three Roots. They abide in all purelands of the Buddhas of the Three Kayas. With

70. khros ma nag mo.

the strength of stainless great exaltation, they have the power of the exalted conquerors who turn the power of wisdom as the source of all miraculous activities and spiritual attainments. Abiding in immeasurable purelands of the Three-Kayas Dakinis, especially in the self-manifesting perfectly pure sacred place of Orgyen Space Activity,[71] it says in the offering of the main sadhana:

> In the gathering of the arrangement of purelands
> and enlightened body,
> For each, there are one hundred thousand Dakinis.
> With ways of dancing beyond thought,
> There are one hundred thousand unchanging Dakinis.
> With melodious voices that pervade throughout all
> directions of space,
> There are one hundred thousand Dakinis who chant
> the songs of goddesses.
> From the space of the conceptionless three entrances,[72]
> There are one hundred thousand Dakinis of the manifestation
> of compassion.
> From the enjoyment of ornaments and the wealth of qualities,
> There are one hundred thousand inconceivable Dakinis.
> Accomplishing the purpose of beings with the four
> miraculous activities,
> There are one hundred thousand spontaneously present Dakinis.
> Jnana Dakinis and karma mudra Dakinis
> Are all surrounded by a retinue of one hundred million Dakinis.

In accord with this offering, the principal and surrounding wisdom Dakinis and karmically manifested Dakinis of one hundred thousand and one hundred million are an assembly of perfectly arranged purelands and enlightened form. Each one manifests countless inconceivable emanations that accomplish the purpose of beings as **those who subdue by any skillful means according to the phenomena of sentient beings with miraculous**

71. o rgyan mkha' spyod, the Dakini pureland of Space Activity.

72. (1) Great shunyata, which is without characteristics. (2) Without wishing. There is no subject or object, so there is no wishing. (3) Without conceptions. Since there are no characteristics, there is nothing to think. These three entrances go with wisdom, so they are called the space of the conceptionless three entrances.

activities, all one hundred thousand Dakinis, may your unconditioned wishes be fulfilled. Thus it is said.

Therefore, in general, both actually arranged offerings and offerings emanated from mind are presented to all Dakinis. Specifically, the appearance of the clarity of the sun, moon, lamps, and so on, as well as the limitless appearance of the light of the enlightened mind of pure awareness, is offered to fulfill the unconditioned wishes of all Dakinis within the space of Dharmakaya. With the support for stainless great exaltation, the red and white amrita of relative bodhichitta and the absolute, unchanging amrita of the enlightened mind of pure awareness, may all the unconditioned wishes of the wisdom Sambhogakaya Dakinis be fulfilled!

From *The Expanse of the Sky Treasure of Dharmata*,[73] in the fulfillment prayer to the assembly of Dakinis, it says:

> The corpse and offerings are mixed indivisibly,
> Extremely filling all of whatever exists of phenomena.
> Whatever glorious desirable qualities arise,
> May they be an ever-increasing infinite offering.

As said, the support for the samsaric habits of all sentient beings is the body of the skandhas. By cutting the body loose with the curved knife of the wisdom of selflessness, the body becomes a great corpse of innumerable tastes and all characteristics. Placed within a kapala that equals the size of the three thousand myriad universes, may these contents completely fulfill the unconditioned wishes of the simultaneously born Nirmanakaya Dakinis. May the emanations of the Three-Kayas Dakinis, the oceanlike assembly of mother and sister Dakinis and spiritual companion Dakinis, receive this offering of enjoyment, and may their wishes be fulfilled. May the further emanations of the wrathful Dakinis of all phenomenal existence be completely fulfilled by the great red rakta. Furthermore, in the pureland of the Immense Ocean,[74] by emanating the revelation of the principal Dakini and retinue, may all wisdom Dakinis and karmically manifested Dakinis who benefit sentient beings be completely fulfilled by these desirable qualities, without anything excluded.

73. *chos nyid nam mkha'i klong mdzod.* Terma revelation of Düdjom Lingpa of the Dakini Troma Nagmo.
74. gangs chen mtsho.

Holders of unobstructed miraculous activity, keepers of pure samaya, Dharmapalas, may your wishes be fulfilled.

As said, those with the power of unimpeded miraculous emanations are primarily the Mahaguru[75] and all Buddhas. The mother of all Buddhas is dharmadhatu Kuntuzangmo, who is the Dakini Yeshe Tsogyal. From that, the manifestation of the reflection of the method of appearance is Mahakala Lekdan, Four-armed Mahakala, Maning, Mahadeva, Shanpa, Damchan, Vasudhara, Dzambhala, Ganapati,[76] and others who are the assembly of male protectors and wealth deities. The natural forms of wisdom are the Dakini protectors of mantra who are Ekajati and the four sisters in her retinue, Goddess Maintaining the Holy Lands of Graveyards, Tseringma and four spiritual sisters,[77] and others who are the assembly of female guardian goddesses. Furthermore, the demon, deva, yama, tsan, raja, mamo, yaksha, naga, and others are all in essence the reflection of the manifestation of wisdom appearing in forms that are both worldly and beyond worldly. In order to protect the teachings of Buddha in general and specifically to guard and sustain secret mantra, with loving-kindness they watch over all practitioners who possess pure samaya and they accomplish unimpeded enlightened activities through miraculous manifestation. By making inconceivable actually arranged offerings and offerings emanated from mind to all these guardians of Dharma, may their wishes be completely fulfilled.

Whatever samaya of the Vajrayana tradition is broken is openly confessed. Generally, there are the outer vows of the Vinaya, the inner bodhichitta, and the secret samaya of Vidyadharas. In particular, there is the samaya of enlightened body, which is broken by not realizing the view of the four mudras,[78] failing to meditate, and so on; the samaya of enlightened speech, which is broken by interrupting the continuity of mantra and daily practice recitation, not practicing the approach and accomplishment rituals at the appropriate time, failing to offer tsok, torma, and so on; and the samaya of enlightened mind, which is broken in general by openly exposing secret teachings of the developing and completion stages, and specifically by openly exposing teachings that have been entrusted to disciples

75. Padmasambhava.
76. In the order they are mentioned, these protectors are mgon po legs ldan, phyag bzhi pa, ma ning, lha chen, shan pa, dam can, rnam sras, dzam lha, and tshogs bdag.
77. In the order they are mentioned, these female protectors are ma mo sngags kyi srung ma 'khor re ti mched bzhi, zhing skyong dur khrod lha mo, and lha sman tshe ring mched lnga.
78. The four mudras are the samaya mudra, dharma mudra, karma mudra, and jnana or wisdom mudra.

who have sworn to guard them, to individuals that do not have the same samaya, who have broken their samaya, or who have reverse view toward secret mantra, and by engaging in inverted, chaotic conduct, and so on.

Not having had the ability to use the five desirable qualities of the skandhas for the benefit of others through skillful means; not realizing the unabandonable five passions as the five Buddha families but just using them in an ordinary way; materializing and not accepting the five nectars but seeing them as dirty or clean; not knowing the five skandhas as the five Kayas and five wisdoms, so being unable to join with this mandala; not accomplishing the five Buddha families because of being forgetful, which causes the result to be delayed: all of these go against the twenty-five branch samayas. Furthermore, there are not complying with the speech of the Vajra Master, disrespecting the consort, harming vajra brothers and sisters, breaking special samaya to accomplish, and so on. In brief, this includes not realizing the five skandhas to be the yab, or male consort, and not realizing the five elements to be the yum, or five wisdom Dakinis, breaking the samaya of the four empowerments of the classes of unsurpassed tantra; and especially, as said in the teachings of the tantras, transmissions, and upadesha of the vajra Dakinis, abandoning the Three Jewels, the four mudras, and others by contradicting the great value of additional samaya; being incapable of abiding in the view of dharmata; being weak in methods of meditation; being unable to climb up the high pass of pure activity and others; and all broken and corrupted vows, mistakes, and contradictions, whatever they may be.

Regarding the view, meditation, and activity, according to the samaya of inner Vajrayana, whatever activity is necessary to benefit pitiful beings must be carried out in order to help them, whether peaceful or wrathful. This activity must be done at the correct time and place. If one is left in a state of doubt from fear and hesitation, one does not climb up the high pass of pure activity. By not conducting the appropriate activity according to time and place but using conventional behavior out of fear that comes from self-attachment, self-protection, and trying to avoid the condemnation of others, one cannot keep this samaya, because one is unable to pass beyond convention for the benefit of liberating oneself and others. To abandon ordinary ego, one must be able to use the right activity without fear, hesitation, or doubt, so that one can engage in whatever wrathful or peaceful behavior will benefit beings, not meaninglessly but at the right time, passing beyond all ordinary conception.

In brief, once entering the mandala of unsurpassed mantra, even though it seems that samaya is properly taken, due to not having profound realization of wisdom mind, one contradicts fearless activity, and so on. Thus, whatever samaya is broken is openly revealed, exposed, and fully confessed without exception with the prayer that it may be purified and completely cleansed. So it is said.

May outer, inner, and secret obstacles be purified in inconceivable, unwavering, flawless wisdom light. These obstacles are not to be interpreted as the inability to fulfill insignificant desires for this life only, but are the obstacles to one's ability and enthusiasm to accomplish the state of fully enlightened Buddhahood. This includes all that is harmful and directly opposed to that goal. Although there are many obstacles, if synthesized, they are categorized as outer, inner, and secret. Outer obstacles occur by not recognizing one's own wisdom nature of equanimity. This causes the appearance of earth to be solid and hard, and the fear of landslides and earthquakes, and so on. Not recognizing one's own discerning wisdom nature causes the wet liquid fluidity of water and the fear of floods, droughts, and so on. Not recognizing one's own mirrorlike wisdom causes the appearance of the heat of fire and the fear of burning, and so on. Not recognizing one's own wisdom of perfectly accomplished activity causes the lightness of movement and the appearance of the winds of jealousy, causing the fear of storms, hurricanes, tornadoes, and so on. The fear of meteorites, weapons, imprisonment by kings or the powerful, enemies including robbers and thieves, flesh-consuming spirits, enraged elephants, wild carnivorous animals, poison, disease, untimely death, poverty, and the inability to acquire that which is desired are the sixteen states of fear.

The four inner obstacles are the demon of the self that binds one to samsara; the demon of the passions, creating attachment and desire as the basis of samsara; the demon of the son of the gods, the deception that provokes obstacles to Dharma based on intoxication by excellent circumstances; and the demon of the lord of death that deprives the body of the life that sustains it.

The secret obstacles are the five passions of desire, anger, ignorance, pride, and jealousy, which are the demons that obstruct the state of liberation. Therefore, the way in which they can be pacified is **in inconceivable, unwavering, flawless wisdom light.**[79] As said, all such obstacles being purified in

79. The unwavering is flawless. Wisdom has no karmic air, so by being overpowered by wisdom, there is no chance to transform and nothing to change. Wisdom is light.

unwavering space are the words that invoke the enlightened mind of compassion. Here, that which is called unwavering is the permanent purification of the passions, so that one never falls into the realms of samsara. It also means the inexhaustible state that is free from destructibility or change. As said in *Revealing the Names of Manjushri:*[80]

> Formlessness, form, and supreme form.

Thus as said, in the formless space of Dharmakaya dwells the formless wisdom Dakini, Kuntuzangmo. The supreme form in the space of Sambhogakaya is not a karmic physical body composed of flesh, blood, and so on. The enlightened form of flawless, clear great exaltation is the intangible manifestation of the Sambhogakaya Dakinis of the five families.

From that, the forms that manifest in the realm of Nirmanakaya, such as Yeshe Tsogyal and others, are the Nirmanakaya Dakinis of compassion, whose ability to accomplish the purpose of beings is immeasurable. Although there are occasions when Nirmanakaya emanations appear in the forms of ordinary sentient beings, this is according to the perception of the objects to be subdued. According to their own appearances, there are never any physical self-defined phenomena. Since the appearance of unwavering clear light is free from depth and edge, it can only be perfectly all-pervasive. **May outer, inner, and secret obstacles be purified in inconceivable, unwavering, flawless wisdom light**. Thus it is said.

May all supreme and common siddhis be accomplished in this life through your enlightened activities. Thus the spiritual attainments are necessary in order to pacify all unwanted illness, demonic possession, obstacles, harm, and so on, from past lifetimes so they do not reoccur. They are necessary to increase life, merit, wisdom, and all positive qualities, and for overcoming all humans and nonhuman spirits with great loving-kindness and placing them on the path to liberation. Also, attainments make it possible to annihilate all humans and nonhuman spirits who have aversion toward the Buddha's doctrine, who intend to harm others, and who are engaged on misguided paths, and to end the ongoing causes and results of suffering. From the door of great compassion, all negativity can be dispelled and all beings can be led to the path. These are the benefits of common spiritual attainments.

80. *'jam dpal mtshan brjod.*

The ability to remain for however many eons of time one desires is the power of life. The ability to abide each instant in immeasurable samadhi with the power to emerge at will is the power of mind. The ability to fulfill all needs and desires for worldly sustenance such as food and wealth is the power of material possessions. The ability to use whatever is desired in all arts, sciences, medicine, and cultural knowledge is the power of activities. The ability to take rebirth in whatever place one wishes in the realms of gods, humans, and others is the power of birth. The ability to transform material substance into whatever sentient beings desire to use, such as turning earth into various precious substances, is the power of aspiration. The ability of male and female Bodhisattvas to emanate and take rebirth withinn the realms of the universe according to their prayers is the power of prayers. The ability to emanate according to what is desired, such as supporting immeasurable purelands in space on one strand of hair, is the power of miracles. The ability to know whatever one wishes from all that is knowable is the power of wisdom. The ability to unobstructedly know with clarity the systems of the terms of all phenomena is the power of phenomena. These are the ten sublime powers.

Also, the unchanging, permanent mandala of the vajra body is free from destruction and vulnerability as the siddhi of vajra life.[81] From the pristine mandala of the natural sound of the unceasing enlightened self-resonance of dharmata, that which is unable to be penetrated by worldly and non-worldly substance in any way, which captivates the minds of sentient beings just through hearing and places them in the irreversible state where they never again return to samsara, is the siddhi of indestructible melodious sound. From the mandala of enlightened mind, the phenomena of samsara and enlightenment, including direction and time, have never been deluded in any way. This is the supreme siddhi of inconceivable clear light. From the inconceivable mandala of qualities, the source of all the glory and qualities of existence and the ultimate state of Buddhahood, the ability to accomplish whatever state is desired, such as higher rebirth as a god or human, or liberation, is the siddhi of accomplishing all that is wished.

Unlike the limitation of fulfilling the aim of sentient beings sometimes and not at other times, to constantly fulfill the aim of all sentient beings is definite activity. Unlike the limitation of fulfilling the aim of sentient beings in some places and not in other places, to continuously fulfill the aim of all

81. Immortality.

sentient beings is pervasive activity. Because all these activities are performed effortlessly and simultaneously, it is the spontaneously accomplished manifestation of activity. The ability to fulfill the aim of all sentient beings according to time and place through these three activities is the siddhi of activity.

In brief, Dharmakaya, Sambhogakaya, and Nirmanakaya are the Three Kayas. Their aspects are discerned undistortedly, which is called the Fully Enlightened Manifestation Kaya.[82]

Even though the aspects of the qualities of the appearance of the Three Kayas are discerned, the essence is indivisible. This is the Vajrakaya or Essence Kaya.[83] These are the Five Kayas.

Always being stainless is the wisdom of dharmadhatu.[84] Always being unobstructed is mirrorlike wisdom.[85] From the beginning, the unconditioned purity of the way of abiding in unconditioned wisdom[86] is the quality of immaculate Dharmakaya. From that quality, the self-radiance of the way that appearances manifest[87] is the immaculate, flawless all-pervasive great exaltation mandala of the Victorious Ones. So therefore, the pure way of abiding in unconditioned wisdom and the way that appearances manifest are evenly pure. This is called the wisdom of evenness.[88] The reason sentient beings do not have evenness between the way of abiding in unconditioned wisdom and the way that appearances manifest is that even though the way of abiding in unconditioned wisdom is pure, they do not recognize the pure way that appearances manifest, so they are deluded in manifestation due to their misinterpretation of phenomena from the conceptualizations of dualistic mind. Therefore, for sentient beings, the way of abiding in unconditioned wisdom and the way that appearances manifest are seen as uneven, so phenomena are seen as impure. For Buddha, the purity of the way of abiding in unconditioned wisdom and the way that appearances manifest are even. Since the way of abiding in unconditioned wisdom is stainlessly pure, its quality is to manifest unobstructedly with flawless exaltation wisdom body, unobscured wisdom speech, and undeluded wisdom mind as the mandala of deities with immeasurable wisdom and immaculate purelands. This unobstructed nature is called mirrorlike wisdom.

82. mngon par byang chub pa'i sku.
83. rdo rje'i sku or ngo bo nyid sku.
84. chos dbyings ye shes.
85. me long ye shes.
86. gnas tshul.
87. snang tshul.
88. mnyam nyid ye shes.

All the immeasurable qualities of phenomena are undistorted. The ability to see all aspects of phenomena at once is the wisdom of discernment.[89] Sentient beings' phenomena are distorted, so they cannot see undistortedly or see all phenomena at once, because of their delusion.

The miraculous activity that is free from attachment and obstruction is the spontaneously present, effortless wisdom of self-accomplishing activity.[90] Whatever ordinary activity sentient beings perform in samsara is ultimately unsuccessful because they are bound by ignorance and its misinterpretations.

From the beginning, the nature of all the phenomena of existence is the five enlightened bodies and five wisdoms, which is the supreme siddhi of the unsurpassed state of Buddha. This is the state of the inconceivable wisdom Dakini. Please may I attain this in this life. I request that you perform enlightened activity and that you accomplish this for us in this life. Thus one prays, **May all supreme and common siddhis be accomplished in this life through your enlightened activities.**

When having tsok, since all practitioners with wisdom are free from dualistic mind, the offering substances also are consumed as wisdom nectar free from conceptualization about ordinary substances. As said:

> From wisdom, having wisdom.

The meaning is clearly said here. Also, the offering of the tsok is said to excel beyond the offerings of the lower vehicles in three ways. The visualized deity is recognized as Buddha. The substance offerings are recognized as the wisdom nectar of siddhi. The mind delights in the manifestation of sole dharmata. These three ways of excelling mean that whoever stays within deity phenomena is abiding in dharmata, so there is no clinging or attachment of mind.

Also, one's own body is fulfilled from the mandala. The mandala is fulfilled from the offering. The yogis and yoginis are fulfilled from the offering substances. All spirits are fulfilled by torma. All the deities of the senses are fulfilled by vajra songs and vajra dance. These are said to be the benefits of the six fulfillments. Also, the inconceivable temporary and ultimate benefits are as mentioned in *The Stages of Vajra Activity:*

89. so sor rtog pa'i ye shes.
90. bya ba grub pa'i ye shes.

The continual perfection of the two accumulations
Is a certain sign of the greatest tsok.

And:

Of merit, tsok is supreme.
In this very lifetime, all desires will be fulfilled,
And in the next life, rebirth will be taken in the
purelands of the Vidyadharas.[91]

Even though the previous result of the karmic body remains, the nature of the mind fully ripens through practice into wisdom deity. Whenever freed from the trap of the karmic body, the body of wisdom deity actually manifests as the fully ripened Vidyadhara[92] of the three characteristics.[93] In *The Splendorous Flaming Wheel of Wisdom*,[94] it says:

By clearly holding the mudra of enlightened body,
When freed from the body's trap,
The mind manifests as the actual form of deity,
And this is called the fully ripened Vidyadhara.

Thus, as said, when the karmic body transforms into the vajra body, then without abandoning the vajra body, joining with the state of Buddhahood with the power over life is the immortal Vidyadhara.[95]

With the body and skandhas,
Having accomplished the state of a Vidyadhara
with the power of life,
Having transcended the concept of a karmic body,
All faults are exhausted in the great state of Vidyadhara.
Whatever occurs, there will be no returning to samsara,
Because, having attained freedom, karmic airs are dispelled.
At that time, one attains the state of the immortal Vidyadhara.

91. Pure awareness holders. There are many categories, aspects, and ways of recognizing Vidyadharas, but all are contained in the four states of Vidyadharas.
92. rnam smin rig 'dzin.
93. The three characteristics are first, the body is a karmic body; second, the mind is already becoming the deity; and third, whenever free from the body, wisdom deity actually manifests.
94. *rngam glog.*
95. tshe dbang rig 'dzin.

So it is said.

Whatever wisdom deity is visualized, one actually becomes that deity, which is called the great pervasiveness Vidyadhara.[96] From *Responding to Requests:*[97]

One's body is the great mudra of deity
Through which the deity actually becomes apparent.
With the wisdom body of thirty-two noble marks,
eighty auspicious signs, and clairvoyance,
This is called the great pervasiveness Vidyadhara.

Perfecting the wisdom qualities of purification and realization is the completely accomplished Vidyadhara.[98] From *Vajra:*[99]

By the development of the power of the state of being a Vidyadhara,
According to the explanations, all stains are purified.
The threefold wisdom state of Buddha
Is the completely accomplished Vidyadhara.

There is no obscuration to purify, because it is the perfectly accomplished, perfectly attained quality of full realization. Thus it is said. This is how all four states of Vidyadharas attain and sustain wisdom body and purelands.

··· —— This *Commentary on the Meaning of "The Continuously* —— ···
Blossoming Lotus Rosary Assembly Palace" Called The Light Rays of the Youthful Sun was composed at the request of many Chinese lamas; Tamang Lama; many Bhutanese lamas; Lama Ngodrub of Western Tibet; Lama Sonam of Northern Tibet, who is always scratching lice on the left side of his head; Golok Lama Orgyen Thinley Kunkhyab, who is always checking young beautiful women's faces and buttocks; and others who abide on the profound path of yoga. Also, this was written for those who

96. phyag rgya'i rig 'dzin.
97. *zhus lan.*
98. lhun grub rig 'dzin.
99. *rdo rje.*

were born to parents having Dharma, who take joy in hearing the sound of Dharma, who are the sprouts of the family lineage, my faithful Asian and Western children. Also, it is for those who have unshakable faith in the one who is the essence of all Buddhas of the three times, the great self-occurring supreme Vajra Master, the Lotus Guru and his Consort, and for those who have blond hair, black hair, white hair, and those of the classes of gods, nagas, rakshas, and others, including all the goddesses of the family that stay here together. Always and for special pujas presenting actually arranged and visualized clouds of wondrous offerings, this inscription of a canopy of white clouds in the space of the blue heavens of the sky was written to fulfill the requests of the previously mentioned vajra family and all male and female practitioners.

As though the colorful Akanishtha Pureland of the Five Buddha Families has reflected on earth, the fields and meadows are brilliant with color and beautified by many lakes, lagoons, and pools. Of the five great continents of this world, the continent named after the sound of falling fruit, Jambudvipa, is the best of them all. Here in this northern land of America, during the time that many inconceivable varieties of fruits such as apples, raspberries, blueberries, and others ripen, this was written by me, Thinley Norbu, at my home, Always Noble Joyful Park, Kunzang Gatsal. By pleasing the all-encompassing Victorious Ones of the Three Roots, may all those I have a connection with, as well as all beings equal to the sky, purify the two obscurations, fully perfect the two accumulations, and attain the Two Kayas.

The Root Texts

༄། །བདུད་འཇོམས་གཏེར་གསར་སྔོན་འགྲོའི་ངག་འདོན་བསྡུས་པ་བཞུགས། །

དང་པོ་སྦྱོར་བ་བློ་ལྡོག་རྣམ་བཞིའི་ངག་འདོན་ནི།

ན་མོ༔ བསླུ་མེད་གཏན་གྱི་མགོན་པོ་བླ་མ་མཁྱེན༔ དལ་འབྱོར་འདི་ནི་ཤིན་ཏུ་རྙེད་པར་དཀའ༔
སྐྱེས་ཚད་མི་རྟག་འཆི་བའི་ཆོས་ཅན་ཡིན༔ དགེ་སྡིག་ལས་ཀྱི་རྒྱུ་འབྲས་བསླུ་བ་མེད༔
ཁམས་གསུམ་འཁོར་བ་སྡུག་བསྔལ་རྒྱ་མཚོའི་ངང་༔ དྲན་ནས་བདག་བློ་ཆོས་ལ་འགྱུར་བར་ཤོག༔

ཅེས་ལན་གྲངས་མང་བརྗོད་ལ་བློ་སྦྱང་།

གཉིས་པ་སྔོན་འགྲོ་དངོས་ལ། དང་པོ་སྐྱབས་སུ་འགྲོ་བ་ནི། མདུན་གྱི་ནམ་མཁར་སྐྱབས་ཡུལ་མཆོག་གསུམ་ཀུན་འདུས་ཀྱི་ངོ་བོ་རྩ་བའི་བླ་མ་ཉིད་གུ་རུ་རིན་པོ་ཆེའི་རྣམ་པར་མངོན་སུམ་དུ་བཞུགས་པར་མོས་ལ།

འདི་བཟུང་བྱང་ཆུབ་སྙིང་པོ་མཆིས་ཀྱི་བར༔ བླ་མ་དཀོན་མཆོག་གསུམ་ལ་སྐྱབས་སུ་མཆི༔

ཞེས་ཕྱག་དང་སྦྲག་སྟེ་ཅི་ནུས་སུ་བརྗོད།

གཉིས་པ་སེམས་བསྐྱེད་པ་ནི། སྐྱབས་ཡུལ་དཔང་པོར་གསོལ་ཏེ།

ད་ནས་བཟུང་སྟེ་འཁོར་བ་མ་སྟོང་བར༔ མ་གྱུར་སེམས་ཅན་ཀུན་གྱི་ཕན་བདེ་བསྒྲུབ༔

ཅེས་བྱང་ཆུབ་ཀྱི་སེམས་ལ་བློ་སྦྱང་།

གསུམ་པ་ཚོགས་བསགས་མཎྜལ་འབུལ་བ་ནི། མཎྜལ་ཚོམ་བུ་དངོས་སུ་བཤམས་པ་དཔེར་མཚོན་ནས།

ཚེ་རབས་ཀུན་གྱི་ལུས་དང་ལོངས་སྤྱོད་དཔལ༔ ཚོགས་གཉིས་རྫོགས་ཕྱིར་དཀོན་མཆོག་གསུམ་ལ་འབུལ༔

ཞེས་མཎྜལ་གྲངས་མང་འབུལ།

བཞི་པ་སྒྲིབ་སྦྱོང་རྡོར་སེམས་སྒོམ་བཟླས་ནི། རང་ཉིད་ཐ་མལ་དུ་གནས་པའི་ངང་ནས།

སྤྱི་བོར་བླ་མ་རྡོར་སེམས་དབྱེར་མེད་པའི༔ སྐུ་ལས་བདུད་རྩིའི་རྒྱུན་བབས་སྒྲིབ་སྦྱངས་གྱུར༔

ༀ་བཛྲ་སཏྭ་ས་མ་ཡ་མ་ནུ་པཱ་ལ་ཡ༔ བཛྲ་སཏྭ་ཏེ་ནོ་པ་ཏིཥྛ་དྲི་ཌྷོ་མེ་བྷ་ཝ༔

སུ་ཏོ་ཥྱོ་མེ་བྷ་ཝ༔ སུ་པོ་ཥྱོ་མེ་བྷ་ཝ༔ ཨ་ནུ་ར་ཀྟོ་མེ་བྷ་ཝ༔ སརྦ་སིདྡྷི་མྨེ་པྲ་ཡཙྪ༔

སརྦ་ཀརྨ་སུ་ཙ་མེ༔ ཙིཏྟཾ་ཤྲི་ཡཾ་ཀུ་རུ་ཧཱུྃ༔ ཧ་ཧ་ཧ་ཧ་ཧོ༔ བྷ་ག་ཝཱན༔

སརྦ་ཏ་ཐཱ་ག་ཏ༔ བཛྲ་མཱ་མེ་མུཉྩ་བཛྲཱི་བྷ་ཝ་མ་ཧཱ་ས་མ་ཡ་སཏྭ་ཨཱཿ

ཞེས་བདུད་རྩི་འབེབས་སྦྱོང་གི་དམིགས་པ་དང་བཅས་ཡིག་བརྒྱ་དང་།

ༀ་བཛྲ་སཏྭ་ཧཱུྃ༔

ཞེས་ཡིག་དྲུག་ཅི་ནུས་སུ་བཟླས་མཐར།

འོད་ཞུ་བདག་སྣང་དང་འདྲེས་རོ་གཅིག་གྱུར༔

ཞེས་རྡོར་སེམས་རང་ལ་བསྡུས་ཏེ་མཉམ་པར་བཞག

ལྔ་པ་བྱིན་རླབས་མྱུར་དུ་འཇུག་པ་བླ་མའི་རྣལ་འབྱོར་ནི།

རང་ཉིད་རྡོ་རྗེ་རྣལ་འབྱོར་མདུན་མཁའ་རུ༔ རྩ་བའི་བླ་མ་པདྨའི་སྐུར་བཞེངས་གྱུར༔

དུས་གསུམ་སངས་རྒྱས་མ་ལུས་འདུས་པའི་སྐུ༔ རྩ་བའི་བླ་མ་མཆོག་ལ་གསོལ་བ་འདེབས༔

འདི་ཕྱི་བར་དོ་གསུམ་དུ་ཐུགས་རྗེས་ཟུངས༔ དུས་གསུམ་རྒྱུན་ཆད་མེད་པར་བྱིན་གྱིས་རློབས༔

ༀ་ཨཱཿཧཱུྃ་བཛྲ་གུ་རུ་པདྨ་སིདྡྷི་ཧཱུྃ༔

ཞེས་བརྒྱ་སྟོང་སོགས་གང་མང་བཟླས་ལ།

སྐུ་གསུང་ཐུགས་ཀྱི་དབང་བྱིན་ཡོངས་རྫོགས་ཐོབ༔ བཛྲ་གུ་རུ་ཀཱ་ཡ་ཝཱ་ཀ་ཙིཏྟ་སིདྡྷི་ཧཱུྃ༔

བླ་མ་འོད་ཞུ་རང་ཐིམ་དབྱེར་མེད་ངང༔ རིག་སྟོང་དོན་གྱི་བླ་མའི་རང་ཞལ་བལྟ༔

དྲུག་པ་འཕོ་བ་ནི།

མགོན་པོ་འོད་དཔག་མེད་ལ་གསོལ་བ་འདེབས༔ ཟབ་ལམ་འཕོ་བ་འབྱོངས་བར་བྱིན་གྱིས་རློབས༔

ཞེས་ལན་གང་མང་བརྗོད་ལ་འཕོ་བའི་འདུན་པ་བྱ།

བདུན་པ་ལུས་སྦྱིན་བསྔོ་བ་ནི།

ད་ནི་ལུས་དང་ལོངས་སྤྱོད་དགེ་རྩར་བཅས༔ མ་གྱུར་འགྲོ་ལ་ཕངས་པ་མེད་པར་བཏང༔
འགྲོ་དོན་རླབས་ཆེན་གེགས་མེད་འགྲུབ་པར་ཤོག༔

ཅེས་སོགས་སྨོན་ལམ་ནན་ཏན་དུ་གདབ་བོ། །

ཞེས་གཉེར་གསར་སྟོན་འགྲོའི་ངག་འདོན་རྒྱས་པ་མི་ཤེས་ཤིང་མི་ལྷོགས་པའི་རིགས་ལ་ཕན་ཕྱིར་སྟོན་འགྲོའི་ངག་འདོན་བསྡུས་པ་འདིའི་གནད་དོན་གོ་བདེའི་
གསལ་འདེབས་ས་བཅད་ཙམ་དུ་འཇིགས་བྲལ་ཡེ་ཤེས་རྡོ་རྗེས་སོ།། །།

A Concise Recitation of the Preliminary Practices of the New Treasures of Düdjom

The Preparation

Reciting the Four Contemplations That Turn the Mind

Homage. I beseech you to know me, Lama, deceitless constant protector.
The eases and obtainments of this precious human rebirth are
extremely difficult to find.
Whoever is born possesses the phenomena of impermanence and death.
The cause and result of virtuous and nonvirtuous actions
cannot be denied.
The continuous character of the three realms of samsara
is an ocean of suffering.
By remembering this, may my mind turn to the holy Dharma.

Thus, reciting as many times as possible, train the mind.

The Main Preliminary Practice

First, Refuge

Visualize that one's root Lama, whose essence embodies the Three Jewels, the sources of refuge, appears in the form of Guru Rinpoche in the sky in front of one.

From this moment until attaining the essence of enlightenment,
I take refuge in the Lama, who is the Three Jewels.

Thus, with prostrations, recite this as much as possible.

Second, to Develop Bodhichitta (Mind of Enlightenment)

Praying to the object of refuge as one's witness:

From now until samsara becomes empty,
I will strive for the benefit and happiness of all sentient beings, who have all been my mother.

Thus, train the mind in bodhichitta.

Third, the Accumulation of Merit through Mandala Offerings

While actually arranging piles of substance symbolizing the mandala:

My bodies, wealth, and glories of all my lives
I offer to the Three Jewels in order to complete the two accumulations [merit and wisdom].

Offer mandalas many times.

Fourth, the Purification of Obscurations: The Vajrasattva Meditation and Recitation

In the state of one's ordinary form:

Above the crown of my head is Vajrasattva, who is inseparable from the Lama.
From Vajrasattva's body flows a continuous stream of crystal moonbeam nectar, and all obscurations are purified.

Sanskrit

OM VAJRA SATTVA SAMAYA
MANU PALAYA VAJRA SATTVA
TENOPA TIK' THRA DRIDHO MEBHAWA
SU TO KHAYO MEBHAWA
SU PO KHAYO MEBHAWA
ANU RAKTO MEBHAWA
SARWA SIDDHI ME PRA YATTSA
SARWA KARMA SU TSA ME
TSITTAM SHRI YAM KURU HUNG
HA HA HA HA HO
BHAGAWAN SARWA TA T'HAGATA
VAJRA MA ME MUNTSA
VAJRI BHAWA
MAHA SAMAYA SATTVA AH

Translation

OM is the supreme mantra, most excellent beginning praise.
VAJRA SATTVA SAMAYA, the tantric vow of Vajrasattva.
MANU PALAYA VAJRA SATTVA, I beseech you, Vajrasattva, to grant me your protection.
TENOPA TIK' THRA DRIDHO MEBHAWA, abide firmly in me.
SU TO KHAYO MEBHAWA, make me totally satisfied.
SU PO KHAYO MEBHAWA, increase perfectly within me.
ANU RAKTO MEBHAWA, be compassionate toward me.
SARWA SIDDHI ME PRA YATTSA, by your blessing, bestow all attainments upon me.
SARWA KARMA SU TSA ME, may I also attain the power of all activities.
TSITTAM SHRI YAM KURU, make my mind virtuous; HUNG is the essence of wisdom heart.
HA HA HA HA, the four boundless wishes of bodhichitta, the four joys, the four empowerments, and the Four Kayas; HO is the exclamation of joy.
BHAGAWAN SARWA TA T'HAGATA, Victorious One who embodies all the Tathagatas.
VAJRA MA ME MUNTSA, Vajrasattva, may you never abandon me.

VAJRI BHAWA, I pray, please make me a vajra holder.
MAHA SAMAYA SATTVA, Great Samaya Deity.
AH is to unite indivisibly.

Recite the hundred syllables while visualizing the nectar descending and purifying, and:

OM VAJRA SATTVA HUNG

Recite the Six-Syllable Mantra as much as possible. Then:

Vajrasattva dissolves into light and becomes one taste
indivisible from my phenomena.

Vajrasattva dissolves into oneself. Abide in meditation.

Fifth, the Swiftly Received Blessings of Guru Yoga

Oneself is transformed into Dorje Naljorma, and in the sky
in front of oneself,
The root Lama of great kindness appears in the form of Padmasambhava.

The complete embodiment of all Buddhas of the three times,
Supreme root Lama, I pray to you.
In this life, the next lives, and between lives, hold me
with your compassion.
May your blessings flow unceasingly throughout the three times.

OM AH HUNG VAJRA GURU PADMA SIDDHI HUNG

Thus, recite this mantra as many times as possible—one hundred times, one thousand times, and so on.

The blessings and empowerments of wisdom body, wisdom speech, and wisdom mind are completely and perfectly obtained. One is collecting or receiving the attainment of wisdom body, wisdom speech, and wisdom mind from the Vajra Master, Guru Rinpoche.

After receiving the four empowerments:

The Lama dissolves into light and is absorbed into oneself.
Abide in indivisible awareness and emptiness, which is
the face of the absolute Lama.

Thus, the Lama dissolves into oneself. Abide in meditation.

Sixth, the Transference of Consciousness

I pray to the Protector, Amitabha, Buddha of Boundless Light.
May you bless me to accomplish the profound path of transference.

Thus, reciting this many times, have the intention to transfer one's consciousness.

Seventh, the Generosity of Giving One's Body and the Dedication of Merit

Now, my body, wealth, and the source of my virtue of all my lives
I give without clinging to all sentient beings, who have all been
my mother.
May great waves of benefit be accomplished without obstacle
for all sentient beings.

... ——— *Thus, this synthesis clarifies the essential meaning of the concise recitation of the preliminary practices. It was written by Jigdral Yeshe Dorje for the benefit of those who do not understand or are unable to practice the extensive preliminary practices of the New Treasures.* ——— ...

༄༅། །མཁའ་འགྲོའི་བསྐང་བསྐུས་པདྨའི་རྒྱུད་མང་ཞེས་བྱ་བ་བཞུགས། །

ཧྲཱིཿ ཚོགས་ཁང་བདེ་ཆེན་པདྨ་འོད། །རྣལ་འབྱོར་བདེ་ཆེན་སྒྲུབ་པ་པོ། །

དམ་རྫས་བདེ་ཆེན་བདུད་རྩི་ཆེ། །སྨད་བྱུང་བདེ་ཆེན་སྤྲིན་ཕུང་འཕྲོ། །

མཁའ་འགྲོ་བདེ་ཆེན་རྒྱལ་མོའི་ཚོགས། །ཐུགས་དམ་བདེ་ཆེན་དབྱིངས་སུ་བསྐང་། །

རིགས་ཀུན་ཁྱབ་བདག་འོད་མི་འགྱུར། །སྣང་བ་མཐའ་ཡས་ཐུགས་དམ་བསྐང་། །

འགྲོ་བ་ཀུན་འདུལ་སྙིང་རྗེའི་གཏེར། །སྤྱན་རས་གཟིགས་ཀྱི་ཐུགས་དམ་བསྐང་། །

འཁོར་འདས་ཟིལ་གནོན་ཐོད་ཕྲེང་རྩལ། །པདྨ་གར་དབང་ཐུགས་དམ་བསྐང་། །

དཀྱིལ་འཁོར་གཙོ་མཆོག་དབྱིངས་ཕྱུག་ཡུམ། །ཡེ་ཤེས་མཚོ་རྒྱལ་ཐུགས་དམ་བསྐང་། །

གང་འདུལ་སྤྲུལ་པའི་སྒྱུ་འཕྲུལ་གར། །འབུམ་ཕྲག་མཁའ་འགྲོའི་ཐུགས་དམ་བསྐང་། །

ཐོགས་མེད་ཕྲིན་ལས་རྫུ་འཕྲུལ་བདག །དམ་ཅན་ཆོས་སྲུང་ཐུགས་དམ་བསྐང་། །

རྡོ་རྗེ་ཐེག་པའི་དམ་ཚིག་དང་། །འགལ་བའི་ཉམས་ཆག་ཅི་མཆིས་བཤགས། །

ཕྱི་ནང་གསང་བའི་བར་ཆད་སེལ། །འཕོ་མེད་འོད་གསལ་ཀློང་དུ་སོལ། །

མཆོག་དང་ཐུན་མོང་དངོས་གྲུབ་ཀུན། །ཚེ་འདིར་འགྲུབ་པའི་ཕྲིན་ལས་མཛོད། །

ཅེས་པའང་ངག་དབང་སྐལ་ལྡན་རྡོ་རྗེས་བསྐུལ་ངོར་ཛྙཱ་ནས་སྤེལ་བ་དགེ། ། །

The Continuosly Blossoming Rosary of the Lotus Assembly Palace

The Concise Fulfillment of the Dakinis

Hrih. In the assembly palace of great exaltation, Radiant Lotus Light,
Maha-yogis and -yoginis are accomplishing great wisdom exaltation,
Offering sublime great exaltation amrita,
Illuminating clouds of wondrous great exaltation.
Great exaltation queen, Yeshe Tsogyal, and your gathering of Dakinis,
May your great exaltation wisdom Dharmakaya mind be fulfilled.

All-pervading lord, the essence of all Buddha families,
holder of unchangeable boundless light,
Buddha Amitabha, may your unconditioned wishes be fulfilled.

Treasure of compassion who subdues all beings,
Avalokiteshvara, may your unconditioned wishes be fulfilled.

Conqueror of all samsara and nirvana who wears a rosary
of bone ornaments,
Supreme Victorious Lotus Dancer, Padmasambhava,
may your unconditioned wisdom heart be fulfilled.

Supreme queen consort of the mandala, abiding in Dharmakaya,
Victorious Ocean of Wisdom, Yeshe Tsogyal, may your
unconditioned wishes be fulfilled.

Those who subdue by any skillful means with miraculous activities
according to the phenomena of sentient beings,
All one hundred thousand Dakinis, may your unconditioned
wishes be fulfilled.

Holders of unobstructed miraculous activity,
Keepers of pure samaya, Dharmapalas, may your wishes be fulfilled.

Whatever samaya of the Vajrayana tradition
Is broken is openly confessed.

May outer, inner, and secret obstacles be purified
In inconceivable, unwavering, flawless wisdom light.

May all supreme and common siddhis
Be accomplished in this life, through your enlightened activities.

. . . —— *This was requested from Jñana (Jigdral Yeshe Dorje)* —— . . .
by Ngak Wang Kalden Dorje.
May virtue increase.

Translated by my [Thinley Norbu Rinpoche's] daughter, Pema Chökyi, Happy Lotus of Dharma, just before the 10th day of the Tibetan sixth month, according to the terma tradition, the great birthday of Lotus-Born Padmasambhava.

Index